Anthony Trollope

ANTHONY TROLLOPE

Acknowledgments

My thanks are due to Balliol College, Oxford, for accepting this book as a project for a research fellowship, and for allowing me time to complete it, to my colleague, Mr. J. N. Bryson, who read the typescript with great care and made valuable suggestions and criticisms, and to Dr. R. W. Cockshut, who first interested me in Trollope. I am also indebted to Mr. Michael Sadleir, whose biography *Trollope: A Commentary* has provided me with much information and food for thought. In particular, I have made use of his bibliography, which is reproduced here by kind permission, of his detailed chronological table of Trollope's life, and of the facts he gives about Trollope's publishers.

Contents

CONTENTS

Preface

ONE TUESDAY morning in the summer of 1943, I took a book out of the school library at Winchester to read during an hour devoted to the study of science. Much as I now deplore my bad manners in reading when I should have been hearing about hydrostatics, I cannot altogether regret my action. For it provided me with my first encounter with Trollope. The book was *The Warden*, and it was the first volume in a finely-bound set of the six Barsetshire novels. Inside in Trollope's own handwriting were the words " From the author—a Wykehamist—to Winchester College." When I later came to read the Autobiography I realised how much was here left unsaid. It must have been a satisfaction to Trollope, remembering the uniform failure of his schooldays, to present himself at last before his old school as a writer of undisputed success. He had not apparently presented any of his books to Winchester until he could present a set that was a monument of his popularity.

To this day the Barsetshire series is far more widely known than any of his other writings. Though I have drawn freely upon them in the first part of this book, none of the separate studies in Part II deals with a Barsetshire novel. Some people may feel that the centre of gravity has been misplaced. If so, it has been done deliberately. For it is part of my thesis that Trollope is a gloomier, more introspective, more satirical, and more profound writer than he is usually credited with being; and further, the Barsetshire series, fine as it is, is not fully characteristic of his genius. Again, this series, so rich in incident and character, is simple in conception. It demands less explanation and analysis than most of his other works.

9

Books like *He Knew He was Right* and *The Eustace Diamonds* are not simple. They have been often neglected, and, when accorded a grudging recognition, they have been even more often misunderstood. These two novels, and several others of Trollope's later period, are among the most complex that I know. If *The Golden Bowl* or *Moby Dick* had never received any critical attention, it would not be surprising if most educated people did not appreciate them very fully.

Trollope's case can be illustrated by that of a distinguished living writer. Mr. T. S. Eliot wrote *The Waste Land* early in his career, and later favoured us with *Old Possum's Book of Practical Cats*. From the author's point of view that is the right order. People are pleased and appreciative when an author of proved subtlety condescends to write light verse. But if Mr. Eliot had written *Old Possum* before *The Waste Land*, it is doubtful if the latter would have been given all the critical analysis and praise that it has received for over thirty years. Trollope is like a man who wrote *Old Possum* first, and then, when he was already becoming *vieux jeu* in the eyes of the young and intellectual, published *The Waste Land*. In the circumstances it is not surprising that his bombshell failed to explode. This book is in part an attempt to rescue Trollope's reputation from the consequences of a tactical error.

Part I surveys the religious, political, and social ideas implicit in his writing, and for this purpose I have drawn on novels of every period regardless of chronology. I have tried to achieve a balance between ideas generally shared by Trollope's contemporaries and ideas characteristic of himself. But nothing is easier in studying the past than to mistake the personal for the general, and the generally accepted for the personal. If, as may well be the case, I have sometimes fallen into one or both of these errors, I can at least claim that I have always been aware of the danger.

We know a good deal more about mid-Victorian thoughts and feelings as a whole after reading Trollope than we did before. Perhaps this is more true of him than of most great novelists. Dickens' books reveal mainly the phantasmagoria of a private dream-world; Thackeray tells us a great deal about a few subjects only; George Eliot is identified with a single highbrow clique. But it should be made clear at once that I do not set up Trollope as the voice of an epoch or as an average man of his day. It is only by giving their full value to his obsessions, his strange fears and bitter memories, that one can sift out any useful material for generalisation.

Part II analyses the most important novels from 1867 onwards, and devotes a chapter to each. The order is chronological, and each chapter reveals a further stage in the steepening curve of the author's pessimism. It is tempting (and possibly useful) to relate this curve to contemporary social changes, but the main reasons for it seem to be psychological and personal.

Thus the first part of the book deals with what was permanent in Trollope, the second part with what was variable, with the gradual development of his art, and the gradual darkening of his imagination and failure of his hopes. The title, *Progress to Pessimism*, may seem unduly paradoxical, but it is not after all so rare that what was painful or even disastrous to a man has proved a blessing to the same man as a writer.

The problem of references has been a puzzling one. It would be pedantic to refer always to first editions, which are available only to very few. My imperfect solution has been to have no regular references, but to give chapter numbers in cases of special importance.

When I have indulged in a guess, as in giving possible reasons why Trollope became gloomier in his fifties, I have tried to indicate clearly that I am guessing. More often I have left the guessing to the reader. For instance, it would be fascinating to connect the relationship of father and son in the novels with the author's personal experience. I have not done this, partly because I do not think that the basic facts of personality can be fully explained, and partly to allow the reader the fun of deciding for himself. His guess is as good as mine.

Main Events in the Life of Anthony Trollope

April 24th,	1815	Born in London
	1827	Went to Winchester College
	1830	Left Winchester and went to Harrow School
	1834	Clerk in the Post Office
	1841	Deputy postal surveyor in Ireland
	1843	Began his first novel (published 1847)
	1844	Married Rose Heseltine
	1852	Began *The Warden* (published 1855)
	1855	Began *Barchester Towers* (published 1857)
Oct. 6th,	1863	Death of his mother, Frances Trollope
	1864	Elected to the Athenæum
	1867	Resigned from the Post Office in order to devote himself fully to writing
	1867	Began *He Knew He Was Right* (published 1869)
	1868	Unsuccessful Liberal candidate for Beverley at General Election
	1873	Began *The Way We Live Now* (published 1875)
April 30th,	1876	Completed his *Autobiography* (published posthumously)
	1881	Began *Mr. Scarborough's Family* (published posthumously)
Dec. 6th,	1882	Died in London

During his life Trollope visited among other countries,
the United States, the West Indies, South Africa,
Australia, Ceylon, Iceland, and most of the countries
of Europe.

PART ONE

*

TROLLOPE AND HIS TIMES

1. *Outlook*

OUTWARDLY NORMAL, Trollope's life had only one eccentricity, he worked abnormally hard. To understand why he did so will take us far towards understanding his nature. " There is no human bliss," he wrote, " equal to twelve hours of work with only six hours in which to do it." This was his considered opinion. Leisure only made him restless. In a letter written from England to Kate Field in Italy, he complained that now he was in England, Italy had a strong appeal for him, but that in Italy, his mind ran on the joys of home. In the Autobiography he records his decision that he must work because he could be happy only when he was working, and in his account of foreign travel he remarks almost as if it were a truism that play is always harder than work. Not that work came easy to him, or he might not have rated its power over the mind so high. When he first began to write he was confident about his literary powers, but doubtful about his industry. At the age of thirty, the past already seems very long to a man as he looks back, and to him it must have seemed a series of idle and wasted years. Long afterwards he would describe with a kind of horrified sympathy the paralysis of the will to work suffered by his friend Thackeray, or by characters of his own creation like Sir Thomas Underwood. However many books he published, and no matter how quickly they were written, he still felt that this paralysis might have been his own lot, and that if it had, the sadness of life would have overwhelmed him.

Apart from the very poor, most people who work exceptionally are moved either by strong ambition or by devotion to a cause.

Trollope belongs to neither class; neither his literary nor official labours served any special cause, and if he can be called ambitious at all, the word only applies in a very specialised sense. The great ambition of his life was to stand well in his own eyes. This ambition was the root from which all his other ambitions sprang, the desire to be in Parliament, to be accepted by the best London clubs, and to write books.

Consider his own description of his daydreams in adolescence. " I never became a king or a duke . . . I never was a learned man nor even a philosopher. But I was a very clever person and beautiful young women used to be fond of me. And I strove to be kind of heart and open of hand, and noble in thought, despising mean things; and altogether I was a very much better fellow than I have ever succeeded in being since."

Apart from the mention of beautiful young women, this is a most unusual catalogue of adolescent ambitions. Most boys, if they considered these qualities at all, would assume that they possessed them. Truly, " ambition should be made of sterner stuff."

His miserable and solitary boyhood, and the feeling that he was a useless thing, which only cumbered the ground, drove his daydreams inwards. He wanted to be loved and to respect himself more than to succeed. When he was a writer of established success he published two anonymous novels. Why did he do this? I cannot accept the explanation of L.P. and R. P. Stebbins in their book *The Trollopes*. They say " his choice of a new personality was obviously due to the overfrequency of his own name on publishers' lists, his wish to exploit a new field, and a desire to air opinions and prejudices which would offend his stable public."

Now it is true that in 1867 and 1868 when *Nina Balatka* and *Linda Tressel* were published anonymously, three other books by Trollope also appeared. But five books in two years was exactly the average that he maintained from 1864 to 1871, when he published twenty books in eight years. One feels that two anonymous publications would do little to affect public interest in this huge output. Nor, so far as we know, had he any reason in

1867 to feel worried about his popularity, for the publisher's payments for his new books were still increasing. He was near the summit of his financial success, but there was as yet no sign of the decline which was to come after three or four more years.

The idea that he became anonymous in order to explore new fields is not very plausible either. It is true that the two anonymous books deal with foreign countries, but so do a number of his others. He even ventured into Roman history without concealing his name. The third reason is the oddest of all. The authors suggest that the public may have been shocked by his " irritation against all organised forms of Christianity." But this was a feeling he had often expressed in connection with Anglicanism and English nonconformity. It would have been strange if the British public after patiently enduring this for many years had become suddenly resentful of criticism of the religion of Nuremburg or of Prague.

No, by ordinary business standards, his action was crazy, and he was well aware that it is the name that sells. But this time of high prosperity and fame was just the time when a man of Trollope's temperament might be expected to rub his eyes and ask himself whether it was all really true. Was he still the same person that had wandered in despair round the fields of Harrow? He wanted to prove to himself that his literary success was not a dream or even a fluke, so that he could be certain he had earned all he had won.

So, all his life, his main motive in working so hard was self-justification. A man who does the work of two need not fear that he will think himself or that others will think him a useless encumbrance. But work had another purpose, it was a sedative for a melancholy temperament. In one way Trollope was the obverse of Samuel Johnson. Each was given to melancholy, and in each congenital tendencies were accentuated by personal misfortunes. Each had a huge capacity for work, and a strong reluctance to begin working. But while Johnson's life is the history of the melancholy idleness of a great mind, punctuated by furious bursts of work, Trollope succeeded in conquering his reluctance to work, and thus, in the main, his melancholy also.

Not completely, however. In his last years, though he still worked hard by ordinary standards, he could not work hard enough to keep his melancholy at bay. He remarked pathetically in a letter that he still wished more than anything else to write, even if no one any longer read his books. This is hardly the remark of an ambitious man, and it certainly is not what it might have been on the lips of Henry James, a confession of devotion to art irrespective of results. It was the voice of a man who dreads being forced to sit down and think. "Success," he wrote in 1860, "is the necessary misfortune of life, but it is only to the very unfortunate that it comes early."

In those last years the only thing except work that was really pleasing to him was sleep; he records with triumph in a letter of 1878, his ability to sleep nine hours without moving, and he comments, " I am beginning to think that the more a man can sleep the better for him." It is safe to guess that if he had lived to be old and lost the capacity to work, the melancholy which was closing in upon him in his sixties would have become intense as it did with Johnson.

But one may ask why, if his ambitions were mental rather than worldly, did he show such obvious zest in recording his literary profits? This has been much misunderstood. More than money itself he desired that satisfaction of knowing that he had proved his capacity to earn it. Thus, when he discovered that the publisher had lost money over his contract for *The Duke's Children* he at once offered to make good the loss, though there was no conceivable moral, let alone legal, obligation. But if the agreed price had been proved too high in terms of the book's popularity, he could no longer feel that his money had been fairly earned. Such money could not contribute to his self-esteem and had better be sacrificed. We must remember, too, that he never at any time intended to publish his autobiography before his death, though his instructions to his son about it are dated more than six years before he died. So far as he personally was concerned, the Autobiography was a private work, written for his own pleasure.

Trinity and the Lord's Supper are not necessary to teach a man to live with his brother man." His religious system subordinated faith to morality and eternity to time. In a most revealing letter he said, " I cannot believe the Old Testament because labour is spoken of as the evil consequence of the fall of man. My only doubt as to finding a heaven for myself at last arises from the fear that the disembodied and beatified spirits will not want novels." One may note in the word ' disembodied ' a further (probably unconscious) watering down of the creeds he repeated in church. But much more serious is the shadowy conception of heaven which the words imply. His heaven is a nineteenth-century version of the underworld of the Odyssey, a land of ghosts.

The two abiding fears of his life, boredom and loneliness, seem to have invaded even the life beyond the grave. There is an obvious failure of imagination here, not a failure to imagine heaven, but a failure to realise that it could be totally different from all he had known. The same failure appears in less momentous matters. He has often been called unimaginative, which is a very inept criticism of him as a novelist. For though his imagination could only operate within hailing distance of what he had known, the same is true of most novelists. In practice this is a very slight limitation for a novelist but a most serious one for a historian. Thus in his *Cicero*, when he was called upon to imagine a society which can be approached only through books, he failed utterly. The book has some merits, certainly; it is clearly and interestingly told, and evidence about facts and motives is often shrewdly weighed. But never for a moment does ancient Rome cease to be Victorian England in disguise. His theological conceptions have the same effect, an even more grotesque one in that case. Life after death is no more than an unwelcome extension of the life we have known. The result is that the only parts of his theology which are fully real to himself are those that seemed to have the warrant of his own experience—conscience—morality, judgment. But the surprising thing is that these attenuated religious ideas are genuinely religious as far as they go. He sees moral problems not in their relation to society, but to the soul.

23

As we shall see, his conception of the thoroughly evil man is not a destroyer of others but one whose spiritual death has left him too weak to harm others.

A good illustration of his religious and moral outlook is provided by his views on celibacy. To him it was either reprehensible or pitiful. It is true that this was no unusual view in his time, but he held it with an intensity which requires explanation. He rejected celibacy as a religious ideal along with every other kind of asceticism, calmly assuming that all asceticism was a form of self-indulgence. This stupid opinion, coming from a man of his insight into character, suggests a suppressed irritation against those whose religious vision was stronger than his own. He wished to believe that his simple ideas of God, a moral code, and judgment after death, formed an all-sufficient religious system, and so he was apt to be angry and uncomprehending about anything, asceticism, sacraments, creeds, or ritual, which gave a hint of unknown experiences.

But if he was puzzled by celibacy as an ideal, he was distressed by the enforced celibacy of the spinster, and the aimlessness of the bachelor. Perhaps unconsciously assuming that everyone's temperament was like his own, he saw unmarried people as the inevitable victims of boredom and loneliness. Work and family life were, he thought, the best remedies for these afflictions; the only other he could imagine was the frantic pursuit of pleasure. As a boy he had walked fourteen miles to a dance and fourteen miles back, and no doubt he had it in him to pursue pleasure with the same abandon as some of his fictional bachelors did. Like Johnson, he found it hard to believe that anyone could be so different from himself as not to be afraid to go home and think. He found tranquillity almost as hard to imagine as heaven. Temperamentally he was sympathetic to those who pursued pleasure endlessly, but their final state might be the same as that of the bored and lonely. Both arrived along different paths at what he felt to be the ultimate evil.

In considering his ideas of evil it is interesting to compare him with two great novelists. The typical evil figure of Henry James

2. *Human Nature*

WHAT ASPECT does human nature bear in Trollope's work? It is not easy to generalise about so many imaginary beings. One cannot say that on the whole they appear either good or bad. In circumstances, wealth, occupation, social class and background, they are too various for any generalisation to be possible. Trollope is supposed by many to be the chronicler of the rural gentry and the cathedral close. But this idea is due to a fact for which he cannot be held responsible—that some of his books are so much better known than others.

There is, however, one unusual omission, which can hardly be due to accident. In all these thousands of pages there is very, very little about children. His last unfinished book, *The Landleaguers*, does contain a ten-year-old boy with a fairly important part in the story. Otherwise, there are no children in all his books with any recognisable character. When they do appear it is usually in order to illustrate some facet of adult character—for instance, the chapter on " Baby Worship " in *Barchester Towers*.

Interesting parallels with Dickens abound in Trollope's life and work, and this is one of the most interesting of all. Both of them had an unhappy boyhood, and a father who could not inspire in his children the normal feelings of trust and security. Yet Dickens never writes better than when his story is seen through the eyes of children, and he has perhaps a larger proportion of children among his best-known characters than any other novelist. I do not offer any precise explanation for this. But the difference in social status may be a contributory cause. Dickens's origins were modest enough for him to feel the pride of the self-made man in thinking of the obstacles he had overcome. Trollope was more unfortunate, for he had the added bitterness of knowing that he was the son of a gentleman, and treated as an outcast by those who should have been his equals. One is far less likely to boast about that. But Dickens and Trollope had one thing in common which may well be in large measure due to their early miseries. Each could depict the ordinary pleasures and comforts of life so vividly as to make them seem like transcendent joys. No one who has always fitted easily into his environment can do that.

For all their large number and wide variety it is possible to detect a few recurring themes in Trollope's characters. The first is self-deception. He is always on the watch for it in the most unlikely places, and when he finds it he reveals it with obvious satisfaction, yet with a curious sympathy. Trollope's books abound in self-deceivers, but they contain few hypocrites. Even Mr. Slope is not a complete hypocrite in the sense that Pecksniff is. Hypocrisy is too clear-cut for Trollope's taste. He is interested more in half-shades. Indeed, he sometimes shows that what is ordinarily taken for hypocrisy is not hypocritical at all. Dorothea Ray, one might have thought, is obviously hypocritical in expressing shocked surprise at her sister's conduct, when her own is indistinguishable. But Trollope always seems eager to extend the area of self-deception, because it fascinates him. And he is prepared to demonstrate that she is unconscious of her own inconsistency. He regards complete sincerity not as an elementary moral rule, but as a most difficult achievement.

Self-deception takes many forms. For Lady Cashel (*The Kellys and the O'Kellys*) it is just a vague, warm, dreamy feeling, arising from mother-love. Told that her dissolute son is coming on one of his rare visits home, she begins to imagine that he will at last marry, live at home, and do his duty by the estate. From this her mind passes to his imaginary heir, and she discusses with her maid the merits of various rooms for her imaginary daughter-in-law's confinement. Lonely, idle, bored, fantasy comes as a pleasant relief to her. " Visions of caudle cups, cradles, and monthly nurses, floated over Lady Cashel's brain, and gave her a kind of dreamy feel that the world was going to begin again with her."

In *The Duke's Children* Lord Gerald Palliser's self-deception is just simple pig-headedness. He has defied the authorities of his Cambridge college in order to watch his brother's horse run in the Derby. He knows that he must catch the nine o'clock train back or he will be sent down altogether. This he and his brother are especially anxious to avoid because of the grief it would cause their father. But Lord Gerald " knew that the special would not start until half-past nine. There were a lot of fellows who were dining about everywhere and they would never get to the station by the hour fixed." And next morning after missing the train he says, " ' Who on earth would have thought that they'd have been so punctual? They never are punctual on the Great Eastern. It was an infernal shame.' "

For others, like Major Pountney in *The Prime Minister*, self-deception is a form of defence against bitter humiliation. He is one of the extras who have managed to obtain a share in the magnificent hospitality the Duchess of Omnium is dispensing while her husband is Prime Minister. Plucking up his courage, he asks the Duke for his support in the parliamentary borough which the Duke and his ancestors have always controlled. The Duke has recently decided regretfully but out of conviction that it is his duty to give up all influence in the elections in the borough. So he turns on the major with great violence, and then sends him a letter directing him to leave the house.

After the rebuke " the major stood for a while transfixed to the place, and, cold as was the weather, was bathed in perspiration." But after he has had time to recover, has parried the first onslaught of ridicule from his friends at his London club, his attitude is different. " There was a mystery; and where there is a mystery a man should never be condemned. Where there is a woman in the case a man cannot be expected to tell the truth. As for calling out or in any way punishing the Prime Minister,

that of course was out of the question. And so it went on till at
last the major was almost proud of what he had done, and talked
about it willingly with mysterious hints, in which practice made
him perfect."

Self-deception reconciled Major Pountney to humiliation. It
rendered Archie Clavering jubilant at financial loss, when his
original object had been financial gain. In his desire to marry
Lady Ongar, a young and rich widow, he decides to bribe her
friend Sophie Gordeloup. He takes her twenty pounds and is then
shocked and astonished by her greed for further payments. But
he has heard that she is a Russian spy, and as he considers the
transactions of the day, his mood gradually changes. " He did
venture to triumph a little when he met Doodles at the club.
He had employed the Russian spy, and had paid her twenty
pounds, and was enrolled in the corps of diplomatic and
mysterious personages who do their work by mysterious agencies.
He did not tell Doodles anything about the glove, or the way in
which the money was taken from him; but he did say that he was
to see the spy again to-morrow, and that he intended to take with
him another present of fifty pounds.

" By George, Clavvy, you are going it! " said Doodles, in a
voice that was delightfully envious to the ears of Captain Archie.
When he heard that envious tone he felt that he was entitled to
be triumphant."

All these passages have an element of comedy. But self-
deception can take more sinister forms than this. There is the mad
obsession of Mrs. Bolton in *John Caldigate*, determined to believe
her daughter's husband is a criminal. There is the crazy vanity of
Mr. Gibson in *He Knew He Was Right*, enjoying the literary merits
of the letter with which he has jilted his fiancée. With him and
with George Hotspur, self-deception amounts to a lie in the soul.
" Then it occurred to Cousin George that perhaps he might bribe
the servant; and he put his hand into his pocket. But before he
had communicated the two half-crowns, it struck him that there
was no possible request which he could make to the man in
reference to which a bribe would be serviceable."

How can this preoccupation be explained? It seems that Trollope's moral consciousness was dominated by the ideas of sincerity and honesty. Both his writings and his conduct suggest this. For he devoted one whole book, *Mr. Scarborough's Family*, to a searching criticism of all the current ideas of honesty, and found them all wanting, while in his dealings with publishers he was scrupulous about keeping every engagement to the day, and indignant with those who failed to do the same. But his indignation did not mean that he thought the exact fulfilment of contracts easy. The higher a man's standard the more likely he is to see the difficulty of attaining it. Conrad, for instance, was obsessed with the problem of personal honour, and regarded a man who had lost it as a maimed creature, though he recognised at the same time that it is uncomfortably easy to lose it. Trollope, thinking complete sincerity to be both very desirable and very difficult, was fascinated by all the degrees of failure. A novelist who thinks that sincerity comes easily to all decent people, is apt to write off the exceptions as obvious hypocrites of little psychological interest.

Another characteristic which consistently haunted Trollope's imagination is endurance, especially endurance in a perverse and unprofitable attitude. " They who do not understand that a man may be brought to hope that which of all things is the most grievous to him, have not observed with sufficient closeness the perversity of the human mind," he says of Trevelyan in *He Knew He Was Right*. When a man of Trollope's nondescript style indulges in this eighteenth-century rotundity of language, it usually means that he is saying something that seems to him very important; and this sentence would have been relevant in a number of his books.

Consider the case of Dr. Harford, the old-fashioned high Tory cleric of *Rachel Ray*. Elderly male Cassandras like him are common in fiction, and surely one can guess pretty well what any of them would have said in 1863 on the question of admitting Jews to Parliament. But with Dr. Harford one is in for a surprise " ' Upon my word,' said he, ' I don't see the use for caring for that kind of thing any longer; I don't indeed. In the way we are going on now, and for the sort of thing we do, I don't see why Jews shouldn't serve us as well in Parliament as Christians.' " He is a man drunk with the odour of the decay of all he values.

In the same book a characteristic passage describes the attitude of the public to Luke Rowan's attempt to produce good beer in Baslehurst. " That idea of a rival brewery was distasteful to them all. Most of them knew that the beer was almost too bad to be swallowed; but they thought that Trappit had a vested interest in the manufacture of bad beer; that as a manufacturer of bad beer he was a fairly honest and useful man; and they looked upon any change as the work, or rather the suggestion, of a charlatan."

In a way these minor instances are more revealing because probably more spontaneous than the examples drawn from full-length characters. But there are plenty of the latter too. Will Belton and Mr. Crawley both endure to the end and both are described with the unmistakable excitement of a man investigating a quality that touches him very deeply. Mrs. Baggett in *An Old Man's Love* is an example of perversity. Proud of her position as housekeeper in a bachelor's household, she does all she can to persuade him to marry his ward. At the same time she proclaims that if he does she must go away and live miserably for the rest of her life, and that she cannot imagine why men are taken in by the facile prettiness of girls. Finally, she is very angry with the girl for presuming to resist a man's choice and refuse him. She maintains all these contradictory attitudes throughout.

Sometimes these qualities of character are so pronounced as to constitute an obsession. It may be no more than a humorous absurdity—for example, the old woman in *The American Senator* who buys a ticket on the railway for her parrot, or it may be the long drawn-out madness of Louis Trevelyan. Things of this kind, though they are commonest of all in his last books, came easy to Trollope before most of his talents were developed. In his first book, *The Macdermots*, the most memorable passages are those that deal with the crazy delusions of old Larry. Speaking to his son who has accidentally killed a man in defence of his own sister and of Larry's daughter, he says, " ' Murther, who doubts but that it was murther? Of course they'll call it murther. Well, he was the only friend you'd left me, and now you've murthered him. You may go now—you may go now—but mind I tell you, they'll be sure to hang you.' "

Later the old man has to give evidence in court. " When the book was handed to Larry Macdermot, on which he was to be sworn, he at first refused it, and when it was again tendered to him, he put it in his pocket, and made the man who gave it him a bow, and was very cross when he was obliged to give it back again." When he is questioned he begins to cry and protest his own innocence, which of course is not in question.

Writing after Thackeray's death of his affection for him, Trollope said that this was something no living man could tell another; at the close of his autobiography he said that he had not spoken of his inner life. Paradoxically for such a prolific writer, he was in some ways inarticulate, and inarticulateness in others deeply interested him. The young man, like John Eames or Lord Silverbridge, who cannot express himself, but who turns out to have plenty of sense, is one of his favourite types. It may be partly a result of his own history, too, that he so often introduces into his novels outcasts, and people who are helpless, or undecided, or despairing. He always identifies himself and the reader with his outcasts; when he is writing of such characters society assumes the aspect of an alien and indifferent power, justified perhaps (for the outcasts have often deserved their isolation), but still forbidding.

Most Victorian novelists needed to feel that their outcasts were innocent before they could place them in a sympathetic light. Usually they are simply the poor and the hungry. Even in *The New Magdalen*, where the outcast is a prostitute, Wilkie Collins contrives to prove that she has been the victim of circumstances, and is not really guilty. But Trollope, perhaps because of personal memories, can endow even Major Tifto, the crooked racing man with the pathos of "Athanasius contra mundum." If such a character had appeared in the work of Collins or Thackeray, he would either have been the villain of the piece or simply a joke.

One of the best of all his psychological studies is of this kind, *Cousin Henry*, the story of a weak and unpopular young man, who is apparently the heir to a large estate. After the owner's death he takes possession and accidentally finds a later will, which leaves all the property away from him. This short book is mainly a record of his mental struggle after the discovery. The struggle is of an unusual kind, for he feels no strong conflicting impulses. He is plunged into misery by his indecision, which is so heavy a burden that any decision would be a relief to him, but none is possible. It is typical of such a nature that he should fear hell as a consequence of his contemplated crime, although he has no real religious belief. Men like him only think things fully real when they become menacing. All the tenants and all his neighbours want the property to go to his cousin, a girl they have known and loved, whereas, he is a stranger and his manner is repulsive. From one point of view the book is an exposure of the moral dangers of being repulsive to others; its main subject is the paralysis of the will. It is as if a brief, hardly recorded battle between conflicting desires has left his soul a no-man's land on which every landmark has been destroyed. His state of mind resembles a prolonged lull in trench warfare. The end of the story is characteristic. He is finally roused from his stupor by the sight of someone about to find the will in the place where the testator had left it. He has not hidden it on all the days on which he has half-hoped and half-feared its discovery. Only when the will is on the point of being found does he decide that he wants to destroy it, and then it is too late. This is Trollope's best study of indecision, inarticulateness, loneliness, and morbidity.

Similar in some respects, but fundamentally different nevertheless, is the case of the old lawyer, Sir Thomas Underwood, in *Ralph the Heir*. He, too, is lonely, though he has a family. He, too, is unable to decide in favour of religious belief or unbelief, and unable to summon the will-power to do what he most desires, to write the life of Bacon. He is shown dozing in his London chambers in the evening, instead of going home to his family (whom he loves in his way), and then after midnight wandering for hours alone round the Temple and Lincoln's Inn. The motives of all this behaviour are not explained until late in the book, but when they are they have all the force of a psychological explanation which is totally unexpected, yet fits all the facts. This occurs in the chapter called " Music Has Charms." Listening half-unconsciously to some melancholy music from the street, he yields to despair and declares to himself that everything is vanity. But as the whole chapter, and particularly its title suggest, these thoughts give him immense satisfaction. If Dr. Harford is pleased by the idea of the social fabric decaying, here is a man who takes pleasure in a despair which extends to life itself, and death and his whole soul.

> " Immensita s'annega il pensier mio:
> E il naufragar m'e dolce in questo mare."

Trollope himself, it would seem, had heard the siren-song of despair, and having resisted it, was able to turn it into art.

Mr. Graham Greene in his book *The Lost Childhood* has stressed similar tendencies in Dickens. Both the similarity and the contrast are instructive. For Mr. Greene is speaking, not of Dickens's subject-matter, but of an impress placed on his books by his personality. If Mr. Greene is right, and I think he is, he is speaking of something of which Dickens was not aware himself, but which the reader can deduce from his works. Trollope had not only felt but understood; and his treatment of the sweetness of despair is a deliberate study of character. So while Dickens's evocation of despair is the more vivid and compelling of the two, Trollope's study is far more revealing psychologically, revealing not so much as in the case of Dickens, the mind of the author, as the human nature he set out to draw.

To find how Trollope deals with problems of conscience, it is interesting to compare *The Warden* with Scott's *Old Mortality.*

Each is a story of a man poised between conflicting loyalties. But while Mr. Harding is central, Morton seems to exist only to illustrate the principles between which he is torn. In *The Warden* the two extreme views, those of the Jupiter and of Archdeacon Grantly, are satirised and condemned. It is suggested that any fair-minded man would have been as moderate, and as uncertain of himself as Mr. Harding was. Like many moderate and liberal men, like Matthew Arnold, for instance, Trollope was apt to assume that every extreme view could merge into his own central moderation, if only people would be reasonable. But *The Warden* is an early work, and Trollope's understanding gradually widened. In the novels written after he was fifty he achieved what was bred in Scott's bones, sympathetic understanding of fanaticism, delusion, and violence. It is true, as we have seen, that from the first he was apt to dwell on obsessions. But it is only in his later works, of the type of *He Knew He Was Right*, that he was successful in showing the inner working of an obsession. In Larry Macdermot or Mrs. Proudie he simply showed how an obsession affected people's outward behaviour. His keenest psychological penetration was confined, till he was over fifty, to normal characters, which, to be fair, is a very wide field. But for Scott from the first the abnormal mind was as easy to decipher as the normal, and excited more sympathy than satire or contempt. He held the balance even between Mause, Claverton, Morton and Balfour. What little satire there is does not prelude respect. One could maintain, certainly, that old Mrs. Maclure, the blind woman who waits at the crossroads to direct the fleeing remnant of the faithful is intended to be the moral touchstone of the book. If so, Scott's ideal is summed up by Tolstoy's description of Princess Mary. " What had she to do with the justice or injustice of other people? She had to endure and love, and that she did." But Mrs. Maclure is only a very minor character, and if she is the ideal by comparison with which the other characters are satirised, satire is only a small part of Scott's purpose. The interplay or religious and political ideas is what fascinates him. In *The Warden* the conflicting ideas exist mainly to exercise an old man's conscience, which is the main subject of the story. And as he shows us the innocence of the man who is so cruelly tormented, satire against the two extreme and rigid ideas becomes very marked. Compared with Scott, Trollope in 1855 seems limited in his sympathies, not because he condemns extremism, but because he does not sufficiently comprehend before he condemns.

3. *Property and Rank*

PROPERTY WAS a subject, in Trollope's time, about which most people felt deeply and thought little; and in his books more is assumed than stated about it.

From the opening chapter of *Dr. Thorne* we learn that the landed powers in Barsetshire are supreme, except in Barchester itself, where the Palace and the Close form " a clerical aristocracy, which is certainly not without its due weight." Trollope was convinced that for all its industry and commerce, England was still the most feudal country in the world.

People to-day are familiar with the idea that property may bring in a very small return, and that its very existence may be threatened. But it is certainly assumed that when the landowner has fought off the demands of the Inland Revenue and submitted to the sufferings of the Rent Restriction Act he is free to do what he likes with what is left. This is not the view of Trollope's characters.

An interesting example of this can be found in *Ralph the Heir*. The plot of this book turns on the fact that the owner of an entailed property has both a natural heir (an illegitimate son) and a legal heir (a nephew). All the old man's ambition aims at remedying the wrong done to his dearly-loved son. But it is hardly suggested throughout the book, certainly not as anyone's considered opinion, that the existence of the entail is a hardship either to father or son. More than this, when the squire attempts to buy the right of succession for his son from his legal heir, Mrs. Brownlow, who represents conventional unreflecting opinion, says, " ' I

38

think it very shocking and very wrong. Such a fine estate, too!'"
It would be easy to misunderstand her objection. It is not
primarily disgust at immorality and illegitimacy. It is an unreasoning sense of outrage that the inheritance of a fine estate can
be affected by bargaining. She feels that the law is being slighted
even by the fairest financial transaction.

Even the young man himself, who hopes to benefit by his
father's bargain, has misgivings. He says to himself that landed
property in England does not belong exclusively to the owner, and
that it would be more consistent with the English order of things
that his cousin should inherit the estate. The squire himself, in
his love for his son, and eagerness to put right at least part of the
harm done by the sins of his youth, alone professes no doubts, but
his continued assertion that if his nephew has anything to sell he
has as much right to buy it as anyone else, has always a trace of
uneasiness about it.

The seriousness of the duties of property is best seen in the
conduct of a man like the old Duke of Omnium. For he is great
enough to neglect them with impunity if he chooses, too selfish to
care about the effects of his actions and omissions on other people,
and too idle to perform his duties simply as a remedy for boredom.
But even he is not a completely free man. He feels obliged to
subscribe to the East Barsetshire Hunt, though he himself only
hunts in Leicestershire. He keeps an agent in order, among other
things, to "do popularity" for him, and he gives an annual
dinner for the local clergy and gentry—none of whom he knows
or wishes to know. All this is not much, but it represents the
absolute minimum that a great lord and landowner felt obliged
to do.

All this is the background for the comedy of *The American
Senator*. The senator himself is Trollope's device for showing us
the conventions of English country life as they might appear to a
visitor from another planet. But the humour is double-edged.
The conventions are shown to be absurd because they are
illogical. The senator's contempt for them is absurd, because he
sees the letter only and not the spirit. He discovers, for instance,

that Captain Glomax works hard at his job as M.F.H., that he receives a subscription of £2,000 a year, but is still out of pocket without being by any means a rich man. " ' If he could make a living out of it, I should respect him,' " says the senator. Similarly he is very indignant at the prejudice against defending one's own property by shooting foxes or by refusing to allow hunting over one's land. The senator, in fact, like any theoretical visitor to a new country, considers the rights and duties of the inhabitants absolute. He holds property sacred and cannot see why anyone should work hard and voluntarily for certain financial loss. But the point of the contrast between the senator and the English characters is that the latter do not consider rights and duties absolute. Property owners have a duty to submit to financial loss for the upkeep of foxhunting. The point is reinforced by other incidents in the book; by old Mrs. Norton who saves her money to redeem the property of her family, though both the responsibility for the past embarrassment and the gain at the future restoration belong to people for whom, personally, she does not care at all. Similarly John Norton, when it is suggested to him that he should leave his property out of the strict male line (which on personal grounds he has every temptation to do), simply says, " ' How could I die in peace were I to rob him? ' " Even the attorney, who normally obeys instructions without question, does not think that he could bring himself to take instructions from a dying man to alienate the property from the proper heir, and this proper heir is no son or brother, but a cousin who has also been something of an enemy.

Even the passionate anger at the killing of a fox is, from one point of view, just a symptom of something which Trollope saw clearly and made some of his characters dimly feel—that if everyone insisted on his legal rights the whole system of rural life, as then organised, must break down. By bringing the honest and ignorant senator into the midst of these subtleties Trollope shows us at once both the haziness and brittleness of the conventions of property and the inadequacy of the outsider's clear-cut argument and distinctions to deal with such complicated questions.

The crucial question which the senator asks about it all is this: Are these conventions imposed on the poor by the rich, or are they agreed in common? It puzzles him that when there are apparently strong grounds for rebellion " there is no backbone of mutiny in them against the oppression to which they are subjected." But Trollope shows us how mixed and muddled are people's feelings on points like these. At one moment people are talking about the " murdering of foxes," at another, " in Rufford there were not a few who thought that Lord Rufford's pheasants and foxes were a nuisance—though probably these persons had never suffered in any way themselves. It was a grand thing to fight a lord . . ." The character chosen to illustrate the general feeling about sporting conventions in all its muddle-headedness and indecision is Larry Twentyman, who owns a bit of property, but is not a " gentleman." A small landowner named Goarly has made an exorbitant claim against Lord Rufford on account of the damage done by pheasants to his crops. Twentyman feels some resentment against Lord Rufford because he has never been invited to shoot on his land. But as a sporting man he feels he ought to stand by the sporting interests; and has a dim idea that if he always sides with the gentry they may accept him as one of themselves. Goarly, the dastard who has murdered a fox, has equally confused ideas. He is intensely proud of his position as an owner of land, and also of being a rebel against the accepted right of property.

All through the novels a distinction is drawn between the squirearchy and the aristocracy proper, usually very much to the disadvantage of the latter. Perhaps Trollope himself had a little of the feeling that it is a grand thing to fight a lord, but he felt too, that the squires were better-rooted and more sociable and therefore more public-spirited in their outlook. Of Mr. Sowerby of Chaldicotes, though himself a worthless man, we are told that his " ancestors had been known in that county longer, the farmers around would boast, than those of any other landowner in it, unless it be the Thornes of Ullathorne, or perhaps the Greshams of Greshamsbury [both untitled], much longer than the De Courcys of Courcy Castle. As for the Duke of Omnium, he, comparatively speaking, was a new man." It is noticeable, too, that while the squires are usually high Tories, the lords are often Liberals, or sometimes altogether indifferent to politics.

Of course there are exceptions to all this—Trollope would never have allowed a whole class of people to be labelled bad or good. There is Lord de Guest, for instance. But when Mr. Dale speaks of the Dales as ever constant, one feels that the squires have a secret that the aristocracy have lost or never possessed; lords are restless, ambitious, or disinclined to stay at home. Lord De Courcy and his eldest son, Porlock, hate each other " as only such fathers and such sons can hate." Porlock himself has a peculiarly aristocratic insolence that no other class could copy.

" ' So your sister is going to be married? ' said Mr. Pallister.

" ' Yes, one has no right to be surprised at anything they do, when one remembers the life their father leads them.'

" ' I was going to congratulate you.'

" ' Don't do that.'

" ' I met him at Courcy, and rather liked him.'

" ' Did you? ' said Lord Porlock. ' For the poor girl's sake I hope he's not a ruffian. How any man should propose to my father to marry a daughter out of his house is more than I can understand. How was my mother looking? '

" ' I didn't see anything amiss with her.'

" ' I expect that he'll murder her some day.' "

Trollope does not neglect to show us the failings of the squires, but he shows them as closely allied to their virtues. Mr. Thorne of Ullathorne, for instance, is so deeply rooted in the soil as to live in a world of his own, dreaming of his ancient blood, armed at all points against the nineteenth century. But he and his sister really believe, do really follow their fantastic code. They are kind to their dependants and tenants. For them the feudal spirit works both ways. In Miss Thorne's eyes, the fact that an illegitimate girl suddenly becomes a great heiress cannot make it right that she should marry the son of the penniless Mr. Gresham, heir of an ancient family. The De Courcys talk about blood too—and in a much more hysterical way. The proposed marriage of Frank Gresham is described as " diluting the best blood of the country and paving the way for revolution." But they are always prepared to capitulate for a price. The penniless and illegitimate Mary Thorne at once becomes " dear Mary " to Lady Arabella when she is suddenly found to be rich. The De Courcys talk about blood in the loud uneasy manner of those who doubt the strength of their case. Nothing can shake the quiet confidence of Mr. Thorne.

It should be noted, however, that even in the eyes of its most ardent champions, rank is never a clear-cut thing. Even Miss Thorne has worries and doubts in deciding where the salt shall be placed for her garden party. As we shall see, this is a symptom of a general confusion. Trollope's aristocracy and squirearchy, whether or not they are happy, do not on the whole question their position in society. The acceptance of an unspoken tradition prevents them from having any views on the effects of wealth. We must go to his *nouveaux riches* if we want to find his own ambivalent attitude to the subject reflected. The most striking remark on the subject is that of the alcoholic railway magnate and former labourer, Sir Roger Scatcherd. " ' When a man has made three hundred thousand pounds, there's nothing left for him but to die.' "

Miss Dunstable and Archdeacon Grantly are two other interesting *nouveaux riches*. Miss Dunstable's position is painful. She is a woman of considerable natural gifts, which are not merely stated, but conveyed to the reader by her talk and behaviour. But her great wealth prevents anyone from recognising them. Her position is comparable to that of the brilliant young politician who might have become Prime Minister if his father's death had not forced him into the House of Lords. And it is worse than this, for a long line of suitors who do not care twopence for her makes her cynical and inclined to doubt whether disinterested love is possible. So the scene in which she tries to prevent Frank Gresham from making an insincere proposal is a poignant one. She actually begs him to say that he does not care for her, and longs for a speech which any other woman would regard as an insult. " Give me one just man," she says in effect, " one who will not invent false feelings, and I will continue to believe in the possibility of virtue and the reality of happiness." For she sees that Frank has only been contaminated and not, like the others, depraved by the desire for a rich marriage. Miss Dunstable is the chosen satiriser of wealth because she possesses it, sees through it, and is herself the focus of the insincerities it leads to. But in *Framley Parsonage* it almost corrupts her, too, as she makes her uneasy attempt to become a great London hostess, though she knows it is not worth-while. This satire on wealth is in a way more effective than the well-worn contrast between rich and poor. For Trollope shows that Miss Dunstable's wealth leads to " nonsense," to words (from her suitors and flatterers) that mean nothing. And no one has ever hated the meaningless more than he did.

It may seem surprising to include Dr. Grantly in the same category as Miss Dunstable. After all, he was the son of a bishop. But the point is that he is trying to set himself up as a large landed proprietor. This, more than anything else, is responsible for his attitude to his son's second marriage. He has an intense conviction that the life of a squire in England is a good life, and it infuriates him to think that a son of his could desire any other in preference to it. Trollope shows us the real basis of what seems like simple snobbery and the normal desire of parents to interfere at every turn with their children, for the father's anger is quickly trans-ferred from its apparent to its real object. The son has decided that if deprived of his usual income from his father he must sell his own house and property, Cosby Lodge. " ' Look here,' says the archdeacon, ' as sure as ever an auctioneer's hammer is raised at Cosby Lodge, I will alter the settlement of the property.' " Mrs. Grantly, anxious to make peace between her husband and her son, gives the latter this wise advice, " ' Say something to your father about the property after dinner.' " It is not really the proposed marriage which is the trouble, but his son's apparent disinclination to be a real country gentleman—what the arch-deacon has only half-successfully tried to be himself. Finally, the great scene of the Plumstead foxes, too subtle to be briefly explained, rounds off the subject. The archdeacon is reconciled to his son because he discovers that his son has at least on one point, and that the most important of all—foxes—the proper instincts of a country gentleman.

But what for Trollope is the moral effect of possessing property? Let us start with the typical examples and move towards the more eccentric. This means starting with Frank Gresham. Here, perhaps, is what Arnold meant when he spoke of the barbarians. Frank is shy, proud, sensible, rambling in speech and illogical in thought, thoroughly matter-of-fact, and terrified of cleverness and solemnity. But his outstanding trait is complete honesty. Consider the unanswerable way in which he quells Mary Thorne's incipient jealousy.

" ' I thought she was always a particular friend of yours.'

" ' What! Who? Miss Oriel. So she is! I like her amazingly. So does Beatrice [his sister].' "

The cleverness of this reply is unconscious, its honesty is somehow impossible to doubt.

Lord De Guest, one of Trollope's most amusing aristocrats, is a model of rural solidity. We see him mainly in the company of his diffident young friend, John Eames. This is the sort of contrast which Trollope reveals with expert skill. " ' Cold pheasant for breakfast,' says the Earl, ' is the best thing I know of. Pheasants at dinner are rubbish—mere rubbish.' " Here is the description of John on his way home after leaving Lord De Guest.

" For some reason, which he could not define, he felt better after his interview with the earl. There had been something about the fat, good-natured, sensible old man which had cheered him, in spite of his sorrow. ' Pheasants for dinner are rubbish, mere rubbish,' he said to himself, over and over again, as he went along the road; and they were the first words which he spoke to his mother after entering the house."

This is the sort of simple-looking passage which might well be pondered by anyone who considers Trollope superficial. Could there be a better or more life-like way of conveying the diffident man's instinctive recognition of a man who has never doubted anything in his life? And no doubt Trollope himself, ever full of self-questionings, felt that there, if they chose to avail themselves of it, was the precious hereditary gift of the aristocrat and the countryman.

But in the plot and especially the ending of *Dr. Thorne* we see the reverse of the medal. In a way it is an ordinary happy ending, with the right people coming into money and getting married. From another point of view it is a gloomy one. For the De Courcys are apparently confirmed by events in the worship of Mammon. They never appreciate Mary Thorne, only her fortuitous inheritance. Though Trollope leaves us in no doubt of his satirical intentions, he allows them to persist in their error to the end—an unusual proceeding in a Victorian novel. Their view, of life, he seems to suggest, is so wrong at every point that every new fact will fit comfortably into it.

Another of the possible effects of property on character can be seen in the business dealings of the old Duke of Omnium with Mr. Sowerby, who, by his extravagance, has gradually mortgaged the whole of his estate into the Duke's power. The Duke, of course, takes no part in the negotiations. In fact, Trollope has managed most successfully to give an impression of the Duke as a silent and invisible " king behind the curtain." No direct statements are made, even by his representative. " Tidings had reached him [Sowerby] . . . that the duke would be glad to have matters arranged; and Mr. Sowerby well knew the meaning of that message."

The Duke is a man who disdains the sources of his own greatness and is the exact opposite of Lord De Guest whose head is full of farming matters. It is the Duke's reticence that is so imposing and so irritating, and as Chesterton observed in connection with the Court of Chancery in *Bleak House*, " Silence is the unanswerable repartee."

The final subjection of all other considerations to rank is found in the wandering and pathetic old Marchioness of Brotherton in *Is He Popenjoy?* Her eldest son, the head of the family, can do no wrong in her eyes, and however justified all her other children are in opposing him, she cannot see it. The story turns on whether the Marquis's son is legitimate and therefore entitled to be called Lord Popenjoy and considered as the heir to the estates.

" ' Are we to call him Popenjoy? ' she asked, with a gurgling voice from amidst the bedclothes. . . . ' Certainly we must,' said Lady Sarah authoritatively, ' unless the marriage should be disproved.'

" ' Poor dear little thing,' said the Marchioness, beginning to feel some pity for the odious stranger as soon as she was told that he really was *to be called Popenjoy.*' "

In this old woman's vagaries are to be found Trollope's judgment on the dangers of respect for rank as a corrupter of intellect and morals.

It would be a mistake to try to detect any political ideas in Trollope's satire on rank and wealth. Mr. Stephen Spender in his interesting remarks on Henry James in *The Destructive Element* has involuntarily shown how tempting it is for the modern mind to interpret the morality of the past in terms of the politics of the present. Trollope and James both saw " black and merciless things behind great possessions," but it was not political evils which they saw. Trollope's satire on wealth has far more in common with Spenser's cave of Mammon than with the political slogan of fair shares; he is concerned with the mental and moral emptiness which follows the acquisition of fortunes, or accompanies the pride of rank.

But these preoccupations seem very inconsistent with his economic individualism. All through the Autobiography and in the personal obiter dicta in the novels, he praises the acquisitive instinct and asserts that civilisation can only be based on men's natural desire to make money. It is true that there is often something uneasy about these assertions; they are made with the vehemence of a man answering an imaginary opponent, but usually the opponent is not allowed to put his case. He does not fully face the contradiction between his theory about the acquisitive instinct and his vision of the evils of wealth. The first was the sincere but superficially held opinion of a man who had studied the subject a little but not deeply, and shared the slightly unreal optimism of contemporary theorists. The second sprang from a profound unreflective intuition fortified by observation and experience.

The conflict between the two can be seen in the ending of *Dr. Thorne*, when Mary Thorne unexpectedly inherits a huge fortune. Her uncle says, " ' Yes, Mary; it is all your own now. To do as you like best with it all—all. May God in His mercy enable you to bear the burden, and lighten for you the temptation.' "

Trollope has been justly admired for his freedom from sentimentality. But here sentimentality has for a moment conquered not only Dr. Thorne, but Trollope himself. The words are unreal —they do not mean what they say, and there is nothing to suggest that Trollope was aware of this himself. This unusual lapse is no accident.

Mr. Humphry House has pointed out that the death scenes in Dickens are sentimental because Dickens's humanitarian religion was unable either to accept or to reject the Christian idea of immortality, and so was very ill-equipped to cope with the thought of death. This passage, written by a man naturally far less sentimental than Dickens, indicates a similar failing. Trollope's religion cannot cope with the idea of wealth; and the imaginary opponent to Trollope's economic individualism would speak, if allowed, with the voice not of Marx or of Chartism, but of the gospels.

Perhaps the concealed conflict in his mind comes into the open here because of the nature of the traditional Victorian plot. (Trollope borrowed the plot of his story from his brother and so it is much more typical of the time than most of his plots). The Victorian novel, for all its maturity, kept an element of fairy-tale, as everyone has noticed who has read about the final destiny of Mr. Micawber. A fortune for the heroine is an accepted way of rounding off a story. Normally, this device has no more in common with a serious discussion of wealth than the equally traditional wedding bells in the last chapter have with the work of the Marriage Guidance Council. But Trollope tried at the last moment to treat a device of plot as a moral problem and so fell heavily between two stools.

The only deliberate and detailed discussion of the conflict occurs in *Mr. Scarborough's Family*. The chief character is a landowner who ignores entails and settlements, saying that " Taxation is robbery and rent is robbery." Everything Mr. Scarborough does is dishonest as the word is usually understood, but he considers himself perfectly honest and seems to have as good a case as any of his opponents, who uphold the sanctity of property and inheritance. Usually Trollope arbitrates between his characters and judges them; on most moral issues there is no doubt where he stands. But he seems powerless to condemn Mr. Scarborough, even when he lies, though lying is a vice for which he had the greatest contempt. It is as if the contradiction in his mind, so long concealed, had at last come into the open shortly before his death, and the strange character of Mr. Scarborough, half-angel and half-demon, was the result. If so, intellectual confusion brought forth artistic power. But this, one of his finest novels, gives no solution to the problems which it raises. It could not, because its author did not know the solution, or rather he knew two, one derived from religion, one from political economy, and he could not reconcile them. *Mr. Scarborough's Family* was a challenge to accepted ideas, but it was also a challenge to one half of the author's mind.

There is a paradox also in his treatment of rank; harmony between observation and theory fails once again. He was very acute at detecting slight social differences. To most novelists a lord is just a lord, but for Trollope there is a clear sociological distinction between an Independent Whig like the Duke of Omnium, and a court Whig like Earl de Courcy. There are several class divisions among the clergy, and at least two or three among the doctors. But his theory about class distinctions is as vague as his description of it is exact. Those of his characters who think about such things have an ill-defined feeling that class distinctions are growing less rigid. It does not make any difference only being a bootmaker now, as one of them says. Miss Dunstable, who is not a " lady " is courted by the aristocracy. But it is also often assumed, for instance, by all the English characters in the Anglo-Irish story *An Eye for an Eye* that differences of rank benefit all classes and society as a whole. To maintain the purity of your class status especially in the choice of a wife is a duty to society as well as to your family and yourself.

But Trollope, and here he is typical of most Victorian novelists, can satirise snobbery and assert the inevitability of class distinctions at the same time. He carries on an endless discussion about rank in which the terms are never defined and no conclusion is possible; he always refuses, when it comes to the point, to say what a gentleman is. He appeals to the understanding of his readers, who were no doubt as confused as himself on the subject. When, at the end of *The Last Chronicle*, Archdeacon Grantly has at last consented to a marriage between his son and Mr. Crawley's daughter, he brushes aside Crawley's references to differences of wealth and position with the air of a man enunciating an incontrovertible proposition of Euclid. " ' We stand,' " he says, " ' on the only perfect level on which such men can meet each other. We are both gentlemen.' " But what does this mean? That they are both clergymen? That they both learned Latin and Greek in their youth? That their fathers were gentlemen? None of these things. It is a purely emotional speech, which the archdeacon would never have made if Crawley's daughter had not charmed him. It is politeness masquerading as sociology.

The word " Gentleman " was useful for middle-class propaganda, because it could be used to include the professional classes in the same category as the peerage, and to distinguish both from the bricklayer. The mid-Victorian professional man still had enough feeling of inferiority to the aristocracy to feel the need for a loud assertion of equality. Some of Trollope's references to this have a surprising ring to-day. It is odd to hear that the average professional man regarded the army as a " hotbed of aristocratic insolence."

Sometimes, however, " gentleman " is used to connote a moral standard, and thus the title is denied to Sowerby, a hereditary landowner. Sometimes it is used in such a way that no meaning can be attached to it at all. Trollope's vague personal thoughts about rank can be summarised thus: class distinctions were necessary, but they were becoming less obvious; this was, no doubt, a good thing, but it did make the whole subject very confusing.

4. Father and Son

AT BEST the relation of father and son in Trollope is subtly out of tune; sometimes it is a flagrant violation of all decency. The rich have the worst troubles; property, inheritance, and entail make a burden too heavy for natural affection to bear. Not that the protagonists generally realise this. For the aristocracy at least, processes of inheritance are too much a part of the natural order to be suspected of influencing natural feelings. It takes a foreigner like Madame Goesler to point out that " it all comes from entail and primogeniture," but little notice is taken of her remark. For her hearers do not feel that quarrels between father and son require to be explained. They are a tradition. Roger Scatcherd, a former stonemason who has attained great wealth, may wonder how he can prevent his son from drinking himself to death when he comes into the money. He is troubled in foreseeing all the possible effects of a large unearned income on a weak character. But the aristocratic fear is that the son may ruin the property, not the property the son.

It seems natural for eldest sons to be in debt. Either law or custom makes them confident that their inheritance will not be alienated. Their present income is often small compared to their expectations, and, apart from an occasional young politician, they are debarred from regular work. The present owners of entailed estates, on the other hand, feel caged with restrictions. Brooding long hours in their studies, they reflect upon the fortunate position of their heirs, who can spend their time in idleness and wait for

52

an ample and inevitable fortune. Even the traditional comfort of the rich in old age is absent; they cannot make anyone dance attendance in hope or fear about the will. Or if they have the legal power to do this, all but the most emancipated would feel disgraced if they so ignored national and family traditions.

The reflections of Lord Trowbridge illustrate a feeling which is seldom explicit but frequently present and influential. " To the mind of the Marquis the heir expectant of all the dignities of the House of Stowte was almost a greater man than the owner of them; and this feeling came not only from a consciousness on the part of the father that his son was a bigger man than himself, cleverer, better versed in the affairs of the world, and more thought of by those around them, but also to a certain extent from an idea that he who would have all these grand things thirty or perhaps even fifty years hence, must be more powerful than one with whom their possession would come to an end probably after the lapse of eight or ten years. His heir was to him almost divine." No one can realise imaginatively what all must know— that the sons also in due time will be confronted with heirs and will probably feel the same sense of inferiority.

It is significant of Trollope's pre-occupations that even when sons are so placed that they have no worries about the inheritance, interested motives still intervene in their thoughts about their fathers. Archdeacon Grantly, kneeling at the bedside of a much-loved and dying father, cannot help speculating whether he himself may succeed to the bishopric and is driven half to hope for his father's death. In this and other cases, selfish and unfilial emotions seem to come involuntarily only to distress the person who feels them. If economic facts or wickedness will not set father against son, fate will take a hand. It is not very probable that a son should hope to succeed his father as bishop. As with Hardy, improbability of plot is revealing about the author's mind.

How much greater are the possibilities of sorrow than of pleasure we see from the relationship between Lord Brentford and his son Chiltern. Brentford is in many ways typical of the Trollopian father; he has a special and unwonted pompous tone for speaking to his son—it is part of the family inheritance, it might seem. Chiltern on the other hand, has inherited a strangely disproportionate terror of being addressed in this way. He even lays plans to take his father by surprise after a quarrel and so escape with only an unprepared and incoherent speech of reconciliation from him. Sons, too, have a special tone in reserve for their fathers. Ordinarily, Chiltern is passionate, angry, affectionate, and given to wild exaggeration, but to his father he writes : " ' For myself, I can only say that, should you desire me to come, I will do so on receiving your assurance that I shall be treated neither with fatted calves nor with reproaches. I am not aware that I have deserved either.

I am, my lord, yours affect.,

CHILTERN ' "

But when all is at last well between the two they cannot express themselves, or even take much pleasure in peace. They are only fully real and important to each other when they are quarrelling. Onlookers know at once that a reconciliation has taken place when the polished phrases give way to uneasy facetiousness. " ' Chiltern kept me standing about,' " says the Earl apologising for lateness, " ' till the east wind had chilled me through and through. The only charm I recognise in youth is that it is impervious to the east wind.' " Anger between them can be magnificent or terrible, but their accord is petty.

The clearest commentary on this mutual antagonism, with its hidden causes and often unexpressed sentiments, is to be found in *Ralph the Heir*. Here the squire's son is illegitimate, and, owing to entail, his nephew is the heir. The normal emotions about inheritance are reversed, and the contrast reveals both sets of feelings more clearly.

The usual grudge which the father feels towards the son as the beneficiary of his death is here turned by Squire Newton against himself. Though he would admit the purely moral guilt of his former brief and irregular union, he feels this guilt exclusively as

54

being an injury to his son. That the boy is illegitimate is a minor matter, for the popularity of the family has induced neighbours and tenants to ignore the fact. But his enforced disinheritance causes the father remorse at every hour of the day. When the hated legal heir runs into heavy debt and so gives the squire an opportunity to buy the reversion of the property, he is over-joyed, imagining that all past realities can be obliterated for himself and for his son by the permanent possession of English earth.

When it seems that the purchase cannot be completed, this exchange takes place between father and son:

" ' One would suppose I was thinking only of myself to hear you talk.'

" ' I know what you're thinking of and I know how much I owe you.'

" ' I sometimes think that you ought to curse me.' "

Ralph cannot bring himself to take the same interest in his possible inheritance as his father does. He has grown up in the consciousness of the fact which will govern his future, and one does not resent first principles. He is never angry with his father, only anxious to allay his self-reproaches. But here begins a vicious circle, opposite to that which spoils the comfort of other families, but equally damaging. When the son is legitimate and the unquestioned heir, the father asks himself questions like these: " Does he know how lucky he is? Does he realise the greatness of his future responsibilities? Is he perhaps wishing for my death? " The son, hurt by these suspicions, increases his opposi-tion to his father, and so further encourages his distrust. But with the Newtons it works otherwise. The father in his remorse at having injured his son, becomes obsessed with the thought of the lost inheritance. The son, anxious to be kind to his father, always minimises its importance when he speaks of it. The father is displeased at what he considers the son's mistaken values, and driven to further self-reproach by the son's charity. So their common desire to be generous drives them farther apart. So in their different ways the two recurring dialogues of father and legitimate son, and of father and illegitimate son end in silence and bitter reflections.

Even when it seems that the reversion of the Newton property can be definitely bought, father and son are not entirely united. When the squire says, " ' Ralph, for the first time in my life I can look you in the face, and not feel a pang of remorse,' " the son feels that this joy is disproportionate. He reflects that it would be more consistent with the English order of things that his cousin should inherit; he feels that names cannot be bought.

A modification in some ways similar occurs when a father's early death has left a son facing a vigorous mother over the barrier of hereditary property. Lady Lufton is regarded by everybody as the ruling spirit of Framley, and is treated by her son (who is a peer, no longer in his first youth, and the owner of the house in which she lives) with a respect which fathers never receive. Both realise, however, that he is the stronger; she is interfering because she recognises his strength, he is generally submissive because he knows he can prevail whenever he is determined. Their financial dealings form a neat contrast with those of angry father and spendthrift heir. Lord Lufton is much richer than his mother, but his extravagance leads him into trouble. His mother is then pleased and proud to come forward with the offer of her carefully husbanded little fortune. Why? Because it is an act of generosity which must win gratitude, while a father who gives a son what would one day be his own in any case, fears ingratitude and perhaps sees passing over him the shadow of the tomb.

When the parson's sister, in her feeling of social inferiority, refuses to marry Lord Lufton without his mother's consent, she unwittingly chooses the only method of winning the old lady to her side. For Lady Lufton's real objection to the marriage is due to the impotent realisation that her son is willing to disregard her wishes. Then a penniless middle-class girl does what no one else could do—places Lord Lufton's destiny once again firmly into his mother's hands. Gratitude for this benefit immediately reconciles Lady Lufton to the marriage. As in her money dealings with her son, she wants power for herself, but the fruits of power for him only.

We are told that Lord De Courcy and his eldest son, Lord Porlock, hate each other " as only such fathers and such sons can hate." What is the fundamental difference between such fathers and sons and humbler ones? Trollope saw family relationships as a series of immeasurable and unpayable debts. At best father and son would have a sense of mingled duty and gratitude, so that any failure of affection would lead to a mild remorse and so to new affection. But landed property alters all that; rights and duties tend to become definite and therefore limited. Lord De Courcy pays his son a large income and is furious at receiving no gratitude. But Porlock's expectations have been crystallised into a legal agreement, and he feels no gratitude at receiving his legal due. When it is delayed he threatens a lawsuit. Similarly John Caldigate is cast from his father's favour for debt. In any other social grade a son would be readily forgiven for debts that his father could well afford to pay. But the determining factor here is the father's hatred of entails. If the law did not compel him to leave his property to his son, his son's debts would not deter him from doing it. But the thought of the entail magnifies the son's fault and turns a small difference into an estrangement.

The obverse of all this is seen in the case of the Greshams. A squire of broad acres has incurred such debts as to leave his son with no prospects. Feeling that he owes his son more than he can ever perform he is stirred to unusual tenderness and cannot oppose with any determination his apparently disastrous marriage. The son, grieved by his father's remorse, does not attempt to exercise an heir's rights, and refrains from reproaches. A lasting irremediable injury is needed to generate affection in these law-ridden families.

Generally the characters are unaware of these influences. The reader hears them burrowing in the earth all the while, and at rare moments of illumination the protagonists catch a glimpse of them. " ' I have only to measure the price,' " says Archdeacon Grantly's son when threatened with disinheritance because of his proposed marriage. Momentarily he realises how much more powerful would have been an appeal backed by no such sanction. The archdeacon himself, when explaining his objections to his son's betrothed, is at a loss. "'I do not know whether you are aware that my son is dependent upon me for the greater part of his income. It is so, and as I am so circumstanced with my son, of course I feel the closest possible concern in his future prospects.' The archdeacon did not know how to explain clearly why the fact of his making a son an annual allowance should give him a warmer interest in his son's affairs than he might have had had the major been altogether independent of him." Such a principle can be acted upon but can hardly be stated; if it were it might dissolve in the sunlight. But even such an indirect and partial expression of the principle as this helps the archdeacon to become more reasonable. The suffocation of filial and parental feeling by law and property is always relieved by any open expression of the latters' claims. But unmentioned, unperceived even, these claims can be deadly.

Everywhere in the social scale fathers tend to get the worst of all battles. Not that there is any open war of the generations. Neither side is conscious of fighting for one period against another, or for reaction or progress. Their assumptions are generally the same, and quarrels often spring from too strong a hereditary likeness. In one only of the numerous conflicts does the spirit of the age appear to take a hand, and this exception well illustrates the rule. In *Marion Fay* Lord Kingsbury, a radical free-thinking magnate, always confident in his principles, is driven to his first self-questionings by his son's determined agnosticism. "'It irks me sometimes,'" he says to his son, "'to think that I should have trained you to ideas which you have taken up too violently.'" The son, in fact, is too great a family traditionalist for the father's comfort, and this is the general rule.[1] The characters think of the future only in terms of themselves and their families. Social change only touches their imagination when it is already accomplished.

[1] Even the signs of filial respect are turned into weapons of domination. When Bishop Grantly heard his son the archdeacon call him 'my Lord' "he shook in his shoes, for he knew that an evil time was coming."

The present is always an absolute, not a stage in development. However often people talk of the country having gone to the dogs it never strikes them that its present condition may be only a stage on the downward or upward road.

The helplessness of fathers and the invincibility of sons is independent of character. In an extreme case a young man of weak character turned out of his father's house without a prospect, an argument, or an excuse, can still cut a triumphant figure and leave his father's righteous anger mysteriously frustrated. The father is Dr. Stanhope, one of the Barchester clergy, who has lived in idleness for many years.

" ' Would it suit you, sir,' said the father, ' to give me some idea as to what your present intentions are? What way of living you propose to yourself ? '

" ' I'll do anything you can suggest, sir,' replied Bertie.

" ' No, I shall suggest nothing further. My time for suggesting has gone by. I have only one order to give, and that is, that you leave my house.'

" ' To-night ? ' said Bertie; and the simple tone of the question left the doctor without any adequately dignified method of reply.

" ' Papa does not quite mean to-night,' said Charlotte, ' at least I suppose not.'

" ' To-morrow perhaps,' suggested Bertie.

" ' Yes, sir, to-morrow,' said the doctor. ' You shall leave this to-morrow.'

" ' Very well, sir. Will the 4.30 p.m. train be soon enough? ' and Bertie as he asked put the finishing touch to Miss Thorne's high-heeled boots.

" ' You may go how and when and where you please, so that you leave my house to-morrow. You have disgraced me, sir; you have disgraced yourself, and me, and your sisters.'

" ' I am glad at least, sir, that I have not disgraced my mother,' said Bertie."

This is more than amusing farce. The father's anger is unreal because he feels the remorse for his son's misdeeds which will never touch their perpetrator. Heredity is strong and upbringing is strong; the strength of sons is that they never think of such things while fathers are haunted and hindered by them.

Sometimes the same result is achieved by opposite means. For Lord Cashel (*The Kellys and the O'Kellys*) regrets for the pleasant vices of his own youth intervene instead of remorse to nullify his wrath against Lord Kilcullen, his son and heir. So Kilcullen, who owes more than £6,000 for his disreputable pleasures, is able to take the lead in the interview, override his father's feeble protests and present him with an ultimatum. Lord Cashel in the end is soothing his son's anger and seizes with eager congratulations on the one bright point in the surrounding iniquity—Kilcullen has at least not raised money on post-obits.

Here, and in several other cases the difficulty lies in the idea that the young man who conducts such a trying interview with such calm intelligence could ever have done all the foolish things which made it necessary. In a writer so notable for psychological consistency, a recurrent failure to maintain it on a single subject must be significant.

On the rare occasions when fathers do get the better of their children, they owe their victory to their weakness. Alice Vavasour is left with all the duties of the home because her father is never happy unless at his club. Sir Lionel Bertram allows his barely adult son to pay his hotel bill in Jerusalem.

We have seen that unawareness of the motives that impel them contributes largely to the troubles of fathers and sons. It is hinted that this might be cured if they were given a wide enough variety of instances from which to generalise. But this too, in the end, will turn out to be a gloomy conclusion because only a stranger like Madame Goesler can gain this material simply by looking about her. What is really needed and rarely granted is personal experience of several cases. For Archdeacon Grantly his wife's father, Warden Harding, is gradually and surely likened in his mind to his own father the bishop.

The process of identification begins in *The Warden* where the warden and the bishop are old and dear friends. They plot mildly and ineffectively together to outwit the bishop's son, the real ruler of the diocese. The archdeacon, his mind wandering to his episcopal ambitions as he watches beside his father's death-bed, is driven, perhaps for the first time in his life, to remorse. But he sees reflected in the face of his father-in-law the grief he ought to feel himself, and so comes to treat him with greater tenderness than ever before. When the warden's death is approaching, the archdeacon is reminded more and more of his father because of the similar course of their last illnesses. The parallel becomes closer when Mrs. Grantly suggests a future holder of her father's benefice, which is in the archdeacon's gift. " 'I haven't thought about it,' " he replies, " ' I don't like thinking about such things while the incumbent is still living.' " He does not reflect at the time upon his own ambitious thoughts at his father's death, but a general understanding of the parallel leads him to feel once again at Mr. Harding's death this unaccustomed remorse.

The effect of all this is to give the archdeacon the illusion of the recurrence, after an interval of years, of an event that can only happen once. There are few conversions in Trollope. Few learn much from the experience of others or from their own. Coincidence and repetition here have just the opposite function to that which Proust might have given them. They indicate the irrevocability of time, and the hopelessness of the attempt to learn anything, before it is too late, by experience. A partial recovery brings into relief a deep conviction that filial understanding is impossible. For the man whom circumstances conspire to teach more than anyone else, learns how he should have treated his father only many years after his death. The stern corollary is that the majority must remain permanently unenlightened.

A brief but notable comic scene from *The Belton Estate* re-inforces the conclusion. If one always learns too late, if at all, from one's own experience, is the experience of the father handed down to the son more profitable? Here we see the result of a father's advice about marriage.

" ' Take my word for it,' continued Sir Anthony, ' that you are much better off as you are than you could be with a wife.'

" ' Do you mean to say that no man should marry? '

" ' No; I don't mean to say that. An eldest son ought to marry, so that the property may have an heir. And poor men should marry, I suppose, as they want wives to do for them. And sometimes, no doubt, a man must marry—when he has got to be very fond of a girl, and has compromised himself, and all that kind of thing. I would never advise any man to sully his honour.' As Sir Anthony said this he raised himself a little with his two sticks and spoke out in a bolder tone. The voice, however, sank again as he descended from the realms of honour to those of prudence. ' But none of these cases is yours, Fred. To be sure, you'll have the Perivale property; but that is not a family estate, and you'll be much better off by turning it into money. And in the way of comfort you can be a great deal more comfortable without a wife than you can with one. What do you want a wife for? ' . . . Sir Anthony went on again, pouring forth the words of experience. ' Of course marriage is all very well. I married rather early in life, and have always found your mother to be a most excellent woman. A better woman doesn't breathe. I'm as sure of that as I am of anything. But God bless me,—of course you can see. I can't call anything my own. I'm tied down here and I can't move. I've never got a shilling to spend, while all these lazy hounds about the place are eating me up. There isn't a clerk with a hundred a year in London that isn't better off than I am as regards ready money. And what comfort have I in a big house, and no end of gardens, and a place like this? What pleasures do I get out of it? That comes of marrying and keeping up one's name in the county respectably! What do I care for the county? D—— the county! I often wish that I'd been a younger son,—as you are.' "

How can a man take seriously advice which implies that he should never have come into existence at all? On this subject the serious and the comic merge into a quiet statement of despair. Samuel Butler's cry is louder but not sadder. Indeed, a comparison with *The Way of All Flesh* is instructive. Trollope presents us with a number of cases and lets the generalisations remain implicit. When drawn they are very wide in their scope. If social institutions such as primogeniture are partly responsible, they are so nearly permanent in English life as to seem like laws of nature. But Butler explains too much. As Mr. Pritchett says, " One is made to feel the pathos of human jealousies, hatreds and humbug. One is tricked into forgetting that they are inevitable." If the revolt against the father involves a revolt against religion, against science, and even against common sense, then the conflict may be different for the next generation. Indeed, the period setting is so powerful that one cannot imagine how the fight would have gone if Ernest's children had been allowed to take a hand. Theobald is altogether too vulnerable, and to be on the defensive would be a new experience for Ernest. Butler has shown us an intense conflict at a particular time and its power of permeating every department of thought. Trollope has placed the subject before us almost free from specifically Victorian influences.

Two associated objections might be made to the treatment of the matter as so far described. It may seem too materialistic and too true to a preconceived idea. If this impression has been given, it will be partly due of course to the generalisation inherent in all literary criticism. But apart from this, are the objections justified? Now Trollope was certainly convinced of the profound influence of money and social position on thoughts and actions. Moreover, a less usual quality—he was fascinated by the working of these influences, and seems to gaze intently at his characters in his anxiety to detect them. It is clear, for instance, that, in his eyes, the Rev. Josiah Crawley would have been a different man if his income and position in life had been comparable to his education and attainments. As a symbol of this, the whole plot of the tale of his sufferings originates in a small cheque given to him out of charity. But this does not mean that the man is utterly dominated by circumstances. He can rise above them and resist and rebuke the power and wealth of the bishop and the moral authority of Mrs. Proudie. It is not materialistic to say that the love of money is the root of all evil. Trollope (who would have found this last a very hard saying) is not materialistic either in his different but equally high appraisal of economic forces.

Nor would it be true to say that all his discussions of the question are too uniform. Take the case of *The Duke's Children*, for instance. Here, in a detailed study, the same laws are still in operation, but the results are novel. The origin of the difference lies in the unusual character of Plantagenet Palliser, Duke of Omnium. His chief ambition has been political, and so the dukedom, when he first succeeded, was a handicap and a disappointment, which forced him to give up the position of Chancellor of the Exchequer. He is very conscientious, and this, combined with his original desire to remain a commoner, has made him think always of the duties and seldom of the pleasures and advantages of rank and wealth. When his sons contract gambling debts and are sent down from the University, when the eldest opposes him in politics, when his daughter is determined to marry an " impossible " person, these peculiarities of the duke dominate his relations with them.

He is never inclined to give way through weakness, but because rank has been a burden to him, he has a suppressed sympathy with the troubles of the next generation. He desires to give way, but his sense of duty restrains him. When Silverbridge, his eldest son, is about to tell him the name of the girl he wishes to marry, he is afraid not of the disclosure, but of the possible wearisome necessity of disapproving. While still determined to prevent his daughter's marriage, he has perfect sympathy with her. " He felt as though he longed to take her in his arms and tell her, that if she were unhappy, so would he be unhappy too—to make her understand that a hard necessity had made this sorrow common to them both." His subconscious wish to throw over the sacred duties of rank leads him to care more for his children in their transgressions than ever before. An instinctive comprehension of their father's motives alters the attitude of the children also. Knowing that he does not, like other property-owners, grudge them money or the reversion of the estates, they are always anxious to please him, even if they are generally unsuccessful.

Where other fathers envy their eldest sons their inheritance, this
one envies something he himself has already lost and his son
already has—the right to sit in the House of Commons. So the
desertion by Silverbridge of the Whig principles of all the
Pallisers is the father's heaviest grief, and the son feels much more
remorse for this act of genuine principle and conviction than for
all his gambling debts. Other sons feel no remorse at supplanting
their fathers in property, because while the father is still alive, the
change has not yet occurred. But in political terms the usurpation
happens a whole generation earlier, and remorse has time to set
in on both sides. So Silverbridge can eventually say to his
brother, " ' You be a credit to the family and all that sort of thing.
Then I'll give up the borough to you. But mind you stick to the
Liberals, I've made an ass of myself.' " This is not a political
recantation—it merely marks the recognition that a father's envy
and regret outweigh any and every political consideration.
Trollope's other detailed study of the relation between father and
son, *Mr. Scarborough's Family*, shows the same laws producing yet
another completely different effect. Once again, property, inheritance, and primogeniture are the key factors, but owing to
the father's cleverness and the circumstances of his early life, he
is able to manipulate them for his own purposes and set his sons
in bewildered opposition to each other. Within the framework
of Trollope's strange, rigid, and apparently materialistic structure
of family life, character and circumstances can afford an endless
variety.

But still the questions remain—probably they are unanswerable in the last resort—why had this one formula such an un-
wearying appeal for him? Why did he see it all in terms of
property? Why is envy so strong in family life, so slight elsewhere?
On the whole, his formula worked for artistic gain. Like the
psychological formulæ of Ben Jonson or of Balzac it showed a
pathway through a large mass of facts, without doing violence to
the unexpectedness of situation and character. Was it then a
deliberate artifice on Trollope's part? Not altogether, it would
seem. Minor scenes, as in the case of Lord de Courcy and

Porlock, little connected with the book's main subject, often have a curious intensity. It is hard not to feel that the subject was a King Charles's Head for Trollope. It is in these minor scenes that we seem to catch the author off his guard, and sense the working of obsession. Perhaps in the more important scenes where art and generalisation are at work, there is still a hidden substratum of obsession. As in Mr. de la Mare's stories and poems about death, obsession and conscious art make a fruitful partnership.

5. *Religion and the Clergy*

APART FROM the extreme evangelicals, most of Trollope's clergy have little concern with religion. They are primarily men with a stake in the country, men with a recognised and honourable position based on education, property, and the habit of reverence paid to them in a conservative society.

Consider, for instance, the rector in *The Claverings* who is typical. He is the uncle of the local baronet and landowner. He has a nice country parish and a comfortable income. He is cultured and idle and keeps a somewhat ill-paid curate to do nearly all the work. But all this, of course, proves nothing. What matters is the way such a man is regarded by Trollope and by the other characters. He is described in a revealing phrase as " awake —though not widely awake to the responsibilities of his calling." So it is with many of Trollope's clergy. They are not vicious or grossly selfish. But they dream the time away in the restrained and virtuous enjoyment of pleasant surroundings. And their parishioners and friends see nothing very reprehensible, certainly nothing surprising in this.

As an example of the lengths to which secularisation could go, consider this conversation between the rector's son Harry and his cousin, the baronet's younger brother.

" ' By the by, Harry, I think you've made a mess of it in changing your line. I'd have stuck to my governor's shop if I'd been you. You'd got through all the d——d fag of it, and there's the living that has always belonged to a Clavering.'

" ' What would your brother have said if I'd asked him to give it to me? '

" ' He wouldn't have given it, of course. Nobody does give anything to anybody nowadays. Livings are a sort of thing that people buy. But you'd have got it under favourable circumstances.'

" ' The fact is, Archie, I'm not very fond of the church, as a profession.'

" ' I should have thought it easy work. Look at your father. He keeps a curate and doesn't take any trouble himself. Upon my word, if I'd known as much then as I do now, I'd have had a shy for it myself. Hugh couldn't have refused it to me.' "

One of the most interesting points in this is the gulf it sets between one clergyman and another. To "keep" a curate is like keeping a servant. This is underlined by the shocked horror shown by the rector when his curate tries to marry his daughter. For Mr. Clavering belongs as much to the squirearchy as to the clergy and regards clergymen of his own type as being distinct from all others.

But in the conversation just quoted there is an obvious element of satire alongside the truth it contains. Archie, throughout the book, is an absurd character. It seems to me that Trollope's aim was to show the implicit ugliness and inconsistency of the rector's pleasant life by letting a rough and stupid character describe it in brutal terms. If such a man as Archie approves of his uncle's way of life, does not that cast a new light on that life? Trollope was not setting up any high ideal of priestly vocation, but he was always ready to put his finger on an inconsistency between theory and practice. It is interesting to notice, too, that the rector suffers troubles of conscience and condemns himself. In these comfortable country parishes religion is not dead, only sleeping. But the clergy have very little authority and what they have is more due to their social position than to their priestly character. Mr. Smirkie, the evangelical clergyman in *John Caldigate*, eager to interfere in the affairs of the squire's family, reflects sadly that clerical interference is hardly possible except among the poor.

Lay patronage is liable to make all but the most determined vicars attentive to the wishes of the great. The Rev. Mark Robarts's escapade in going off to enjoy himself at Gatherum Castle is interesting for two reasons. Though he has some slight pangs of conscience about the neglect of his parish, his main worry is that Lady Lufton, his patroness, will disapprove. And though he is prepared to risk this temporarily, her permanent withdrawal of countenance is an idea too terrible to contemplate. Nor does this feeling appear to be inspired by a purely selfish desire to keep on the right side of rank and wealth. Robarts is not a deliberately selfish man though he can be both thoughtless and extravagant. It is as if he recognised Lady Lufton as the legitimate keeper of his conscience.

The other point about Robarts's visit interesting from this point of view is the attitude of the rest of the Duke's guests towards him. They almost contrive to ignore the fact that he is a clergyman. In every way secularisation seems to be complete. But here again we are shortly to get a surprise, when Robarts is admonished by Mr. Crawley, who for all his self-pity and bitterness is a minister of the gospel and regards Robarts's conduct as a betrayal of vocation. The appeal to religious values is like a voice from another world.

But Mr. Crawley with his poverty and his vision is far away on the fringes. Until accident brings him to the centre of the picture, his more fortunate colleagues usually contrive to forget him and his like. So the clerical life is apparently very serene. The close at Barchester is a place of long evenings of quiet contentment. When Mr. Harding dined with old Bishop Grantly, which he did every other day, it meant staying with him from three o'clock until ten. But where so many casual readers have made a mistake is in thinking that this idyllic life is regarded by Trollope as normal and safe. On the contrary, it seemed to him a survival. Perhaps he fell into the same error about the calmness of the years before he was born as we are apt to do about his time.

In the interesting collection of articles called *Clergymen of the Church of England*, he makes this comment on deans and the anomalies of their appointment. " How English, how absurd, how picturesque it all is——" Once an institution has been called picturesque its existence is seriously threatened. And we may notice that the pleasant old-fashioned clerical life only exists in the country and in the cathedral cities. Trollope has other worlds besides the Barsetshire one. One cannot imagine Mr. Harding having much to say to Melmotte of *The Way We Live Now*. In writing of Barsetshire itself he was certainly not uncritical, but what he calls " the sweet medieval flavour of old English corruption," would later seem almost laudable to him, as his vision darkened and Melmotte and his like began to grip his imagination.

In his treatment of evangelicalism, Trollope is open to a charge which does not often lie against him—the charge of prejudice. Not that he is alone in this, for several of the most eminent writers of the time erred in the same way. Consider this passage, for instance, from Thackeray's *Vanity Fair* [Chap. 33].

" A mature spinster, and having but faint ideas of marriage, her love for the blacks occupied almost all her feelings. It is to her, I believe, that we owe that beautiful poem

> Lead us to some sunny isle
> Yonder in the western deep,
> Where the skies for ever smile,
> And the blacks for ever weep, etc.

She had correspondence with clerical gentlemen in most of our East and West Indian possessions, and was secretly attached to the Rev. Silas Hornblower, who was tattooed in the South Sea Islands."

Opinions may be divided about whether this passage is amusing. What is clear, I think, is that it is a great contrast to Thackeray's normal, slow, subtle, deliberate satire. In *Vanity Fair*, Thackeray seems to set himself up as a High Court judge over human life. As a rule he conducts himself like a judge, and

Vanity Fair for a satirical work is singularly free from pettiness. But suddenly on this one subject the judge throws away his wig and gown and cocks a snook from the gutter.

Of course I am not concerned to deny that much Victorian evangelicalism was very open both to serious satire and to vulgar laughter. But what is interesting is the outraged and immoderate way in which the satire is applied. It would seem that evangelicalism had a much greater appeal to its satirists than they were prepared to admit. A normally calm man does not become wild with anger just because he sees something amusing or reprehensible. Men like Thackeray (and Trollope) saw a challenge in evangelicalism, an implied criticism of their own standards. Their tone in speaking of it is similar to that of Macaulay on the subject of monasticism. And here, perhaps, is the key of the problem. It was not any particular religious system, but asceticism in any form which was mainly responsible for this obscure irritation that so many eminent writers shared.

Thackeray and Dickens, on the whole, did not face the problem. For they assumed, generally at least, that their evangelical characters were hypocrites. As long as this is so, all is well. Feigned asceticism need be no challenge to the most worldly. But it is doubtful whether this escape from the difficulty satisfied even those who devised it. They are always contrasting the religion of their evangelical characters with some vague undefined ideal of " true " or " real " Christianity. But what this may be we are never told. By implication we are allowed to guess that it lays great stress on one or two of the moral precepts of the gospels, such as the duty of forgiveness and of generosity, to the exclusion of others. It concentrates, in fact, on those moral qualities which the ordinary good-natured man of the world usually imagines himself to possess. Beyond this they resort to the same kind of legerdemain in dealing with the nature of religion that was practised more skilfully and even more perversely by Matthew Arnold in *Literature and Dogma*. They are less precise than Matthew Arnold was because they are not as clever as he in dealing with ideas, and because it is easier in a novel than in

71

any other kind of work for a writer to evade the problems which he has raised.

Trollope was just as unfair to the evangelicals as Thackeray or Dickens, but he was more honest in facing the challenge that they made. For he was not prepared to use hypocrisy as a complete explanation. It would seem that he had three main objections to the practical working of the evangelical creed. He was indignant at the attempt to deprive people of reasonable pleasures, he disliked people who would not be reticent about their feelings, and most of all he resented the claim to guide people in every detail of their lives. There is the making of a serious case here, but usually Trollope prefers to use other methods to discredit evangelicals. Sometimes he gives them physical defects, and particularly humiliating ones. Mr. Slope has a moist, sweaty palm, Mr. Maguire in *Miss Mackenzie* a horrible squint. These things are presented in such a way that misfortune seems culpable. Often he suggests that faults of individuals can be attributed to the system. The pomposity, banality, and greed of Maguire, the unnatural feminine domination exercised by Mrs. Proudie and Mrs. Stumfold of Littlebath (in *Miss Mackenzie*), the gloomy, solitary mania of Kennedy in the political novels, all are made to cast a slur on Low Church ideas. All this is in contrast to his treatment of politics, where individual shortcomings are never made the pretext for an attack on political parties or ideas.

Two novels, *Miss Mackenzie* and *John Caldigate*, have a more Low Church setting than any of the others. The world of evangelical Littlebath is narrow to the point of claustrophobia. War is carried on against the outside world by means of spying and scandal. It is rumoured that the local High Church curate, thwarted in his desire to have candles in his church, keeps a pair on an inverted box in his bedroom. Someone has spied Lady Ruff teaching her maid picquet on a Sunday afternoon. It is a little corner of leisure, modest affluence and boredom. Religion, in spite of its severity about some kinds of amusements, is a comfortable drawing-room affair. Mr. Stumfold preaches to the converted and offers them tea and cake. Stumfold himself is drawn more convincingly than most of his kind in Victorian fiction. He pretends to be very daring.

" ' But I'm not going to have anything more to say to Peter and Paul at present,' he declared at last. ' You'd keep me here all night, and the tea will be spoilt.' Then they all laughed again at the absurd idea of this great and good man preferring his food —his food of this world—to that other food which it was his special business to dispense. There is nothing the Stumfoldian ladies of Littlebath liked so much as these little jokes which bordered on the profanity of the outer world, which made them feel themselves to be almost as funny as the sinners, and gave them a slight taste, as it were, of the pleasures of iniquity."

But the depressing thing about these gatherings is the lack of variety in the people who attend them. The clergy simply cannot find enough middle-aged spinsters with moderate incomes to join their inner circle. There is rivalry between Stumfold and his assistant, Maguire. When they quarrel and the latter threatens to set up an independent church he boasts that he will force Stumfold to leave the neighbourhood. Their competition is like that of tradesman—tradesmen in a very specialised line. There are not enough souls to go round.

But, together with all this caricature, Trollope did make one serious analysis of the evangelical mentality at its most forbidding, in the character of Mrs. Bolton in *John Caldigate*. On the whole, Trollope's contemporaries did not attempt this, and for the seriousness of his treatment and his understanding that religious ideas really can influence lives, Trollope deserves credit. Thackeray and Dickens were superficial on this subject, and Trollope is reverting, whether consciously or not, to the better tradition of Scott, and *The Confessions of a Justified Sinner*, later continued by George Eliot. A character like Mr. Chadband is not really influenced by religious ideas ; sentiment takes the place of dogma and his pious phrases are only the means by which he chooses to impose himself on the world. It is possible to imagine him remaining essentially the same and yet choosing some political nostrum or some quack medical doctrine for the purposes of his deception. All this is no disparagement of Dickens, who after all, did what he set out to do with Mr. Chadband; he created a memorable and amusing character; Trollope was aiming at something different.

Mrs. Bolton is a strict evangelical, who devotes herself to preventing her daughter Hester from marrying. In particular, she opposes the suit of John Caldigate, who has been a wild youth, wasted part of his father's fortune, gone out to Australia as a gold miner, and returned a rich man.

Trollope shows us that her fear of losing her own daughter is her dominating motive, but that at the same time her religious scruples are entirely sincere. More than that, it is religion which gives her the motive power to resist the marriage. A woman of different religious views could never be possessive in just the same way. There is a terrible passage describing her prayers at the wedding, which she attends unrecognised, refusing to take part in the celebrations. Because out of every hundred ninety-nine must perish, she dare not pray for the husband. One must restrict one's demands on God to a minimum to have any hope of being heard. But in her arguments with her daughter there lies a concealed fallacy. She says the man is bad because she believes that all human beings are corrupted by original sin. But having proved her point in this way, she begins to speak of him as if he were bad in the ordinary sense in which the world uses the word, and much worse than other people. So her daughter, who largely shares her mother's religious assumptions, scores a dialectical victory. Thus we see that Mrs. Bolton's religious ideas are not inevitably destructive in themselves, only when mixed in a certain way with personal passions. But we see at the same time that these religious principles are a temptation to surrender to the passions.

When Hester's husband is accused of having a living wife in Australia and of having made a bigamous marriage with Hester, Mrs. Bolton is triumphant. But again we are conscious of this concealed fallacy, for all men are not bigamists, not even all irreligious men. Mrs. Bolton speaks as if some such calamity were inevitable when her daughter married. In fact, her religious grounds of opposition can really be reduced to personal feeling or just to a guess that this particular marriage would turn out badly. After this accusation the Boltons try to keep their daughter away from her husband, first by persuasion, then by force. The imprisonment scene is a very powerful one. Hester refuses to go to bed, and the two women sit up all night in the hall behind the locked doors and windows. The irony of Mrs. Bolton's attitude, as her efforts to persuade Hester to abandon her husband fail, is thus described: " To Mrs. Bolton the worst of it was that this cloudiness had come upon her daughter—this incapacity to reason it out—because the love of a human being had become so strong within her bosom as to have superseded and choked the love of heavenly things." She does not realise that the very same explanation holds about her own conduct. And once again Hester is able to show that on Mrs. Bolton's own principles it is her duty to stand by her husband whatever he is accused of.

The all-night vigil is a scene that can hardly be described except at length, as Trollope has described it. One can just note how cleverly the ideas of physical cold and the spiritual arctic of the Boltons' house and religious system mingle with and reinforce each other. In the end Hester's obstinacy conquers and Mrs. Bolton's last words of defiance, when she can no longer remain awake and no longer bear her daughter's suffering, reveal at last the basis of her religious arguments.

" ' Let me go,' said Hester.

" ' I will not let you go,' said the mother, rising from her seat. ' I, too, can suffer. I, too, can endure. I will not be conquered by my own child.' There spoke the human being. That was the utterance natural to the woman."

This moment in the book is a great surprise, and yet an entirely logical one. The psychological portrait is consistent throughout.

Her reaction to the proofs of Caldigate's innocence of bigamy is characteristic: " Post-marks indeed—when her daughter's everlasting life was the matter in question." But she had not made this confusion between the importance of things used in evidence and the importance of the facts they prove when the evidence had seemed to go the other way.

The two stock types of Victorian evangelical in fiction are Mr. Chadband and Wilkie Collins's Miss Clark. The first is a hypocrite and character part, and so the author's treatment of him involves no judgment on evangelicalism as such. At the most, the inattentive reader may think that it has been slightly discredited by association, as it were. He may feel that there is something about evangelicalism which makes it a suitable mask for rogues and hypocrites, but the more thoughtful will realise at once that ideas cannot be judged by the character and conduct of those who do not sincerely hold them. Trollope's Emilius is of the same kind. Miss Clark, on the other hand, is fully identified with her religious system. Collins's pitiless exposure of her character is intended to make us think " so this is what this infamous Bible-cum-tract Protestantism brings people to."

The vast majority of evangelicals in novels of the period will fit into one of those two categories, but not Mrs. Bolton. For in her Trollope made a study of the imperceptible blending of religious and personal motives to form a harsh and rigid pattern. He does not hold her religious system responsible for her possessiveness, he only shows it as providing her with an opportunity to deceive herself about her own motives. From this point of view, her persistent illogicality is very important, for it shows how far she unconsciously strays from the tenets of a Calvinistic system which is logical above all things.

But sometimes, as in the case of Pritchett in *The Bertrams*, this mingling of motives results in simple burlesque. " ' Oh, Mr. George, we are grass of the field, just grass of the field, here to-day and gone to-morrow; flourishing in the morning and cast into the oven before night! It behoves such frail impotent creatures to look close after their interests—half a million of money! ' " As we have seen the problem suggested here, the conflict between religion and avarice was too much a personal one for Trollope to be able to analyse it calmly until near the end of his life. For once he fell back on the convenient explanation of hypocrisy, and imitated his great contemporaries by trying to drown a difficult moral problem in a sneer.

Similarly facile is the assumption, common to Dickens, Thackeray, and many lesser writers, and partly shared by Trollope, that religion is a matter of temperament. The young lady who takes to religion and good works when she is jilted occurs altogether too often in Victorian fiction. She becomes a symbol, almost an explanation, of all religion. You were an evangelical because you had been disappointed, or were naturally gloomy; you were a Catholic because you were born in Ireland, or because you were credulous and fond of ritual and submission to authority. With the important exception of George Eliot the more eminent novelists were weak in religious psychology but unwilling to leave the subject alone. They did not grasp the cardinal fact that the same religion can appeal to people of opposite temperaments.

Trollope would have maintained (as he explained at the end of *The Last Chronicle*) that specifically religious issues were out of place in fiction. But this does fully square with his practice. He tells a great deal about the religious ideas and feelings of Kennedy or Mrs. Proudie. But when in *Castle Richmond* he describes Herbert Fitzgerald kneeling down to pray at a crisis in his life, he breaks off with the words, " I will not make his words profane by repeating them here." His sense of propriety about religion operated in the same unfortunate way as the more widespread ideas of propriety about sex. The more worthy of reverence a religious attitude seemed to him, the more reluctant he was to speak of it in a mere novel. And so indifference and fanaticism are stressed; normal religious feelings and practices are passed over with a few hurried words.

As one would expect, he was even more reluctant to be precise about religious doubt. He was perfectly at home with an atheist like Brattle the miller, or an old-fashioned cynic like John

Caldigate's father. They were out of date and remote from contemporary anxieties. But he was chary of being explicit about doubts which were new and dangerous. It is surprising how little the great nineteenth-century controversies echo in Trollope's pages. Wilkie Collins could put these words into the mouth of one of his characters. " Oh, the new ideas, the new ideas, what consoling, elevating, beautiful discoveries have been made by the new ideas! We were all monkeys before we were men, and molecules, before we were monkeys! And what does it matter? And what does anything matter to anybody? "

Collins was no very intellectual writer, but evolution is seen here as obviously relevant to problems of everyday conduct—marital fidelity, for instance. Trollope's characters are apparently unaware of Darwin's existence. It is vagueness that mars *The Bertrams*. Here for once Trollope took as his main subject religious doubt and the failure of spiritual ambitions. Bertram himself, when a friend tells him of forensic triumphs, " spoke of the joy of some rustic soul saved to heaven in the quiet nook of a distant parish." His visit to the Holy Land is symbolical of his search for spiritual satisfaction. He is half-attracted and half-repelled by what he finds there, but as he watches two Greeks praying, he is filled with envy of their unquestioning faith, and realises that he cannot fully share it. The book is the story of the lure of the unattainable and of disgust at the actual.

But the book is unsatisfactory because the religious problems are never explicit. Bertram never seems to know what he is doubting or why. It seems at times as if religious doubt has become an end in itself, and the uncertainty which follows is a shield against industry or decision. There is the same self-indulgence in doubt, the same self-conscious honesty as was to be expressed some years later by Tennyson in the sonnet he wrote for the first number of *The Nineteenth Century*.

> For some, descending from the sacred peak
> Of hoar high-templed Faith, have leagued again
> Their lot with ours to rove the world about;

And some are wilder comrades, sworn to seek
If any golden harbour be for men
In seas of Death and sunless gulfs of Doubt.

Certainly an excellent novel might have been written with such a character as a hero, but not by Trollope. For to write it, it would have been necessary to detach oneself from the hero's problem, or else to identify oneself with him. Trollope could do neither. His natural melancholy made it difficult for him to devote his mind to theology, and he was not gifted with the power of analysing ideas. He felt certainty on a few points such as the existence of God and the reality of judgment, but otherwise he was perplexed and reluctant to admit his perplexity. *The Bertrams* was published between *Dr. Thorne* and *Framley Parsonage,* and so was in the middle of the Barsetshire series. Whereas in these, which deal with the externals of religion, Trollope seems to understand all his characters, Bertram's state of mind often seems a puzzle to him. He was not often vague, but if he had understood George Bertram, he would have come nearer to understanding the character that no novelist can altogether fathom —himself.

Most of Trollope's characters are incapable of connected thought on religious questions. Let us compare a passage in *The Claverings* with a very famous passage, written not very long after it, but in a very different and distant country. In the first, Sir Hugh Clavering is urging his brother to marry a rich widow who has been suspected of infidelity during her marriage. For both of them money is the real object.

" ' I don't suppose there was anything really wrong, eh? '

" ' Can't say, I'm sure,' said Sir Hugh.

" ' Because I shouldn't like——'

" ' If I were you I wouldn't trouble myself about that. Judge not, that you be not judged.'

" ' Yes, that's true, to be sure,' said Archie, and on that point he went forth satisfied."

In the other passage, Dostoevsky's Smerdyakov is maintaining

79

that it would not be a sin to renounce one's faith when threatened with martyrdom.

" ' For as soon as I say to those enemies, " No, I'm not a Christian, and I curse my true God," then at once, by God's high judgment, I become immediately and specially anathema accursed and cut off from the Holy Church, exactly as though I were a heathen, so that at that very instant not only when I say it aloud, but when I think of saying it, before a quarter of a second has passed I am cut off. . . . And if I've ceased to be a Christian, then I told no lie to the enemy when they asked whether I was a Christian . . . seeing I had already been relieved by God Himself of my Christianity by reason of the thought alone, before I had time to utter a word to the enemy.' "

At first sight both these passages seem like similar examples of the devil quoting scriptures. But the contrast in length (Smerdyakov's argument is much longer than the part quoted here) is a sign of a more important contrast. Smerdyakov is using his dialectical skill to confuse the faith of his hearers, and sees through his own sophistry. His purpose requires that his hearers shall comprehend the religious ideas which he is standing on their heads. But the passage in *The Claverings* reveals a mental vacuum. Religious ideas have disappeared leaving only a few half-remembered Biblical phrases in their place. The phrases no longer have a definite meaning, but they are on call when a sudden pang of uneasiness demands soothing. Their real meaning and implications are of no more importance than logic in a lullaby.

There is a curious and instructive scene in *Marion Fay* in which a clergyman is contemplating murder. One would have thought that this could only be explained in one of three ways. Either the man was a complete hypocrite, with no religious belief, or he was conquered by a surge of passion, or he experienced terrible mental struggles between his faith and his inclination. But the actual state of affairs is different from all these. The man quietly turns the idea of murder over in his mind, and his scruples are too vague to deserve the name of conscience. " It was as is some boggy-bo to a child, some half-belief in a spectre to a nervous woman, some dread of undefined evil to an imaginative and melancholy man." Though he seems to have no fixed beliefs, he is no hypocrite, for he has never thought seriously about his duties as a clergyman. The oddest thing of all is that all this is recorded without a trace of surprise or a suspicion of satire.

At first sight Trollope's religious world seems singularly free from Victorian anxieties. But this impression is only partly accurate. Archdeacon Grantly may be a High Churchman of the school of Samuel Johnson, rather than of Pusey; Bertram may never have heard of geology, but the Victorian anxiety about religion is there none the less. Over and over again the novels implicitly ask the question which Trollope himself asked in connection with the Colenso case, " Who would not stay behind if it were possible? " The natural corollary of this nostalgic tone is the idea that the Church of England is dying. The old religious ideas may be lovable but are they justifiable? Religion is always on the defensive; doubt is in the air, though it may never achieve intellectual formulation. Even the pleasant, opulent, idle atmosphere of the Clavering rectory is not free from unquiet dreams. Harry Clavering says to his father, the rector:

" ' The truth is, I do not feel myself qualified to be a good clergyman.'

" ' It is not that you have doubts, is it? '

" ' I might have them if I came to think much about it.' "

Unbelievers are apt to regret the pervasive influence of doubt as much as others do. Lord Hampstead, the agnostic radical aristocrat of *Marion Fay* says, " ' That is the worst of what we are apt to call advanced opinions. . . . I never dare to tamper with the religious opinions of those who are younger.' " And his companion replies, with the air of one uttering a platitude, " ' They, none of them, know what they believe, nor do you or I. Men talk of belief as though it were a settled thing. It is so but with few; and that only with those that lack imagination.' "

The word " advanced " in Hampstead's remark is a danger signal. For so many Victorian minds, obsessed with the idea of progress in a straight line, it was hardly imaginable that a process would ever be reversed. Whatever was advanced was bound to triumph; Trollope could be as nostalgic as he wished. "Who would not stay behind if it were possible?" He could not challenge the inevitable. It is sometimes forgotten how little the great Victorian doubters put forward in the way of argument. Tennyson might dabble in geology, Arnold in Biblical criticism, but their main argument, or feeling disguised as argument, was that the modern mind had begun to doubt and so must inevitably doubt more and more. T. H. Huxley could write of religious dogmas, "The modern world is slowly but surely shaking off these and other monstrous survivals of savage delusions, and whatever happens, it will not return to that wallowing in the mire." This passage illustrates the emotional, unreasoning character of much Victorian doubt and propaganda against religion. But it is important to remember that few of the doubters were aware of this. Emotional though it was, the disbelief expressed by Huxley or the doubt portrayed by W. H. White in the *Autobiography of Mark Rutherford* were not (like say, Swinburne's anti-religious outbursts) romantic expressions of defiance, careless of reason and argument. Huxley and the fictional Mark Rutherford represent emotion masquerading with the utmost sincerity as argument. Huxley, it is true, produces many serious arguments on points where religion seemed to him to trespass on the territory of science, and there he often showed himself to be a fine reasoner and controversialist. But when it comes to a specifically religious issue, he is reduced to remarks of this kind: "'And the spirit of God moved upon the face of the waters.' I have met with no form of the nebular hypothesis which involves anything analogous to this process. And he dismisses the cornerstone of all orthodox theology, the Fall of man, without any argument as 'monstrously improbable.'"

Mark Rutherford is even more revealing about Victorian doubt, because it is not a crusade against religion, but the story of loss of faith. The curious thing about the book is that, after reading it, all the detailed description still leaves one wondering how the loss of faith came about. There is very little argument, and what there is is obviously irrelevant. For instance, it is suggested that biological evolution provides an argument against the immortality of the soul, because, if all progress is from lower to higher, the lower forms are unlikely to survive. Here again we have one of the most characteristic expressions of the uncertainty of the period —an unanalysed emotion buttressed with the appearance of argument. But it is in this same book nevertheless that we find perhaps the most revealing description of the processes by which faith was lost. " It often happens that a man loses his faith without knowing it. Silently the foundation is sapped while the building stands fronting the sun, as solid to all appearance as when it was first turned out of the builder's hands, but at last it falls suddenly with a crash."

When we speak of Victorian ideas of progress and Victorian optimism, we should remember their obverse side. Evil things as well as good seemed to many as if their career must continue unchecked with the precision of Newtonian physics and the remorseless gradualness of Darwinian biology. For Huxley the decline of religion was an aspect of progress, and therefore both desirable and inevitable. To Trollope and to Tennyson and Arnold it sometimes seemed equally inevitable, and the imaginary certainty of their knowledge of the future was a source of bitter pain.

6. Death

IN HIS treatment of death Trollope is strangely unlike his contemporaries. He has no special tone in which to speak of it. It is one event in a series which may be sad, ironical, peaceful, or terrifying. The difference will be obvious if we consider, say, the death of the heroine's mother in *North and South*. The description is a different kind of writing from the chapters which surround it; it is Mrs. Gaskell's organ-music voice. Against this, take the death of Major Caneback in Trollope's *The American Senator*. The major has had a hunting accident. " The major was quite certain that it was all over with him. He had broken so many of his bones, and had his head so often cracked, that he understood his own anatomy pretty well. There he lay quiet and composed, sipping small modicums of brandy and water, and taking his outlook into such transtygian world as he had fashioned for himself in his dull imagination. If he thought then that he might have done better with his energies than devote them to dangerous horses, he never said so. His voice was weak, but it never quailed; and the only regret he expressed was that he had not changed the bit in Jemina's mouth."

Trollope goes on to describe the feelings of the other people in the house—their mild sympathy for a man none of them had known well, their fear that a ball may have to be cancelled, their wish that the man was dying anywhere else. He describes the irrational guilt felt by the owner of the horse Caneback had been riding, and the use made of the shock of the affair by a girl to increase the tempo of her intimacy with the major's host. It is the death of an average man, surrounded by people of average sensibility and sincerity. There is no sentiment and no satire. The mystery is expressed by being played down.

Trollope's death-scenes are unusual in Victorian fiction because they introduce death as something to be faced and experienced. Often, as in the passage quoted, they do this in such a calm, undramatic way that one is apt to forget how unusual this is. But if we turn to the 138th letter in *Clarissa Harlowe* we shall find the contrast neatly pointed: "'Die did you say, sir? Die! I will not, I cannot die! I know not how to die! Die, sir! And must I then die? Leave this world? I cannot bear it! And who brought you hither, sir?' (Her eyes striking fire at me): 'Who brought you hither to tell me I must die, sir? I cannot, I will not leave this world. Let others die who wish for another! Who expect a better!'"

Reading this, we are at once aware of something alien to nearly all the leading Victorian novelists. Yet Trollope, exceptionally, has preserved this tradition of looking death in the eye. As a rule, in Victorian fiction, death is a spectacle, not an experience, or even a future threat. No doubt there are exceptions to this, but the exceptions have a way of proving only apparent. For instance, we are given an insight into the thoughts of Paul Dombey as he approaches death. But just before he dies, Paul is allowed a vision of his mother who died far too soon after his birth to be remembered even vaguely. By making the unknown dead visible to the living, the moment of death is annihilated. All terrors disappear if the mystery can be brought over to this side of the gulf. Paul's last words are, "'The light about the head is shining on me as I go.'" It is customary to refer to sentimental Dickensian blank verse. But it is more to the point to notice that in these last words, the point of view shifts back to the survivors. This is an onlooker's comment, rather than the voice of the dying. The subject has become object, and in the last resort death as an experience has once again been transformed into death as a spectacle.[1]

[1] Public opinion would have regarded a death's head, suggesting future death, as morbid, but sanctioned elaborate mourning, and the concentration of attention upon deaths already past.

Dickens's method here is to suggest a mystery (by the symbolism of the waves and the river), and then at the last moment to resolve it by something very like a trick. Trollope suggests the mystery by negative means; by showing how people ignore, deny, or avoid it. Where other Victorian novelists induce the reader to identify himself with the onlookers, he preserves an impartial scrutiny of sufferer and onlookers together. Dickens portrayed death in many forms with great artistry, and runs the gamut from sentiment to necrophily, and from necrophily to horror. Nevertheless, it is paradoxically true that Dickens encourages us not to consider the nature of death, by concentrating on the deep feelings with which people gather round the dying and the dead: Trollope invites us to consider it by showing us the inadequacy and evasion of the survivors.

Consider, for instance, the death of Sir Hugh's infant son in *The Claverings*. Different as all the relatives are, they have in common the inability to face the situation. The grief-stricken mother is distracted from her grief by wondering how her hard, unsympathetic husband will take the death of his heir. The baronet's brother, who has become heir presumptive, shows his inadequacy thus: "'We are all like grass,' said Archie, 'and must be cut down in our turns.' Archie, in saying this, intended to put on his best behaviour. He was as sincere as he knew how to be." After all, what could he say? To say nothing would also have given offence. The bereaved father, in response to the consolations of his uncle the rector, says, "'My boy has gone, and I know that he will not come back to me. I shall never have another, and it is hard to bear. But, meaning no offence to you, I would sooner be left to bear it in my own way. If I were to talk about the grass as Archie did just now, it would be humbug, and I hate humbug. No offence to you. Take some wine, Uncle.'" The rector is profoundly shocked by this speech, but his own feeling about the death is no more than conventional.

Harry Clavering, the rector's son, accidentally finds himself putting on the correct funeral demeanour only because he is thinking of different troubles of his own. On the day of the funeral he has a furious quarrel with the boy's father. After calming down, he feels a natural revulsion at this incongruity. But even then his mind dwells only on the moral sordidness of the affair and not on the dead child.

They are all watching each other to find someone who will take the lead, explain the event to them in its full significance or terror or beauty. Each is vaguely disturbed by the failure of all the others, but cannot attempt to repair it. They all feel smaller after staring with unseeing eyes at a question mark. They can neither ignore it completely nor give it a value, and they are irritable and unfriendly because they have betrayed their in-adequacy to those who have shared this frustrating experience.

A difficult problem for the novelist is the death of a character who is naturally insensible to any of death's implications. In the case of Roger Scatcherd, in *Dr. Thorne*, the difficulty was overcome in a characteristically indirect method. The man has brought himself to death with drink, and impatiently rejects the admoni-tions of his friend, Dr. Thorne, and listens with polite unconcern to the parson. He is not afraid. But his son also is killing himself with drink, and the father can see his own insensibility for a moment with an objective eye, as it is mirrored in that of the son.

A more complicated case is that of Mrs. Proudie. This celebrated death has caught the imagination of readers, but has never perhaps been analysed. People have obscurely felt that it is very surprising, without being able to say why. Are not fictional characters all as mortal as real? Like the death which ends *The Turn of the Screw*, this death is surprising because it reinterprets a whole past series of events. We see at last that Mrs. Proudie's power to dominate has all the time been derived from her husband not only from his position as bishop, but also from his personality. When once he feels himself disgraced and no longer has the power to offer his usual feeble, vain resistance to her authority, her heart is broken. Weak as he was, he was the pulse that kept her going. She is killed by his apathy.

But this psychological subtlety is combined with several aspects

87

of death, including a straight description of the corpse, when Mr. Thumble found it: " The body was still resting on its legs, leaning against the end of the side of the bed, while one of the arms was close clasped round the bed-post. The mouth was rigidly closed but the eyes were open as though staring at him." Trollope allows death to present several incongruous aspects at the same time. He was doing what Scott, for instance, had done. In the second chapter of *The Bride of Lammermoor* the death of Lord Ravenswood presents many different facets. There is sociology in the account of the funeral feast, but, on the other hand, a suggestion of disturbing universality in the idea of the dead man as a " partner in the corruption " of his ancestors. A sympathetic, misty landscape and the ruined tower have still wider implications, while the strange quarrel interrupting the burial service, the countenances, " more in anger than in sorrow," and the timidity of the officiating priest impart a grim humour to the proceedings.

The variety and ambiguity of this account are alien to the single-mindedness of most Victorian thought. Thackeray, for instance, deals generally with the reflections aroused by contemplating death from a distance. His characters have a way of dying far from the scene of the story. A characteristic example is the brilliant account of Esmond's visit to his mother's grave (" I felt as one who had been walking below the sea, and treading amidst the bones of shipwrecks "). Subtle as this account is, it deals with a single aspect of death—the delayed influence after death of a forgotten woman. In *Lothair* the death of Theodora is an inspiration to the living and nothing more. In *Middlemarch* the significance of Casaubon's death lies in one fact—the emphatic importance it gives to the thoughts which were in the mind of his wife at the time. Many of the most memorable Victorian death scenes, for all their artistry, have the effect of a spotlight in a theatre, intensifying vision, but isolating one person or action from everything else.

It is significant that it is usually the very guilty like Fagin or the very innocent like Little Nell whose deaths are most stressed, Fagin's thoughts about death can be described in some detail because he is to be hanged, and so the reader, not being a member of the officially criminal class, regards himself as a spectator. Everything conspires, in most Victorian novels, to suggest that death is something abnormal and specialised. By stressing the variety of death, its ordinariness as one event of a series, and its impact on those who face it, Trollope was unusual. As we shall see, his religious faith, though like that of other leading novelists of the time very attenuated, was unlike theirs in being completely firm. Dickens, Thackeray, George Eliot, and others, were abnormally sensitive about death. They dwelt on it with the loving care of people who must manœuvre their subject into exactly the right position. The reader (and perhaps the author) must only be allowed to see it in a glare of light. The subject is handled with awe or else (especially in the case of criminals) with a savage satisfaction.

Nothing could point the contrast more clearly than the two railway deaths—that of Carker in *Dombey and Son*, and of Lopez in *The Prime Minister*. Dickens makes the train an instrument of cosmic retribution, a being with a personal life of its own, gradually attracting its victim with the fascination of horror. Trollope's train is just a train and the effect is achieved by showing the ordinariness of all the concomitants of a suicide's violent end—Lopez's conversation with his wife about the drying of clothes, his breakfast, his casual remarks to people at the station.

Trollope betrays neither attraction nor distaste for the subject of death. This in itself, though unusual in the period, was not unique. The same robustness of feeling can be found, for instance, in the last chapter of *Mr. Sponge's Sporting Tour*, when Lord Scamperdale laments over the sudden death of Jack Spragger.

" 'Oh, what a tr-treasure, what a tr-tr-trump he was. Shall never get such another. Nobody could s-s-slang a fi-fi-field as he could; no hu-hu-humbug 'bout him—never was su-su-such a fine natural bl-bl-blackguard; ' and then his feelings wholly choked his utterance as he recollected how easily Jack was satisfied; how he could dine off tripe and cow-heel, mop up fat porridge for breakfast, and never grumbled at being put on a bad horse."

Brilliant as this scene is, it is isolated. Surtees is no exception to the rule that each Victorian novelist tends to see only a few aspects of death, unusual though his point of view is. But for Trollope, as for Scott, death was protean.

For his satirical effects Trollope relies on a background of religious belief. It is taken for granted that after death comes judgment. Occasionally this is definitely stated, as in the account of the miser's death in *The Bertrams*, and of the old bedesman Bell in *The Warden*. More often judgment stands unmentioned in the background, deepening what is stated with an implied touch of satire, or of horror, or of comfort. In many cases, it is only when characters are dying that we are shown how much or how little religion means to them. The truly religious man, like Harding, the fanatic like Kennedy, the atheist, like Brattle, all these are rare. For the most part their thoughts are very vague. " ' Somebody says somewhere that nobody can live upon bread alone,' " says Mountjoy Scarborough, and his remark epitomises the shadowy religious world of most of the characters. Religion is a habit, or a half-forgotten memory of childhood, or a vague confidence or fear, or an unconvincing posture before an unknown universe.

The novelist's own attitude to all this is not easy to analyse. He was inclined to be impatient of dogma. Anglican though he was, he never subscribed to the idea of a church as anything more than an association of not very like-minded people. Yet in the death scenes, his treatment of the religious vagueness of his characters is definitely satirical, and he sometimes conveys a judgment on a whole life by this satire. The fact is that though so little dogmatic, Trollope was not vague about all religious ideas. He was near to being that very rare bird, the adherent of the theologian's " natural religion." He believed in God, in a moral law, in judgment and immortality, and in very little else. But unlike most such people he believed these things with an unchanging conviction. In a letter written on 4th April, 1879, he said, " The necessity of the supremacy of man [over woman] is as certain to me as the eternity of the soul. There are other matters on which one fights as on subjects which are in doubt—universal ballot, public education, and the like—but not as I think on these two." Natural religion is always apt to shade off into natural doubt; so far as we can tell, Trollope never doubted. This single fact gives scope for all the satire upon characters whose religious ideas are similar to his own, but who do not hold them with certainty. To Trollope this difference was crucial beyond all doctrines. Thus it comes about that he comes very near to Newman's attitude to religious certainty, in spite of the contrast of their two creeds. Indeed, Newman's critique of popular religion is an apt description of the dilemma of Trollope's characters as death approaches. " Since, too, they have no certainty of the doctrine they profess, they do but feel that they *ought* to believe them, and they nurse the offspring of their reason, as a sickly child, bringing it out of doors only on fine days." (*Difficulties of Anglicans* IX, 7.) Trollope perhaps was anxious to show more dogmatic believers that he, too, could be definite when the small but strong citadel of his faith was under fire.

So much for belief. What of feeling? We might expect to find a coherent attitude to death, if anywhere, in *The Fixed Period*. In this book written about two years before his own death, death for once became the central subject. As a novel *The Fixed Period* is a failure; as a study of death it is very puzzling. The plot turns upon an attempt in an imaginary part of the Antipodes to introduce compulsory euthanasia at the age of sixty-eight. The book is different in many ways from everything else that Trollope wrote. It is set in the year 1980; there is no attempt at realism, and the characters are for the most part lay figures with comic names. The story is told in the first person by the main character, who has nothing in common with the author. Generally, Trollope is accustomed to give his own opinion in little asides, and even to treat the reader as a confidential friend privileged to know in advance the secrets of the plot. On the very few occasions when his stories are told in the first person, the narrator is a thinly-disguised version of himself. But here for once, the ubiquitous personality of the author is excluded by a talkative, untrollopian narrator. No view of death is implicit in the book, apart from the obvious one that men will not be dissuaded from fearing death by any system. Trollope was on his guard as never before. We learn from his other books what he believed about death; here where we might expect to learn what he felt about it, we learn nothing. Death which is so actual in the other novels, becomes here only a vague subject for endless debates. No one actually dies within the pages of the book. It is as if the elaborate precautions against a personal confession have deprived the subject of all its human implications.

Perhaps, after all, this is not surprising. His strength in the other novels, was that he treated every death in a different way. By choosing this subject for *The Fixed Period*, he had challenged himself to generalise. The book with its unreal humour and absurd mechanical inventions is a prolonged evasion of this necessity.

7. Politics

TROLLOPE'S POLITICAL world is easy-going. Not many of its inhabitants believe political ideas or political measures to be supremely important. For most of them the game is the thing, and party loyalty is like any other kind— a matter of taking a side and sticking to one's friends. A man's political convictions are mainly due to a combination of tradition and chance, and any exceptions to this are apt to cause sorrow and heart-burning. When young Lord Silverbridge, in *The Duke's Children*, under the influence of his intellectual young friend Tregear, decides to desert the family tradition and become a Conservative, his father is extremely distressed. Now the Duke of Omnium is an intelligent man of progressive views, and a hard-working politician who has been Chancellor of the Exchequer as a commoner in his twenties and Prime Minister in middle life. One would have thought that such a man with his strong political conscience would have been grieved by his son's political error. Not a bit of it. The thing that annoys him is that his son of all the Pallisers should be the one to desert the family tradition and disgrace his great Whig ancestors. In ordinary life the Duke has the greatest respect for Conservatives, but in his own family they are as out of place as if his butler were to sit down to dinner with him.

To make matters worse, his daughter is in love with this same penniless Tregear and when she pipes up timidly, " I suppose it's as respectable to be a Conservative as a Liberal," " I don't know that at all," said the Duke angrily.

93

If tradition comes before conviction with a conscientious man like this, the same is *a fortiori* true of the average. Lord Grex, who is as traditionally Conservative as the Duke is traditionally Liberal, is annoyed to find that Silverbridge is coming over to his own side, and can see no motive but contrariness for such a change. " It's just the sort of thing for a son to do in these days. If I had a borough, Percival [his heir] would go down and make Radical speeches there." For him, of course, as for most elderly people in Trollope, the world is rapidly going to the dogs.

Men who have no such family traditions, like Melmotte, the financier, in *The Way We Live Now*, usually select their political allegiance at random or for reasons of ambition. And for Trollope the sadness of politics arises from this. For a man's supporters know so little about him and usually believe so much more than he does in the principles he preaches. Of Melmotte, his greatest villain, he says plausibly enough, " Honest good men, men who really loved their country . . . shed their money right and left . . . to have this man returned to Parliament." And after we have seen for several hundred pages what sort of a man Melmotte is, these ordinary words come home with some force.

With a few exceptions such as Mr. Monk, Trollope's politicians have no more convictions than are strictly necessary. It is the public who drive them to commit themselves tardily and unwillingly. Mr. Bunce, the radical householder and landlord of Phineas Finn, sees through the claims of the parties to initiate policies. In reply to the claim by a Conservative for his party that it repealed the corn laws and brought in household suffrage he replies, " I think I've been told all that before; them things weren't given by no manner of means, as I look at it. We just went in and took 'em. It was hall an haccident whether it was Cobden or Peel . . ." And in this sentiment he has his creator on his side. On the other side, Frank Gresham, the real old high Tory country squire who doesn't meddle much in politics, is equally convinced that true Conservatism in Parliament is an impossibility. " A Conservative in Parliament is, of course, obliged to promote a great many things of which he does not really approve. Mr. Gresham quite understood that. You can't have tests and qualifications, rotten boroughs and the divine right of kings back again."

From the point of view of political conviction, Mr. Bunce and Frank Gresham stand like the two immovable legs of the Colossus while the ordinary politicians with their comings and goings and their compromises play about underneath. Each is sublimely aware that though the needs of the political game may cause events to lean a little towards the desires of one or other of them, no real political creed in its consistent entirety is ever likely to be considered practical by professional politicians. For their world is one of comfort, slow compromises, and weariness. " They advocated reform as we all of us advocate doctors." They endure the agonies of sitting until the 11th of August, they enjoy the princely but strictly political hospitality of Lady Glencora, they go to the Universe Club ("its attractions were not numerous, consisting chiefly of tobacco and tea. The conversation was generally listless and often desultory. . . . But the thing had been a success and men liked to be members of the Universe "). Finally, they dash away to the grouse and country joys in August and try to forget about politics, if possible, till February.

The aristocratic patronage which the Reform Bill was supposed to have destroyed still flourishes, but is decently veiled. Lord Brentford makes a point of not going near Loughton in election time; on one solitary occasion in the course of several volumes he refers in his rage to " my borough." It is as if an account of a fashionable wedding in the Court Circular had included a report of what the bridegroom said to the bride after they had left the reception.

Trollope saw the rotten borough system as absurd, but not as a reason for great indignation. In one of his best pieces of irony he made his conscientious semi-radical hero, Phineas Finn, owe his election to two separate borough-mongering lords—and one of them a lifelong Tory. Lord Tulla sends Phineas to Parliament because " they've given the deanery of Kilfenora to a man that never had a father, though I condescended to ask for it for my cousin." When tradition and loyalty are more important than conviction in determining political allegiance, it is natural that pique should sometimes lead a man to change sides.

When politics and social life are so intermingled, it is inevitable that women will have a large share in the political game. It is a trite reflection, but none the less true, that the effect of votes for women, women in Parliament, and endless books and speeches about the equality of the sexes, has been, to judge from Trollope's account at least, to reduce the political influence of women. Women, it is true, especially unmarried women, are officially supposed not to concern themselves with politics. Violet Effingham is rebuked by her aunt simply because she says that she likes young men to be Liberals, not on the grounds that this is a mistaken opinion, but because she should have no opinion about politics. But it is women who see and ridicule the elaborate male pretences—Marie Goesler, for instance, asking Phineas Finn if he is Lord Brentford's member. This Phineas " excused by remembering that the questioner had lived so long out of England," but we know she is right. Indeed, the women are usually too clever for the husbands in the Cabinet. After a strenuous campaign by Lady Glencora and Madame Goesler the Duke of St. Bungay found that he had a very low opinion of Mr. Bonteen, but did not know why, and eventually the unfortunate man was denied the high position that had been promised him. Phineas Finn's political success is mainly due to his popularity with the wives and daughters of the Whig aristocracy. But this is only one side. Politics are a delicious amusement for women of wealth, but for Mrs. Bunce it is different. The shilling a week that her husband pays to the Union is the grievance of her life. To her way of thinking politics are all very well for those that can afford them. They merely distract the ordinary man from his duty to his family.

Parliament appears in these books as interesting, magnificent, desirable, and fundamentally futile. One is never likely to forget, as one reads Trollope's descriptions of it, his own enduring ambition to be an M.P. He writes in the Autobiography of his

" almost insane desire " to sit in Parliament. This phrase sums up his attitude because it reveals both the strength of his ambition and his understanding that it was a foolish ambition. So he describes the worthless and criminal George Vavasour passing the little lamps and the policemen at the entrance of the House as if he were a man entering a promised land. He describes Phineas Finn's maiden speech, the excitement, the nervousness, the horrible feeling of failure, as if it had been an experience of his own. He repeats again and again that a seat in Parliament is the highest aim an Englishman can have. I think the position appealed to him particularly because it was at that time unpaid and could still be made to carry the flavour of disinterested and patriotic public service. Of course, no one thinks in this way of Parliament now. But the most remarkable thing about Trollope is his balance. And like Pope in *The Rape of the Lock* he belittles in order to magnify and magnifies to belittle. He shows us the insincerity of the political battle. He was a man who liked words to mean what they said and so he was annoyed by many of the most revered ceremonies of the party game. It irritated him that the Prime Minister should one day do his best to blacken the character of the Leader of the Opposition and the next advise the Queen to send for him.

Two things he managed particularly well—the grand parliamentary manner of men like Daubeny and the little busy twittering party managers, the Ratlers and Robys and Barrington Erles who arrange everything, never deviate from the party line, and thoroughly respect the similar people on the opposite side. Daubeny's eloquence is magnificent, but hollow. Indeed, the satire against him is unusually bitter. For Daubeny the battle is a display of wits, and he is prepared to introduce a revolutionary disestablishment bill to allow his party, the Conservatives, to stay in office. The neat reversal of the positions of the two parties which results from this bill illustrates Trollope's feeling that they really agreed well enough. But if they agree on politics they agree even better about abuses. This is amusingly shown in the Browborough trial in *Phineas Redux*. The Conservative candidate is prosecuted for bribery by a Liberal Attorney-General, and allowed to get off very lightly. Everybody knows that Browborough is guilty but everybody sympathises with him, particularly M.P.s on both sides who " knew very well what had taken place at their own elections." Browborough, of course, escapes, though bribery is proved against his agents, but Trollope provides a delightful and illuminating epilogue when the matter is discussed in the smoking-room of the House by the party managers. Roby belongs to Browborough's party, Ratler to the Attorney-General's.

" I was very glad that the case went as it did at Durham," said Mr. Ratler.

" And so am I," said Mr. Roby. " Browborough was always a good fellow! . . .

" You must acknowledge that there was no bitterness in the way in which Grogam did it."

" We all feel that," said Mr. Roby, " and when the time comes, no doubt we shall return the compliment."

In some ways this is the key passage of the whole political series. The old ways are failing, no doubt, but no one wishes to hurry the process. " The thing can't be done all at once," as Mr. Ratler says. Both sides understand each other and will move no faster than they are forced to do by the electorate. The party hacks have mixed feelings. Things are not quite what they were, but they will probably last our time without any serious changes. Trollope is one of the greatest creators of these little, ordinary, grey characters. And for those who really desire self-knowledge— their number is never large—Trollope can be recommended. It takes an exceptional person to see his own failings in Iago or Mr. Pecksniff. It is comparatively easy to see them in the Ratlers and Robys.

In this, as in many things, Trollope was typically Victorian up to a point, and then added an unexpected personal twist of his own. He expressed the normal feeling about politics of an age when parliamentary reports were really read, and portraits of Gladstone or Disraeli presided over the home lives of thousands.

At the same time he hinted, delicately but definitely, that politics were a sham and settled nothing.

The heads of the political novels are Phineas Finn and Plantagenet Palliser, Duke of Omnium. Phineas is not one of Trollope's more memorable characters, but he was extremely well chosen for his function in the story. He is honest, good natured, weak and adaptable, and thoroughly likeable. Moreover, he has real political convictions. He is shocked and surprised when Fitzgibbon answers his expression of political faith, " the country gets nothing done by a Tory government," with the brief gems of his experience. He says, " I never knew a Government yet that wanted to do anything," and, " The country gets quite as much service as it pays for—and perhaps a little more." In scenes like this Phineas is used to express the author's own indignation about the cynicism of politics. He is honest enough for that, but he is weak enough to become involved in turn with every political abuse. He owes his election in the first place to the fact that a peer had quarrelled with his brother, later to a woman's influence and finally to the discovery of his opponent's bribery. He is seduced by the gutter press (" You can't do without a horgan, Mr. Finn "), by the desire for office and the grandeur of great acquaintances. One after another all these influences, ambitions, and pleasures betray him and he discovers the hollowness of each only then. When the gutter press turns against him he tells himself that a member of Parliament should be altogether independent of the Press.

But in spite of all this he is prepared to resign for a principle and his gesture, when at length it comes, has a great satirical effect. For he has been shown to us in his weakness and his honesty as an ordinary man. His resignation seems a natural and not a supremely fine act. So it shows up the average politician all the more. For the political world is shown as one where very few will willingly give up anything they can lay their hands on.

Phineas Finn's honesty is the rough-and-ready kind of the man who will not desert his colours. The Duke's honesty is a different thing altogether. He is the T. E. Lawrence of Trollope's political scene, the self-questioning man of action, whose conscience will never be quiet, but very seldom presents things to him in a clear light. " As a matter of course the Prime Minister blamed himself." It is typical of Trollope's method that he should place such a man in the thick of the borough-mongering system, just as he had made the lovable Mr. Harding the man who profited by the abuses he attacked in *The Warden.* The process by which the Duke gradually renounces the family interest in the borough of Silverbridge is traced with great delicacy. In *Can You Forgive Her?* when he is still Mr. Palliser and sits for the borough himself, he is described receiving the first news of the general election while he and his wife are travelling in Switzerland.

" ' Sophy tells me that you are returned for Silverbridge,' she said at last.

" ' Who? I! Yes; I'm returned,' said Mr. Palliser, speaking with something like disdain in his voice as to the possibility of anybody having stood with a chance of success against him in his own family borough. For a full appreciation of the advantages of a private seat in the House of Commons let us always go to those great Whig families who were mainly instrumental in carrying the Reform Bill."

For such a man the voluntary surrender of his privileges in Silverbridge costs a great deal. Trollope suggests this indirectly but very cleverly. Soon after he has made his decision Major Pountney, who is staying in his house on his wife's invitation, asks him for his interest in the election at Silverbridge. The Duke is sore from the struggle of putting his convictions before his instincts and family traditions. And so he turns on the poor major with a disproportionate fury and makes him leave the house the same day. Trollope has shown us the Duke for hundreds of pages as a mild, shy and courteous man. This sudden explosion tells us all we need to know about his state of mind.

This is only one of the numerous irritations which, in Trollope's view, the truly conscientious man must suffer if he takes a hand in politics. As Prime Minister, the Duke is driven nearly to despair by worries, doubt, and self-reproach. Here, as so often, Trollope records his final judgment in an indirect way, that may easily pass unnoticed by those who think of Trollope as too simple a writer to need careful reading. In his loneliness and sorrow, surrounded in his own house by squads of political guests invited by his wife, the Duke makes friends with an unpolitical old maid, Lady Rosina de Courcy. They go for quiet walks together and have dull conversations. But the Duke finds these walks a great relief because " She was natural and she wanted nothing from him. When she talked about cork soles, she meant cork soles."

All those who have experienced the horrors of intrigue and affectation, whether in politics or university life, in business or at cocktail parties, will feel about these moving words as Johnson did of Gray's *Elegy*. It is a sentiment to which " every bosom returns an echo." It is also Trollope's considered condemnation of the political world he had created.

Mr. Bott, the Manchester school M.P., is of interest because of the curious reversal of class distinction which operates in his relationship with the Duke. A foolish, insensitive, self-opinionated man, he is a person the Duke might have been expected to find excruciating. But Bott, Trollope suggests, is tolerated and even approved by the Duke because their backgrounds are so different that they have no common standards by which to criticise each other. And the friendship of the humble is always a sop to the uneasy conscience of the aristocratic reformer.

The Duke of St. Bungay is an excellent foil to Plantagenet Palliser. Here we have the ordinary political nobleman, untroubled by any self-questioning. He has an average intelligence, average conscience, and a more than average patriotism. He is useful, he does not overrate himself, he is not ambitious. All his life, Trollope tells us—and here we return to the idea of politics as a solemn game, which we have noticed before in the parliamentary descriptions—he has been in and out of office like a man cutting in at a whist table. He " enjoys both the game and the rest from the game." With a vague, half-serious regret he says at the dinner-table to a lady urging him to vote for the ballot, that he has tried to be a Radical, but has never got beyond

Whiggery yet. Like the Beveridge Report for certain old men in 1945, it was a thing he would have liked to believe in. He would have liked to follow the way the world was going, but the accumulated mental habits of half a century were too strong. Richard II's description of John of Gaunt fits him perfectly. He is "time-honoured." He had sat in conclave with THE Duke, he had congratulated Sir Robert Peel. . . . The party game has been a large part of his life and he is not the man to question what he has known so long.

" ' I would not wish to see every Lord-Lieutenant of a county a Whig.' In his enthusiasm the old Duke went back to his old phraseology. ' But I know that my opponents when their turn comes will appoint their friends to the Lieutenancies, and that so the balance will be maintained.' "

" To maintain the balance "—a modest ambition, and as long as it is fulfilled the old man will be happy. But Trollope allows one hint of prescience to be mingled with his self-satisfaction, and this landmark of the time before Victorian improvement realises that he is one of the last of his kind.

" There must surely have been a shade of melancholy on that old man's mind as, year after year, he assisted in pulling down institutions which he in truth regarded as the safeguards of the nation; but which he knew that, as a Liberal, he was bound to assist in destroying! It must have occurred to him from time to time that it would be well for him to depart and be at peace before everything was gone."

Indeed, there is plenty to worry him. Turnbull, the rich Radical merchant, thunders away night after night as if reform were a process that need have no limits. Quintus Slide on the *Morning Banner* devotes himself with equal zeal to the support of each party in turn and to indiscriminate calumny of politicians' private lives.

" ' It's my belief that there isn't a peer among 'em all as would live with his wife constant, if it was not for the Press—only some of the very old ones who couldn't help themselves.' " After this you might as well have Lord Northcliffe at once. Lucky for the old Duke that he was not sensitive to such things.

Trollope did not wish to leave us in doubt about the way in which his imposing political structure was supported. The first political character to be introduced in *Can You Forgive Her?* (with which the political series begins) is Mr. Grimes, the publican, who helped George Vavasour in his election campaign. For him politics means bribery at elections in the Chelsea districts. Like the constituents of Andover a generation before when Florence Nightingale's father was a candidate, he " took the view that the possession of a vote had always meant hard cash."

" It's the game I looks to," he says. " If the game dies away it'll never be got up again—never. Who'll care about elections then? Anybody'd go and get his self elected if we was to let the game go by! "

For all his morality and his high view of what politics ought to be, Trollope, like Chaucer, clearly enjoyed and, in a way, admired his own rascals. He realised the man's sense of tradition, the soundness of his nightmare logic, and his moderation. (" But the Chelsea districts aren't dear. I don't call them by any means dear. Now Marylebone is dear—and so is Southwark.") He relished, too, the man's perfectly genuine unselfishness. As long as there was money going, Grimes did not mind whether he got much of it himself. But for all Trollope's and the reader's enjoyment—and again there is a parallel with Chaucer—he was angry about the degradation of politics. It is no accident that Mr. Grimes appears in the series before all the cabinet ministers and the K.G.s. He is the basic political character.

There is not a great deal of actual doctrine in the novels. What there is is mainly a series of attacks on the sincerity and consistency of Conservatism. He makes two main points, neither of which, oddly enough, is yet altogether out of date. Conservatives are prepared to adopt any revolutionary measure, when it suits them; but in their hearts they are always dreaming of a return to a mythical past era of glory.

" At that time," he says in *The Bertrams*, speaking probably of the early fifties, but writing near the end of the decade, " men had not learnt thoroughly by experience, as now they have, that no reform, no innovation—experience almost justifies us in saying no revolution—stinks so foully in the nostrils of an English Tory politician as to be absolutely irreconcilable to him. . . . Let the people want what they will, Jew senators, cheap corn, vote by ballot, no property qualification, or anything else, the Tories will carry it for them if the Whigs cannot. A poor Whig premier has none but the Liberals to back him; but a reforming Tory will be backed by all the world—*except those few whom his own dishonesty will personally have disgusted.*"

Similarly he blames Peel for repealing the Corn Laws and makes the Conservative Prime Minister, Daubeny, bring in a bill for disestablishment. All this angered him, but the Utopia of the past merely amused him, and he can be very amusing about it. This passage, for instance, in *The Way We Live Now* (1875):

" Who knows what may be regained if the Conservative Party will only put its shoulder to the wheel and take care that the handle of the windlass be not mended! Sticinthemud, which has ever been a doubtful little borough, has just been carried by a majority of fifteen. A long pull, a strong pull, and a pull altogether —and the old day will come back again. Venerable patriarchs think of Lord Liverpool and other heroes, and dream dreams of Conservative bishops, Conservative lord-lieutenants, and of a Conservative ministry that shall remain in for a generation." And in the same book he speaks with scorn of a political master (presumably Disraeli), who explains that progress can only be expected from those whose declared purpose it is to stand still.

There is no doubt that Trollope thought the triumph of Liberal principles inevitable. In one way he has proved wrong. But in another way he was right. For by Liberalism he meant the narrowing of the gap between high and low, and the Conservative idea (a little unfairly) he thought of as the improvement of the people, maintaining the same ratio between high and low as at present. He was not oblivious of the main argument for Conservatism at all times—that parties of the Left are eaten up from

the left. He did not agree with it, but he put it into the mouth of
Tregear, the young man who seduced Lord Silverbridge from his
family tradition of Liberalism. Tregear is one of Trollope's few
theoretical politicians—Mr. Monk is the only other of any importance—and he (interesting in the England of 1880) is a Conservative because he fears that Liberals are really, without
knowing it, playing the game of the Socialists and Communists
who will follow them.

It is always interesting, after trying to interpret a novelist
from his novels, to turn to what he has written as a direct expression of opinion. If we go to the sixteenth chapter of the Autobiography, we shall find plenty to surprise us. First of all we learn
that " of all studies the study of politics is the one in which a man
may make himself most useful to his fellow-creatures." What a
contrast to the political life of the novels where, as people talk
lugubriously, during Cabinet crises, about the Queen's government having to be carried on, we find that it does not greatly
matter whether it is carried on or not. It is a great contrast, but
perhaps, after all, not such a surprising one. No one is so critical
as a lover, and no agnostic so angry about the abuses of the
Church as a reforming pope.

In this chapter Trollope expounded his political theory of
" Conservative-Liberalism " and the gradual diminution of in-
equalities which he recognises as inevitable. Then he goes on to
describe his experiences as parliamentary candidate for Beverley
in 1868. Everything happened as it was prophesied beforehand—
" You will spend £1000 and lose the election. Then you will
petition and spend another £1000. You will throw out the
elected members. There will be a commission and the borough
will be disfranchised." So he went into what he calls the most
wretched fortnight of his manhood, forewarned but undeterred.
Here we may note the abiding sensitiveness of his character. He
felt an insult, and still more an injustice, as a wound. He writes
in the Autobiography of a punishment he received at school for
something he did not do. " All that was fifty years ago, and it
burns me now as though it were yesterday." So it would seem

that the tenacity of his parliamentary ambitions was largely due
to the sarcastic words of his uncle, when he was in his twenties.
" As far as he knew few clerks in the Post Office did become
Members of Parliament." The deep self-distrust and the power
of endurance, both natural to him and both fostered by an
unhappy adolescence, must have made these words a terrible
challenge. Trollope would have agreed with Mr. Eliot, " this
thing is sure that time is no healer."

Trollope's experiences at Beverley were, as he said himself,
the basis for the election chapters of *Ralph the Heir*. He goes further
and says that Beverley and Percycross are one and the same place.
For this reason any reader who has previously subscribed to the
stock idea of Trollope as a photographer and no artist, would be
wise, if he wishes to be just, to consider these chapters carefully.
Now the easiest way for those who doubt if Pope is a poet to
convince themselves of the truth is to compare the verse descriptions of Atticus with the prose one on which it was based. They
will find that the prose passage has not merely been polished,
improved, heightened. It has been transformed. So with
Trollope, these chapters which are so closely linked with personal
experience provide one of the most striking examples of his art.

The hero of Percycross, Sir Thomas Underwood, who suffered
with Trollope's own sufferings, is a Conservative, perhaps because
Trollope thought it more fitting that the two main characters with
whom he is associated should be Conservatives also. The first is
Mr. Griffenbotham, who has represented Percycross for years,
content to share the spoils with a Whig in a two-member con-
stituency. He is a professional politician with no nonsense about
him, has been accustomed to pay his way, and hates petitions.
Sir Thomas may talk about purity and political principles. Mr.
Griffenbotham knew better.

" Mr. Griffenbotham was very good at canvassing the poorer
classes. He said not a word to them about politics, but asked them
all whether they did not dislike that fellow Gladstone, who was
one thing one day, and another thing another day. ' By God,
nobody knows what he is.' "

His treatment of Sir Thomas is abominable. He had never wanted to have another Conservative candidate. But with typical fairness—and typical subtlety—he emerges in the end as a pathetic figure. For when the threat of a petition arrives, and he is afraid he will lose his seat after having been at the head of the poll, he breaks down. Experienced, bored, and gouty as he is, Parliament means everything to him. He is not interested in politics, he never speaks, he is used to pay heavily for his seat, but " such as was the life, it was his life, and he had no time left to choose another."

The other character—an even more memorable one—is old Mr. Pile. For him the glory of England is departed because Sir Thomas and his like will no longer agree to buy their voices. Not that he wants money for himself, but it defeats his sense of justice that a poor man shouldn't have his due. Purity makes him sick, and purity and pickpockets are about the same.

" ' Things have come to that in the borough, that I'll meddle and make no more. I did think it would last my time,' added Mr. Pile almost weeping."

Pile and Griffenbotham are at once monuments of a past period and examples of the emptiness and the illusions of old age. Sir Thomas and the Radical bootmaker Moggs are introduced to Percycross as a pair of doves into a nest of vipers, and have a sort of fellow-feeling in spite of their political differences. Moggs is so high-minded in his theory of the independence of the voter that he will not even canvass. Sir Thomas refuses to use his influence to win a position in the Post Office for a brainless man of forty.

He says, " ' I understand these things are given by merit.' Mr. Trigger smiled and Mr. Griffenbotham laughed outright." Of course they are both defeated, fleeced, and saddened. Trollope's political creed would hardly admit of the triumph of virtue. But, indeed, as long as he is speaking, old Mr. Pile almost persuades. " I hate Purity, I do. I hate the very smell of it. When I see the chaps come here and talk of purity, I know they mean that nothing ain't to be as it used to be. Nobody is to trust no one.

There ain't to be nothing warm, nor friendly, nor comfortable any more."

I am not claiming for Trollope that he shows a profound insight into political theory. But he did not try. The ideas which are discussed at party conferences and worm their way through a thousand semi-literate election addresses are not and never have been profound. They are scraps and catchwords culled from a jumble of systems, backed sometimes by large inarticulate feelings. Why should we quarrel with him because he thought political success due to " an epicurean concourse of atoms " or because many of his characters are of the kind who are " weighed down by their own incapacity and sink into peerages? " Trollope gave us a pageant of average politicians and showed what politics meant to each, and how their convictions were mingled with their traditions and their ambition. He revealed with subtlety variations of prestige and the unpredictable influence of personalities in a party or a Cabinet. And finally he evoked with memorable distinctness the everyday details of the life he had desired but never known, the House, the smoking-room, the Reform Club, and Brooks's, and the brittle splendour of the great Whig houses nearing the end of their greatness.

The obvious comparison is with Disraeli; and the following passage which appeared in the *Times Literary Supplement* on 11th April, 1952, is relevant to it.

" Why has the political novel so often attempted, so often, if not always, been a failure? Perhaps the answer to the problem lies not in the scale but in the nature of politics. The political concept, to put it cynically, is an artificial simplification of reality. The novel is a different form of fiction. When the two are brought together, when the framework of one is made to enclose the other, it leads to the old and insoluble problem of the picture within a picture. . . . Politics should remain a subject for satire or fantasy, not for realism."

Everyone has noticed how often Disraeli's most brilliant discussions of political ideas seem like mere episodes, and give the same disagreeable feeling as the picaresque story within a story.

The passage quoted gives an interesting explanation for this. And nearly every reader of Disraeli has remembered the scenes about Tadpole and Taper while forgetting the feast of political ideas. In fact, Disraeli's most successful scenes are those which do not deal with political concepts at all. Tadpole and Taper are not capable of understanding such things. And so one might argue that if one accepts the generalisation quoted about political novels, these scenes are immune from that criticism.

But such scenes are exceptional in Disraeli's work. They are the most important part of Trollope's political books. Disraeli's are novels of ideas and success-stories. Trollope's are primarily the record of politics as a game, an occupation, not a theory. Of course when Trollope does attempt political theory, he is far inferior to Disraeli, but fortunately the attempts are few. Though each will trespass into the other's ground on occasion, the main lines of the contrast are clear. For instance, readers of Disraeli get a very slight impression of the House of Commons, or the political clubs which are so vividly portrayed by Trollope. Why? Because political ideas are best thrashed out by two or three people in a small room. But the House of Commons and the political clubs make the best background for politics as a profession, a solemn game, and day-to-day experience, and Trollope's pages smell of the House of Commons.

Again, Disraeli's satire is much more sociological than personal. He pauses to laugh at Lord Monmouth, but he is much more interested in the satirical effect of the vast contrast between the Two Nations whose very existence side by side is a condemnation of English life. Trollope's satire is moral and refers to individuals. It consists in such things as the divergence between Palliser's instincts and considered thoughts about differences of rank. Thus Tadpole and Taper are satirised against a standard of ideas which they ought as politicians to understand, but do not. Trollope's Roby and Ratler, whose position as party hacks is very similar, are condemned by a standard of sincerity, goodwill and public service. Tadpole and Taper fail as politicians, Roby and Ratler as men.

Disraeli was born over ten years before Trollope and his first three political novels were published more than twenty years before *Phineas Finn*. But Disraeli the political idealist looks forward, Trollope the recorder of tradition looks back. It is sometimes difficult to believe, when reading the two side by side, that the gap is really so great. And this remains true even when Disraeli is dealing with actual historical measure and dates. For they are only a background for the things which in his view should follow the realisation of his own ideals.

Trollope thought Disraeli's novels unreal. Disraeli might have replied that in his sense Trollope was not a political novelist at all.

8. Love

VICTORIAN WRITERS do not as a rule explain or analyse the onset of love. The feelings it excites, its influence on human destinies, its dramatic consequences, its slow decay, all these are exhaustively treated. But its source is obscure; we are told much about the feelings and actions of David Copperfield and Dora, but no reason for their choice is suggested. But we see why, how far, and with what reservations Richardson's Clarissa and Lovelace are attracted to each other.

The Victorian novel owes much to the ancient English tradition of stage comedy. Two young people meet, fall in love in a moment, are separated by artificial obstacles, and are finally united. Trollope uses a plot of this kind in *Rachel Ray*, where the obstacles are so slight that even with some dilatoriness on the author's part they are barely enough to keep the book going till the end. The weakness of the obstacles here and in other cases testifies to the strength of the convention. Victorian readers might be very concerned about the reasons for Hamlet's delay, but few of them would have wondered at the delay of lovers in novels of their own time, whose conventions they seldom questioned.

Now, on the stage, love at first sight is generally a device to save time. But the Victorian novel is usually a leisurely affair and does not need such a convention. Yet it is nearly always retained. Are we to regard it as purely vestigial? Technical traditions certainly die hard. But here we are dealing with something more than a technical tradition. Disraeli, whose lively thoughts were certainly not confined by literary conventions, says

in *Henrietta Temple*, " There is no love but love at first sight."
He seems to have retained this conviction all his life.

A poem worth studying in this connection is Browning's " By
the Fireside." Here an affectionate married couple who have
come together

> " Just for the obvious human bliss
> To satisfy life's daily thirst
> With a thing men seldom miss,"

are united in a moment with an infinitely stronger bond by the
power of the Italian landscape. As Browning says with a sim-
plicity which is either magnificent or absurd, according to the
point of view, " the forest had done it."

For Trollope love at first sight seemed too stagey and improbable. Yet he was no more prepared than his contemporaries
to delve into the processes of choice. So choice, as often as not,
is passed over in the narrative and recorded only when accomplished. He does not stress the idea that choice cannot be
analysed; he simply leaves us to infer it from his silence. For
him it is not mysterious, merely unknown. Sexual choice is a first
principle on which the stability of the family and ultimately of
society depend. It is like the law of gravitation, a necessary
condition both of the real world and of all fictional worlds. He
would not have appreciated why Patmore, Browning, and
Meredith treat the subject with a quasi-religious reverence and
are so eager to create mystery.

A common idea, assumed more than stated, is that a love which
aims at marriage is meritorious, and that it is somehow separable
from the sexual instinct. This is partly why Trollope habitually
treats the period of engagement as the happiest of all. He even
calls the married state the " bread and cheese " of love, by comparison with what went before. When Clara Desmond in *Castle
Richmond* gives reasons for postponing her marriage, Trollope
regards it as an understood thing that any girl of seventeen would
wish to do this, so as to enjoy more fully the intervening period.
There seems to be an assumption in many novels of this time that

physical desire is a male peculiarity, and that even men can transcend it when they are in love. Perhaps, though this is only speculative, this accounts for the emotional importance of little girls in the novels of Dickens and in the lives of men like Lewis Carroll and Ruskin. For it is doubtful whether women will ever agree to be treated for very long as ineffectual angels. It is notable that no such idea of them is to be found in the works of the women novelists of the time. Their heroines indeed tend to have their animal natures developed at the expense of all their other faculties.

An extreme case of male reluctance to allow women physical status is provided by Ruskin, who told his wife on his wedding night that he had thought women's bodies were different. Probably he had formed his ideas of them from nude paintings. No doubt such aberrations may occur in any period, but in this one they assume a greater literary importance. In some ways the most successful way out of the difficulty was found by Patmore, who, while stressing the physical, implied that love had a separate and unattainably high spiritual soul. In the words of the married lover:

> Because, though free of the outer court
> I am, this temple keeps its shrine
> Sacred to Heaven; because in short,
> She's not and never can be mine.

But Trollope's heroes were not meditative enough to have it both ways and for them " When all is won that hope can ask," the bread and cheese period of love must set in.

When Trollope treats love from the point of view of his male characters, he often seems to identify himself with them. Especially in the books written in the forties and early fifties when the memory of his hopeless youth was strongest, he would break off from the description of a proposal into a personal rapture on the glory of being accepted by a woman. For Trollope was one of those rare men who had once doubted whether any woman would even look at him. But when the mind through which the story is seen is a woman's, the picture is different. His aim then is to be a social historian as well as a psychologist. He takes into account not only women's romantic feelings, but their need for marriage to bring social position and occupation, and their horror of dying as spinsters.

These facts, which are much more prominent in his later than his earlier work, are not normally introduced with an air of condemnation. In other novelists of the time they are seldom evident except in the case of women of depraved character, like Becky Sharp; or in the case of a character whom the writer does not wish altogether condemned, like Myra Roehampton in Disraeli's *Endymion*, there is a compromise. She marries Lord Roehampton, without any strong feeling for him, because of his wealth and his political position. But she does it to advance her brother and not for herself. Trollope allows that normal and virtuous women must make calculations too. When he does condemn a girl like Arabella Trefoil in *The American Senator*, it is for lying and unfaithfulness, not for obviously wanting a husband. And the attack is as much against the system and education which tempt her to behave thus, as against herself.

But Arabella Trefoil belongs to the darker world of the novels of the seventies and early eighties. None of the many contrasts between Trollope's early and late work is more striking than the contrast in his treatment of love. In his early and middle works it is normally a source of joy and if unhappy, brings a worth-while sorrow. In such works as *The Way We Live Now* and *An Old Man's Love* it is a destroyer, and the lucky ones are those who cannot feel it at all.

Like many of his contemporaries, Trollope loved to moralise about love. Some of his ideas not only seem strange to-day, but would have seemed strange to almost every generation earlier or later than his. But these transient views of the question were, paradoxically held as unquestioned truths. The main eccentricity of this moral system lies in the moral value which is given to feelings. To fall in love is in some way a virtuous art, and it becomes more virtuous still if it outlasts rejection and loss of hope.

Love makes a man of John Eames and of Larry Twentyman in *The American Senator*. With these two, indeed, being a rejected lover becomes almost a life-work, and serves to enhance their reputation with their friends. The feeling of Mr. and Mrs. Fenwick in *The Vicar of Bullhampton* about their friend Gilmore is typical. " They both felt that he was showing more of manhood than they had expected from him in the persistency of his love, and that he deserved his reward." It is almost as if some one had taken the solemn game of courtly love and turned it into a serious commonplace of everyday.

The corollaries of this idea are what one would expect. Bachelors are dangerous and those that are not actually disreputable, or chicken-hearted creatures who cannot face life, are comfortably nourishing a hopeless and lifelong passion. An example of the last group is Roger Carbury, a figure of virtue, surrounded by the multiple villainy of *The Way We Live Now*. Generally speaking, it is, as Trollope says, as if the matter admitted of no argument, " manifestly a man's duty to live with a woman." But to marry without love is sinful—one of the few acts about which Trollope uses this word with its suggestion of explicitly religious sanctions. What may be the duty of the man who finds that he simply does not love anybody is an unanswered question. In general, Trollope is well satisfied with the standards which most of his male characters follow by instinct. But he finds right conduct for women a more difficult problem. " It seems to me," he says in *The Bertrams*, " that it is sometimes very hard for young girls to be in the right. They certainly should not be mercenary; they certainly should not marry paupers; they certainly should not allow themselves to become old maids. They should not encumber themselves with early, hopeless loves; nor should they callously resolve to care for nothing but a good income and a good house. There should be some handbook of love, to tell young ladies when they may give way to it without censure."

Some of Trollope's girl characters take these exacting standards of choice and behaviour very seriously. There is an echo of Arthurian jousting in this remark of Gertrude Woodward in *The Three Clerks*: " ' I would have a competitive examination in every service. It would make young men ambitious. They would not be so idle and empty as they now are.' " But balancing this, there is a general feeling among the female characters that men, of course, are rather wicked and don't go to church as women do, and that nothing but a woman's love can redeem them from a dissipated and useless life.

These ideas will be found diffused through his novels, but two problems of the relations between the sexes claimed his special attention. In *The Vicar of Bullhampton* he deals with the fallen woman, and in *The American Senator* with husband-hunting.

The Vicar of Bullhampton has many of the usual weaknesses of the problem-novel. The author's interest here was more in the social question than in its artistic treatment. His preface is a plea for freedom to treat these things in fiction and a criticism of the existing practice of society. In *Can You Forgive Her?* Trollope had written two brief and effective scenes about Burgo Fitzgerald's meetings with a street girl, who is introduced simply to illustrate Burgo's wretchedness. The point lies in the contrast between their origin, appearance and status in life, and the similarity of their feelings and prospects.

But now he set himself a much more difficult task; a whole book requires more detail and a more precise background than Trollope would allow himself. Any reader of *David Copperfield* must be struck by the vagueness of the surroundings, the life, and even the feelings of Martha, the fallen woman. Vagueness is especially noticeable in a writer like Dickens with his immense zest for vivid detail, and great gift of memorable characterisation in a short space. Vagueness of background mars *The Vicar of Bullhampton* also, as it is likely to mar any book whose author feels that he is wandering near the limits of which is permitted by the taste of the public.

Carry Brattle herself, the fallen woman, is shown only in her misery and regret, after she has been deserted. She is bitterly ashamed, but unable to repent. The difficulty of repentance when everyone around her regards her guilt as irreparable, is one of Trollope's more telling points. Her shame is such that she is unwilling to touch the hand of the clergyman Fenwick who tries to help her, and is incredulous when told that his wife feels any sympathy for her. As Trollope is unwilling to go into details about her life, he is no doubt wise to give her only a small speaking part in the book. Unfortunately, as Carry cannot be the heroine, he felt impelled to introduce an irrelevant hero and heroine. On these Trollope's own disarming comment is enough: " As I have myself forgotten what the heroine does and says—except that she tumbles into a ditch—I cannot expect that anyone else should remember her." The main merit of the book lies in the effect on the other characters of Carry's illicit love, but he does also succeed in conveying the aimlessness of her life, and the emptiness of her hours, after society has rejected her. There is the dilemma of Fenwick, the clergyman, who tries throughout to help her spiritually and materially. When she says, " ' Nobody loves me now,' " his first thought is to tell her that God loves her. But he finds that he cannot bring himself to speak thus to a woman who is almost friendless. Instead he says that he and his wife love her, feeling as he says this that religion and charity are pulling him opposite ways.

There is the unconscious irony of Carry's respectable relations whom Fenwick tries to persuade to help her. " ' There never wasn't one of the Hugginses who didn't behave herself;—that is of the women,' added Mrs. George, remembering the misdeeds of a certain drunken uncle of her own, who had come to great trouble in a matter of horseflesh." And her husband sums up the proud, respectable lower-middle-class philosophy with the words, " ' A boy as is bad ain't never so bad as a girl.' " But Trollope is not content with satirising this very normal attitude. He shows the effect on people with pity and imagination like Fenwick.

Fenwick is an independent, generous man, and inclined to be hot-headed. He is the sort of man who likes to be in a minority and in arguments, and inclined to assume that the weaker party in a quarrel will always be in the right. This side of his character is carefully built up in the description of his feud with Lord

Trowbridge, who owns most of his parish. This is how his attitude to Carry and her seducer is described: " Her fall, her first fall, had been piteous to him rather than odious. He, too, would have liked to get hold of the man and to have left him without a sound limb within his skin—to have left him pretty nearly without a skin at all; but that work had fallen into the miller's hands, who had done it fairly well. And, moreover, it would hardly have fitted the Vicar. But as regarded Carry herself, when he thought of her in his solitary rambles, he would build little castles in the air on her behalf, in which her life should be anything but one of sackcloth and ashes. He would find for her some loving husband, who should know and should have forgiven the sin which had hardly been a sin, and she should be a loving wife with loving children."

His attitude is by no means unique. Mr. Benson, the minister in Mrs. Gaskell's *Ruth*, protests that he finds it impossible to forgive the fathers of illegitimate children, though he and his sister treat Ruth herself and her child with the most generous charity and sympathy. He even refuses the financial help of the penitent father for the education of his son (although the boy's mother is by now dead), and he refuses indignantly. There is a partial parallel too, in *David Copperfield*. But Trollope tries to analyse this attitude. He shows that Fenwick, in resisting the popular view of Carry, is really imitating it in reverse. He does not see that if two rational beings commit a sin together, they must both be responsible for it. He sees that the man escapes most of the blame in most people's eyes, and that Carry's punishment is very heavy. Hence, by an instinctive retrospective piece of false reasoning, his indignation against the man is as strong as possible, against the woman he has none. In making this distinction he goes near to a tacit admission that women are not really responsible for their actions, that is, not fully human. From one point of view, the book is a striking study of the pitfalls of generosity and of the subtle influence of public opinion on those who pride themselves on ignoring it.

It is one of the drawbacks of most problem novels that the

characters lack individuality. This is true of Carry herself and of most of her respectable relations, but not of all. Fanny, her sister, comes to life at any rate for a moment after Carry's final return home in her misery and wretchedness. Watching Carry asleep there, Fanny recalls the envy she has felt in the past for her beauty. This recollection, combined with the thought of the pass to which her beauty has brought her, makes her decide always to be kind to Carry and never to judge her.

Their father, the miller, typical in some ways of the ordinary outraged parent of fiction, is yet a character one remembers. The ordinary processes of life, and the ordinary reputation of an honest man, are not just the foundations of life to him, they are life itself. " To pay his way was the pride of his heart; to be paid on his way was its joy." He has no religious belief, and it is no good talking to him of repentance. He knows that disgrace before the world is irretrievable. But whereas most of Carry's other relations accept this fact half-uneasily, conscious of other more humane standards, which they have not the strength to follow, to Brattle the world's standard is a sort of substitute religion, accepted with all a believer's zeal. " Beyond eating and working a man had little to do, but just to wait till he died. That was his theory of life in these his latter days." It is characteristic of him that, though he is terribly distressed when his son is accused of murder, his relief when the charge is shown to be false, is moderate. When he finally forgives Carry, he is still consistent, never allowing himself to forget that they are all permanently disgraced by what she has done. Brattle's atheism, unusual as it is in Trollope's work, is important. For he has discarded sin as meaningless and received in return an irrational and vicarious guilt, for which there is no remedy.

The most interesting point in the analysis of forgiveness is the fundamental similarity it reveals between the apparently opposite attitudes of Fenwick and Brattle. Fenwick forgives too easily, or rather half-condones; Brattle can hardly bring himself to forgive at all. But each is unduly influenced by public opinion, one negatively, the other positively. Each sees Carry's act as a momentary stain, not as a moral act reaching out in its causes and consequences into past and future. Fenwick underrates its importance because it is past and momentary; Brattle overrates it because it is past and therefore irrevocable. For Fenwick her repentance is scarcely necessary, for Brattle it is futile; and so once again theoretical opposites meet in practical agreement. Pity and anger are alike in denying to their object responsibility and a full human status.

In his study of background and consequences in *The Vicar of Bullhampton* Trollope made a notable, but partial success. He did not do what he set out to do, and though many people will consider his views about fallen women eminently sensible, he could not turn them into art.

Though husband-hunting appears as one would expect in a number of his books, Trollope made only one full-length study of it, in *The American Senator*. Lord Rufford, the pursued man, is apparently made for the part. He is young, very rich, slightly weak about women, but with some feelings of honour. Arabella Trefoil who pursues him is already assured of a man with £7000 a year when she starts trying to catch Rufford, whose income is clearly far larger than this. Most of the time he is simply the quarry and the chase is presented from the woman's point of view. But the glimpses that we are given of Rufford's point of view are interesting. He expects to be chased and does not blame Arabella for that. He has never promised to marry her, and any assurances of love he has given have been in response to her questions; and he has kissed her. When she demands marriage and claims that he promised it, he hesitates for a moment, knowing that he must marry some time, and that it would, at any rate, make an end to being pursued. He decides to resist, but he still feels that a good deal is due to the lady. "Though he should resolve to pass five years among the Andes, he must answer the lady's letter before he went." He consults his brother-in-law, who insists that he must agree to everything short of marriage, which may be demanded of him. So Rufford is subjected to a series of harrowing interviews with Arabella's relations, and finally with Arabella herself, and promise to pay £8000 on the suggestion of Arabella's mother, Lady Augustus Trefoil. This Arabella refuses. His code of conduct seems clear to himself. " ' I have been a fool and I own it. But I have done nothing unbecoming a gentleman.' " And this is a " wicked," idle lord, who hates to be anywhere but in a railway carriage on a Sunday. In the interviews with the relatives, he cannot bring himself to say that he has been pursued, and that Arabella is lying; he can only keep repeating that there has been an unfortunate mistake. He is calm and apologetic when Lord Augustus is insulting him freely. His despair when a new interview is demanded is comical. Though he is keenly alive to the value of money, he feels that £8000 is a cheap price to pay for avoiding more interviews. The curious, vestigial chivalry which is mixed with Rufford's contempt for women is well suggested, and it is on this that Arabella relies and she almost succeeds.

Arabella herself, the heroine and villainess of the story, is presented, in a variety of conflicting ways. She is condemned, pitied and at the same time, her pursuit of Rufford is given a kind of sporting interest of its own. In the background is an implicit condemnation of the system which makes a rich husband seem to her the only object worth her attention. But husband-hunting as a social problem is never obtrusive, as is the corresponding problem of *The Vicar of Bullhampton*, and this time no solution is suggested. Nor, if the system is bad, is that held to be any excuse for the free acts of individuals.

When she is first introduced, she is engaged to Morton, she has been at the game for years, and she is almost in despair. " ' Talk of work,' " she says, " ' men's work! What man ever has to work as I do? ' " We see the constant vigilance required for the game of winning one man without losing a grip on the less desirable but safe and moderately wealthy one. When she arrives at her uncle's house to meet Rufford, and when it is essential to keep her engagement a secret, she is distressed to see a politician's wife in the party, because she connects her with the Foreign Office to which her fiancé is attached. This is just one of a number of small strokes by which Trollope skilfully conveys the torture of having to look out of the corner of one's eye at every hour of the day, on the watch for things one can never admit to noticing. It is the mingling of apparent spontaneity and real calculation which is such an effort. Continually she is forced to remember that time is short and that ill-natured matrons younger than herself are saying that she was behaving in just the same way ten years ago. But the winning of Rufford, at the terrible risk of losing what she has already, becomes an obsession. " Aut Cæsar aut nihil," she says, although she does not care for him. When he seems to have rejected her finally, her thoughts at first return to Morton, and the assured prosperity he offers her. But, " Then again arose to her mind the remembrance of Rufford Hall, of all the glories, of the triumph over everybody. Then again was the idea of a ' forlorn hope.' She thought that she could have brought herself to do it if only death would have been the alternative of success."

The works which Trollope wrote from 1868 to 1882 contain a series of studies of monomania, Louis Trevelyan, the Hotspurs, father and daughter, Mr. Scarborough, and several others. All these are leading characters in their respective books. There is also the occasional one-phrase character-part, like the old woman in *The American Senator* who books a seat on the railway for her parrot. Both these groups, very different as they are, invite comparison with Dickens. Of the woman with the parrot, we can only say that she is very amusing, but that Trollope clearly cannot stand comparison with Dickens on Dickens's strongest ground. Trollope's characters of this type reveal only a fraction of the fertility of invention, the unexpectedness, and the life that Dickens achieved. But in the first group, the serious full-length studies of the effect of one obsession on a whole life, the comparison is rather in Trollope's favour. Whereas, for instance, the Richard of *Bleak House* seems to change too, suddenly before our eyes, in Louis Trevelyan we see and understand the logical consequences of an abnormality originally slight. Trollope is a master of gradualness. It is notable, too, that the abnormalities of these characters with their grotesque results are made of the same stuff as ordinary human passions. Arabella Trefoil begins by wanting a rich husband. Louis Trevelyan wishes to be master in his own home, Mr. Scarborough to do what he likes with his own property—all very natural aspirations. They are the monomaniacs of everyday life. Here, perhaps, are Trollope's finest achievements, when the passions of ordinary life move by a natural process to grotesque self-destruction. As studies of the gradual disintegration of a life, these portraits rank with Dickens's masterpiece in this kind, old Dorrit.

At a crucial point in her campaign to win Rufford, Arabella hears that Morton, still engaged to marry her, is seriously ill. Her behaviour on hearing this is the high point of her story, and a good illustration of Trollope's method of irony, which is a somewhat unusual one. Most novelists use their plots to convey their ironical intentions; in *Candide*, in *Rasselas*, in *Tess of the D'Urbervilles* it is usually a sudden, unexpected event which disproves the theories or falsifies the expectations of the characters. Now Trollope, as we see in the Autobiography, seriously underestimated the importance of plot. He lost a great deal by this; some of his finest achievements are marred by irrelevant subplots. But it may be that in the matter of irony he gained. In this case, Arabella discovers that her selfishness has been incomplete. She feels a genuine grief for Morton, rushes to his bedside and tells him that she has been engaged to Lord Rufford. This is untrue, but she has made her lie for her own purposes and she sticks to it and repeats it when it can do her nothing but harm. This scene has been prepared by her endless lies and unfeeling passion: " There certainly was no man for whom she cared a straw; nor had there been for the last six or eight years. Even when he was kissing her she was thinking of her built-up hair, of her pearl powder, her paint, and of possible accidents and untoward revelations. The loan of her lips had been for use only and not for any pleasure which she had even in pleasing him. In her very swoon she had felt the need of being careful at all points. It was all labour, and all care—and alas, alas, all disappointment."

Coming where it does, her action at Morton's bedside seems to me to show ironical powers of a very high order, and it is essentially irony of character.

Throughout the story, Arabella is exhibited in contrast to her mother, Lady Augustus. The contrast is founded on a strong basis of similarity and identity of interest. They have both devoted their lives to the cause of a splendid marriage for Arabella. But Arabella's touches of humanity are inexplicable to her mother. Bound to the same course though they are, there is no sympathy between them. One is reminded of Florence Nightingale's " moloch of family life." Trollope uses the same device that Balzac did in *Cousin Pons*, where a very simple-minded character is placed against his friend who is so simple-minded as to make Pons seem almost worldly wise. Here Arabella has become almost inhuman, her mother is the finished article, and is completely so. But here, too, there is irony of character. For Lady Augustus, inhuman though she is, is devoted to a cause which, if successful, will leave her more miserable and lonely than ever. Her story ends in despair, when Arabella finally does marry. Thus involuntary unselfishness wrecks the selfish calculations of them both.

The end of Arabella's own story is inconclusive. She marries far below her former ambitions: " She was almost stunned by the change in the world around her. She need never again seem to be gay in order that men might be attracted. She made her promises and made them with the intention of keeping them. . . ." It is hinted that she may not be able to do so.

Considered simply as a social recorder Trollope is strangely contradictory when he deals with courtship. Some things, it is true, recur again and again; for instance, men in proposing marriage very often say " Give me your hand," or, " There is my hand. If you will give me yours . . ." or some near variant of these. But this may be no more than a personal idiosyncrasy of Trollope's own. But if one looks in Trollope for the answers to any of the questions that anthropologists would ask, one finds only confusion. Time and again axioms of proper conduct will be stated by one of the characters as an unquestionable dogma, and accepted by everyone else, only to be completely contradicted elsewhere. At one moment a kiss will seem practically equivalent to a written promise of marriage, at another, and in the same class of society, it will be accepted as meaning nothing. Now a man will be held to have done very wrong in not speaking to a girl's parents before herself, at another time everyone will accept without question his right to speak to her first. But one thing does seem to be generally agreed: a girl's parents have a right to prevent her from marrying a man they disapprove of, but must not force her to marry. And, as one would expect, when young people are not often alone together, tiny indications of affection assume great importance. " Linda had thought that whenever he shook hands with her since that memorable walk, she had always felt a more than ordinary pressure. This she had been careful not to return, but she had not the heart to rebuke it." This passage from *The Three Clerks* is typical of many.

Trollope's treatment of love is at its best when it occurs for the sake of something else. His interest in the subject was too vague and general for him to produce a precise analysis of the appropriate feelings. His stock plot, much too often repeated, of the woman hesitating between two men, is perfunctory. But he can use love with very great indirect effect. I will give two examples. One is the story, discussed elsewhere, of the old Duke of Omnium and Madame Goesler, where the effect is satirical. His desire to marry her is the last half-noble infirmity of a man who has always been powerful, ignoble, and irrationally admired. Madame Goesler realises that she will be ostracised if she marries him, and so refuses, for prudential and not for personal reasons, one of the men of highest rank, power and wealth in the country. This is one element in a detailed satire on power.

The other example is *Sir Harry Hotspur of Humblethwaite*. This, as we shall see, is not primarily a love story at all, great though the space is which the love story occupies. Its plot is simple, Sir Harry, a great landowner of old family, loses his only son and heir. He is left with a daughter, for whom he tries to arrange a marriage which will preserve the property for future male heirs. She refuses his choice, but falls in love with her cousin, George Hotspur, who is now the heir to the title, but a man of very bad reputation. Sir Harry vacillates for a long time, between his desire to unite the property and the title, and his fear of George as a husband for his daughter. Finally, such clear evidence of George's cheating at cards is discovered that Sir Harry finally forbids the marriage. The book ends with Emily's death.

Trollope succeeds here in the difficult task of making Emily's love convincing. She is the kind of woman for whom the sanctity of her own first choice outweighs everything. She is slowly convinced by the overwhelming evidence that George is a liar and a swindler, and has had a mistress all the time he has been professing love for herself. She is, as it were, a moral heretic, pushing the virtue of fidelity to the point where it becomes deliberate blindness. It is not his power over her, but her own power over herself which brings her life and her father's hope to disaster. Opposed to Emily's desperate fidelity is her father's obsession with his name and property. (The clash between them is heightened by their family likeness.) This, too, is presented as the exaggeration of a quality in itself good. For there is no self-seeking in it and no regard for wealth as such. Sir Harry knows that he does not want a man of noble rank and great property as her husband. He wants a man for whom the Hotspur property will be the care of his life. If his character were satisfactory, he would be thankful to accept George Hotspur, a penniless man with many debts, because the title must go to him and " to be head of the House of Hotspur was . . . a much greater thing than to be owner of Humblethwaite and Scarrowby." On this point father and daughter are agreed.

The book is one of the few examples in Trollope of a single, simple plot worked out logically from beginning to end. There is no extraneous matter, such as disfigures some of his best plots, for instance, in *Mr. Scarborough's Family*. The morality of the book is interesting for two reasons. The moral criticism is implied by the inevitable stages of the story itself. Only near the end in one sentence is the implicit judgment expressed in this account of Sir Harry's thoughts. "Did not the lesson of every hour seem to tell him that throughout his long life he had thought too much of his house and his name?" One of Trollope's greatest faults as a novelist, like Thackeray whom he so much admired, was chattiness. But it was a fault that grew less serious as time went on. In several of his books after 1870, as here, there is very little.

The other interesting thing about the moral criticism is the kind of vices involved. Based on personal fidelity, and family responsibility, they were for Trollope *splendida vitia*. Like Dickens with the character of Harold Skimpole, he was here dealing with the very vices which might spring out of his own temperament and his own moral values. The ability to do this is the last triumph of the satirist, and it is absent from some of the very greatest satirical works—like *Gulliver's Travels*. *Sir Harry Hotspur* is the story of the destructive power of truth and single-mindedness, the tragedy of the pure in heart. In this book, for the first and only time, Trollope set out to measure the power of love, not as a passion, but as an idea. The last chapter makes havoc of the guiding principles of Sir Harry's life. He goes to live abroad out of solicitude for his daughter's suffering, and so abandons all his duties as a baronet and landlord. He disinherits his nephew and so abandons the sacred law of primogeniture. But the fetish of primogeniture though once conquered is not exorcised. Instead of leaving his property to a man who would really care for it and continue the traditions he has cherished, he feels constrained to leave it to the next man after his nephew in the natural line of succession. This happens to be an earl of immense wealth and landed property, who will never live at Humblethwaite, and for whom the new possessions will only be a burden. So in his old age Sir Harry is driven to trample on all his idols in turn and cannot even being himself to preserve the identity of his estates by being consistent in his inconsistency.

But with Emily the result is different; her idol, too, has become impossible to worship, circumstances have shattered the primary assumption of her existence. But she can still remain true to her shattered ideal, when her father with the same integrity and determination cannot. Thus Emily's decline and death contain something of the moral strength of martyrdom; her father's death when it comes will only be a pitiful consummation of defeat. Amid all the busy, superficial, and seemingly endless flirtations of his numerous books Trollope has left this one very impressive monument to a type of love strange to his generation— a lord of terrible aspect hard as hell and stalwart as the grave.

PART TWO

★

PROGRESS TO PESSIMISM

Introductory

TROLLOPE'S LIFE can conveniently be divided into three periods. The first, which ended about 1847, was a period of suffering, self-reproach, and daydreaming. Though the dreams always seemed impossible of fulfilment, there was nothing napoleonic about them. To be liked, to make a good living, to have a family, to feel justified in one's own eyes, would seem to many people modest ambitions. It was in these long years of boyhood and adolescence—for his maturity was delayed to an unusually late age—that the foundations were laid for the successes of the middle period which extends roughly from 1847 to 1868. Trollope had many literary gifts; but perhaps one, a direct result of his early experiences and dreams, has been the main cause of his popularity in his lifetime and in the twentieth century. Because the most ordinary pleasures had once seemed to him like whispers of an impossible paradise, he was able in his middle years to depict them with a strange mixture of detailed precision and visionary splendour. He never lost the heightened interest in these things which most people only have when they are ill or subjected to a rigid discipline.

The last period, from about 1868 to his death in 1882, is one of retreat, questioning, and satire. The leading books of this period deserve a detailed analysis, because they constitute his greatest achievement, and reveal, as the earlier ones do not, his deepest preoccupations. The change from the optimistic middle period, to the steadily-growing pessimism of the last corresponds with a decline in popularity.

The wheel would come full circle. The pleasures and successes which before 1847 had seemed unreal because unattainable, gradually drifted into another unreality. What, in the last analysis, was their moral nature? Were they so desirable after all? More and more his mind came to dwell on the ambiguity of things. Simple ideas like love and honesty turned out to be complex, and perhaps deceptive. The anger of a man who in his brightest times had well known how to be angry, was now turned against the agreed ideas of society. Unexpected objects for his pity came into view. These feelings brought him to his finest achievements.

1. The Story of a Reputation

THE HISTORY of Trollope's literary reputation is more complex and more interesting than has generally been realised. We are familiar with the textbook account: Trollope admired and read in his lifetime, then, owing to the views on literary methods and rewards expressed in the Autobiography, execrated and afterwards forgotten; then revived as the 1930s and 1940s sought by the fireside an image of the security and abundance they had lost. On the face of it, the place assigned to the Autobiography in ruining his reputation is strange. Could it ever really have seemed like a messenger of guilty secrets from the grave? Were the æsthetes really so influential and was the public ever so very easily shocked? Was it really news to Trollope's former admirers that he worked fixed hours and regarded writing as a craft? Such preliminary doubts are confirmed by a study of the way his books were received by reviewers in the sixties.

To understand what happened it is necessary to distinguish between esteem and popularity. When Trollope's popularity was at its height and his earnings greatest, esteem was already waning. In 1869 the *Saturday Review* accused him of " superstitious adherence to facts " and could see no difference between *He Knew He Was Right* and all his previous books. Reviewing *Phineas Finn* a few months earlier the same journal said blankly, " approval fades into dislike and interest into tedium." In 1863 contempt had been masked but still present: " There is a brisk market for descriptions of the inner life of young women, and Mr. Trollope is the chief agent for satisfying that market." Even *Framley*

133

Parsonage in 1861 was only " as good a book as is often written by a clever and pleasant man in the intervals of business." To find genuine praise we have to go back as far as 1857 and *Barchester Towers*. In these reviews of the 1860s the appraisal of Trollope is not much different from that made at the nadir of his fame by Frederic Harrison in 1911. Faint praise is mixed with accusations of photography, vulgarity, and failure of imagination.

It is not surprising that Trollope had a bad press in the sixties. He had committed two serious faults in the eyes of most reviewers. He had become a best-seller and he was writing several books a year. His reviewers in such periodicals as *The Athenæum* and the *Saturday Review* have the air of men who knew it all before. They scarcely need to read the book to form a judgment. The conception of Trollope as just another best-seller was fostered by the deceptively lowbrow air of his writing. This is often refreshing to later generations, but irritating to contemporaries of intellectual pretensions.

As time went on the Barsetshire novels, with which he had made his name, became a handicap to Trollope. Reviewers awaited with ennui, faithful followers with delight, another and another book in the Barsetshire spirit, even if the name had been abandoned. Confronted, from 1867 onwards, with books of a different air and atmosphere, they were puzzled, irritated, or simply contemptuous. If *He Knew He Was Right* could not convince them that something new was being attempted, what could do so? *The Athenæum* reviewing *Dr. Thorne* in 1858 had declared the death-bed of Sir Roger Scatcherd equal in its way to those in Richardson's *Clarissa*. In 1875, it devoted about one-eighth the space to *The Way We Live Now* formerly given to some of the Barsetshire novels and could only say, " Poor as the novel is, there are clever scenes in it." The review of *The Prime Minister* said simply, " We cannot say we like Mr. Trollope's ministers and M.P.s half so well as the clergymen and country doctors of his earlier novels." Thus once their topical interest was gone a sharp decline in the novels' popularity was already in the logic of events, before the Autobiography was thought of.

When Trollope went out of fashion he did not cease to be read; he merely ceased to be discussed. It was dowdy to read him in 1910, but a slight feeling of shame did not deter everybody, any more than it prevented people, at a later date, from reading Kipling.

Already in 1925 *The Times Literary Supplement* was speaking of this period of dowdiness as past, and in 1927 gave him high praise in a front-page article. In 1922 an acute appreciation had appeared in the *New Statesman*. Mr. Michael Sadleir's biography in 1927 was important to his reputation, but not revolutionary. In 1932, Hilaire Belloc wrote that it was fashionable to say that he was in fashion, but indicated that he was not being read much more than before. The real boom, commercial and popular, followed the outbreak of war. In revival as in decline a change of esteem preceded by years a change of popularity. This process was not always understood by those who set it in motion. For an appreciative discussion of the political novels in *The Times Literary Supplement* of 1937 said: " Trollope's little burst of popularity in the twenties has already waned."

Every well-known author is liable to be attacked in one of two ways. If he is like Milton, a great established name in literary text books, and a writer one was made to read at school before real appreciation was possible, attacks upon him are generally learned and uncompromising. His enemies approach him with the devout rage of iconoclasts. Wordsworth's attack on Pope, T. S. Eliot's upon Shelley, and Dr. Leavis's on Milton, are all of this kind. Such attacks, under the guise of dethroning a single author, often aim at a whole kind of poetry or even an attitude of mind. When they are successful they may herald a general revolution of taste.

In the case of Trollope and his like, criticism takes a different line. " His like " here means writers who never aspired to the highest literary honours, who have been enjoyed by the fastidious, but have been read by them without effort as entertainment. Such writers are the founders of no schools and a change in their valuation will not much affect the reputations of others. The critical are apt to shrug their shoulders and say, " Very good of course, only perhaps a little dull." So did Dr. Thorne reply to Lady Arabella's embarrassed remark that it was a fine day, by saying that it was fine only perhaps a little rainy. In such remarks the criticism always sounds more sincere than the praise.

Trollope's most damaging critics are apt to be professed admirers. Frederic Harrison, whose friendship and admiration for the author were certainly genuine, wrote, " His work has most of the merits and some of the weakness of the best photography. It is almost painfully realistic—painting men and women as he knew them in everyday life." And a little later he uses the still more damning epithet " pedestrian." That was in 1911; but Professor Bradford A. Booth, a learned and genuine admirer of the present day, says substantially the same when he quotes from Lowell on Grote, " honest incapacity for imagination is . . . singularly soothing." Though, in my opinion, such criticism is mistaken, it is not absurd. There are certain writers, like John Webster, who would never be called pedestrian by anyone who was not being deliberately paradoxical. But Tennyson, who is not pedestrian either, might well be called so.

It is difficult to answer such general criticism, and the dissatisfaction expressed often turns out to be curiously vague. In Harrison's comment " everyday " is a suggestive word, but has no precise meaning in the context, and does not every novelist use what he knows of men and women as his material? The question is, what use does he make of this material? If Harrison meant that Trollope dealt only with people as they appear in society, then one can be content to say that he was wrong. In books like *Cousin Henry* and *Sir Harry Hotspur* he probed into a series of subtle contrasts between appearance and reality. It is true that the political novels which were Harrison's immediate subject necessarily deal much with people in large groups in the House of Commons and in the political salons. But even here we have a detailed and delicate study of the relationship between Plantaganet Palliser and his wife. If Trollope saw this in the life around him, he must have been an X-ray photographer.

An essay contributed to *Essays and Studies, 1920* by George Saintsbury, deserves close consideration—not because it is a specially distinguished piece of criticism, but because it illustrates so clearly certain paradoxes about Trollope's reputation and the nature of his appeal. It would seem at first sight that Saintsbury was peculiarly well fitted for the appreciation of Trollope. He was not the man to be overcritical of casual artistic methods. He had a keen sense of enjoyment, and was not afraid to enjoy what had been admired before him by people of mediocre literary perceptions. Both author and critic prided themselves on being fine old crusted English characters. Trollope, who knew in his heart that this was not the truth about himself, would have approved of Saintsbury for approaching his ideal. Most important of all, Saintsbury could bury himself in a book and treat its characters almost as real people, which is just what Trollope did when writing.

For Saintsbury the novel was a form of conviviality. He loved to hear the author's voice as if from the other side of the hearth. He wanted to discuss the characters with a friendly author until they came to life, to complain (as he does in this essay) that some of them are prigs and want kicking, to point out that whatever the author may think, Kate Vavasour is " a much nicer girl " than her cousin Alice. If Trollope could have been present in the flesh, he would have enjoyed the dialogue and might have approved the criticisms. He would have felt a bond with anyone who could enter into the spirit of his own imaginary world, and no minor criticisms and disagreements would have clouded his gratitude.

One thing he would not have realised. To treat fictional characters as if they were real, however valuable to creation, is fatal to criticism. Ironically, Saintsbury's inability to perceive anything beyond Trollope's superficial effects is due to following a critical method very like Trollope's own. The result is just what one would expect. Typically, he tells us that *The Way We Live Now* is " rather dreary." In making this judgment his mind insensibly slides from the kind of society treated by the novel to the literary merits of the treatment. His view or the contrast between Trollope's work before 1868 and after is a simple one. " The majority," he says, " of the characters of the new books were themselves new; and it must be a very odd taste indeed which does not decide that the old were better." For him, Trollope, especially in the Barsetshire novels, offered a passport to memories (or perhaps to illusions) of a spacious and sunny mid-Victorian land. He did not wish to be distracted on the way by disturbing images. Perhaps Trollope, too, would gladly have been spared the bitter vision that issued in the harsh story of Melmotte and the despairing defeat of Louis Trevelyan. Saintsbury dismisses them with the irritation of a eupeptic man afflicted with un-accustomed nightmares after a good dinner.

As a general test of all fiction, Saintsbury asks the question, " Are the folk of the novel such that you have or feel that you might have met them in your life or in theirs? " What he does not say, but his detailed judgments reveal, is that he also wants the characters to be such as he would enjoy meeting. So his choice can be summed up in a simple contrast. Books which are crowded, gay, extrovert, humorous, he likes. Books which deal with madness, guilt, indecision, loneliness, despair, he condemns. This involves the corollary that he likes many of the books of the early and middle period, few, if any of the last fifteen years of the author's life. The often-repeated story of Trollope's declining powers in the seventies has no greater foundation than this very natural preference. In rejecting such a criterion, we should remember how very popular it is.

Sir Hugh Walpole had more excuse for taking a similar view; he was a novelist himself. The same excuse can be made for Trollope's own critical failure in his book on Thackeray—a failure also partly attributable to the pain caused by loss of a friend. Trollope's attitude to his own characters is certainly infectious. Many a reader has been struck by his remark that he still lives much in company with Mrs. Proudie's ghost and has felt that it contains more truth than absurdity. Walpole exhibits in a severe form the occupational disease of the novelist turned critic. When he criticises Trollope for not making Barchester Cathedral into a symbol, one cannot help thinking of the way he used his own cathedral in the novel he called after it. But he ought to have realised that Trollope was not trying to do the same thing as he was himself. A cathedral may be a most valuable symbol, as Kafka and others have shown, but the fact is not relevant to the criticism of a novel which uses no symbolism.

In Walpole's remarks upon *Mr. Scarborough's Family* the novelist supersedes the critic. He describes old Mr. Scarborough as dying " smiling sardonically." Now this end might well be thought in character for Mr. Scarborough. All through the book he has been a bitter, sneering old man, astonishing everyone by his barefaced wickedness. If Walpole had been writing the novel no doubt he would have died smiling sardonically. But Trollope saw him differently. He made him betray here and there a sign of hidden tenderness and a hint of idealism in all his scheming. One does not blame Walpole for missing this; it is very easy to miss things. But it is reprehensible in a critic to build such a vivid idea of another author's character that, to preserve this fictitious consistency he should be forced to alter the plain facts which the author tells us. Trollope describes Mr. Scarborough's end thus: " But now, in his last moments, in his very last, there came upon him some feeling of pity, and, in speaking of his son, he once more called him ' Gus.' " He goes on to beg his elder son to provide for the younger and with his last words begs him to give up gambling.

In many passages where no actual misstatements are made, there are signs of the same urge to collaborate instead of criticise. He tells us, for instance, that Lily Dale " should have turned to Eames " after her failure with Crosbie. It is not clear whether this piece of retrospective advice is addressed to Trollope or to Lily Dale herself, considered as a real person. It may be that he did not know himself which he meant.

Walpole uses the word " modern " as an epithet of unqualified praise, and is delighted when he feels able to apply it to any part of Trollope's work. Here one must sympathise with him, for he conceived himself to be conducting a difficult defence of dowdy mid-Victorianism before a mocking and sceptical intelligentsia. Moreover, this attitude has an insidious appeal to nearly all of us, so that we find ourselves adopting it before we are aware. Still, full appreciation is impossible if we are always thinking in terms of the " cause of nowadays and the end of history."

Where Saintsbury had seemed offended by the later and less cheerful books, Walpole seems to be puzzled. For before he begins to discuss them he has made a general statement which makes understanding difficult. " Trollope's spirit," he says, " is too unmorbid, cheerful, and humorous for any general twilight atmosphere. . . ." It would be interesting, and might be very instructive to know why he thought so. Did he assume that people who work and play hard and behave in a hearty manner are always of this kind? Or was he thinking in terms of income tax and the prosperity of the middle class? Or did he feel that the Victorians did not have to cope with Freud and all the confused prophetic voices of the twentieth century? Since we know that Walpole read and studied the Autobiography, and was acquainted with all the novels, it is hard to see how he could have come to this conclusion without some such preconceived idea.

Trollope's criticism of his own work would be of little interest if it were not an author's self-criticism. He has no discernible critical principles, and his preferences among his own books seem arbitrary. All his life he was an incurable dreamer, though he left himself little time to dream, and may have feared that his dreams might become too powerful over him. He was exceptional in not needing leisure and solitude for his dreaming; he had had enough of those in his youth to last a lifetime. In the fifties and sixties when his most celebrated, though not necessarily his best, books were written, few men could have had less time for reflection. For, as he tells us more than once with angry emphasis, he was not dreaming as his pen moved rapidly across the pages in the solitude of early morning. Imaginary characters and incidents, more real to him than his actual experiences, must have formed themselves in his mind at other times. He must have dreamt over the whist tables, while still playing a hard game. He must have dreamt while enjoying to the full his angry arguments and his foxhunting.

In criticising other novelists he unconsciously assumed that every novelist ought to be like himself in this. Because he did not understand the assumption he was making he was often at a loss to explain his own judgments of his contemporaries. He was very severe on Disraeli, but could not define his charge of " falseness "; he felt obscurely that Disraeli had thought up his characters by an intellectual process, instead of encountering them, in the proper way, in the visionary wanderings of the mind. And, though he was entirely out of sympathy with Dickens, he recognised in him with fellow-feeling a peremptory and dominating imagination.

But at the same time he was continually harping on " truth to life." Once again he did not reflect very carefully upon the implication of his words. He was simply impatient of any form of exaggeration. The unusual strength of his feelings and especially of his fears led him to regard exaggerated and high-flown sentiments as a sign of defective feeling. Wild beasts that are allowed to roam freely are not likely to be the strongest or most dangerous. Trollope could have understood Samuel Johnson's remark that he would eat his dinner on the day of a friend's execution; he would have guessed that Johnson said this because bereavement struck him with unusual force. Sensible on the whole as these ideas are, they led him to be unjust to Dickens. He failed to see that exaggeration was an essential part of Dickens's whole method and necessary to his imagination. The spell that his own working methods exercised on his critical judg-ment is revealed when he seriously rates as slow work Thackeray's production of *Pendennis*, *Esmond*, and *The Newcomes* in four years.

It is amusing to see Trollope, with the air of one enunciating a platitude, contradict Aristotle and call the plot of a novel un-important. Once again, he was generalising from the experience of his own inner world, where personality and speech were vivid, and events were shadowy. But why did he generalise so boldly? Sympathetic with most weaknesses, why had he no patience with authors who found writing difficult? Because he had once felt himself an outcast he did not wish to feel that he was peculiar even when the peculiarity was creditable. He would have liked to believe that everyone had an inexhaustible literary treasure house in his own mind, if he chose to use it. His anger at writers who were forced to sit staring at the wall is in defence of his own ordinariness. His self-deception has partly deceived posterity.

Judging as he did, Trollope was bound to be capricious about his own work. He judged by the vividness of his own memories; it did not occur to him that memories are influenced by many factors, irrelevant to literary merit. His criticism of *Ralph the Heir* is simply that he has forgotten most of it, and this seems to him a damning criticism. If he had not himself been the author, he would have been more charitable. Sometimes it is possible to guess the reason for an unlikely preference. His fondness for *The Three Clerks* may be due to associations with his own first success in life at the Post Office and (as he seems to hint) to romantic memories as well. On the other hand, his idea that *The Bertrams* is on a par with *Dr. Thorne* seems merely perverse until we reflect that, if we knew enough about his state of mind when writing them, it might seem no more than natural.

The mid-Victorian period was a time of unusual dissociation between creation and criticism. A number of distinguished writers—Dickens and Tennyson are obvious examples—imagined and recorded things of which their own everyday mental faculties took no account. They had no need to complain of being misunderstood, for they did not understand themselves. The same failing is well illustrated by Trollope's appraisal of *He Knew He Was Right*. " I do not know," he says, " that in any literary effort I ever fell more completely short of my own intention than in this story. It was my purpose to create sympathy for the unfortunate man who, while endeavouring to do his duty to all around him, should be led constantly astray by his unwillingness to submit his own judgment to the opinion of others. The man is made to be unfortunate enough, and the evil which he does is apparent. So far I did not fail, but the sympathy has not been created yet. I look upon the story as being nearly altogether bad."

One could not have a clearer case of the opposition between Trollope the creator and Trollope the critic, between the originality of the one and the conventional dullness of the other. He cannot appreciate his own best work. He is hamstrung by the tradition that demands real heroism of a novel's central character. As a novelist he had escaped from the idea, which vitiated much mid-Victorian criticism of real and of fictional characters—the idea that right conduct is always easy, and that deviation from it is therefore despicable. Indeed, his tone in speaking of the book is very like that of the more unsympathetic reviewers. The *Saturday Review* complained that Trollope made us feel a hearty contempt for both husband and wife, and regarded their weakness of character as a damning criticism of the work as fiction.[1]

In part, the jejuneness of Trollope's criticism is deliberate. He would not in any case have been a critic of special talent, but the desire to be as normal as possible prevented him from probing deeply. He was obviously reluctant to disagree with public opinion even on such an open question as the relative merits of Dickens, Thackeray, and George Eliot. But he could, when the matter at stake interested him personally, perceive the inconsistencies of the public taste. He says, for instance, that he received many letters begging him to let Lily Dale marry John Eames, but he remarks acutely that the writers of these letters were really interested in her just because she would not.

His ideas on the moral effects of fiction were over-simple. He was right judging the question important. Those who have thought it unimportant have usually confused deliberate moralising with the implicit moral judgments which every book about human beings must convey even against the author's will. But he did not allow for the complexity of the reader's response. After all, Carlyle has in all probability influenced more people against hero-worship than he has in favour of it. Trollope tends to assume that every reader will accept whatever he is given. Once again his practice was subtler than this theory.

[1] Of another character in this book the same review says, " If a man has so little vigour of mind that he really cannot decide whom he wants to marry, we do not take much interest in following his fortunes."

One one occasion the disproportion between his creative and critical gifts leads him to claim too much for himself. Speaking of *Nina Balatka* and *Linda Tressel*, he says " Prague is Prague and Nuremberg is Nuremberg." Perhaps they are, as far as physical accuracy goes. But, just as he did not appreciate the depth of his own understanding of English culture, he did not realise his failure to understand other cultures. If he had comprehended his own best achievements he would not have been satisfied with the superficial foreignness of these two minor works.

A few considerations of general critical interest emerge from this study of an author's reputation. The first is that best-sellers are the most difficult of all subjects for contemporary criticism. People may quote Johnson's remark about concurring with the common reader, but how many critics either in the nineteenth or the twentieth century have genuinely subscribed to it? The obscurely felt distinction between highbrow and lowbrow has vitiated modern criticism of nineteenth-century literature as surely as the schism between classic and romantic led Matthew Arnold to underrate Pope. The second, allied to the first, is that habit is crucially important in reading and reviewing. Once reviewers and public become thoroughly accustomed to a writer's manner, he will have the greatest difficulty in impressing them favourably with anything new. Even the former disparagement of Shakespeare's romances is partly to be explained in this way. The fable that Shakespeare was a tired old man before he was fifty illustrates how far some critics will go rather than admit that he was entitled to write serious plays unlike *King Lear* and *Macbeth*. If such misunderstandings can occur about a writer whose every line has been studied and weighed, how much more about less revered writers. A curious modern example is the schizophrenic attitude to Kipling (now partly repaired). He seems to have been admired either for the craftmanship, subtlety and disillusionment of his Indian stories, or for the thumping rhythm and sentiment of his verse. But in fact even his best stories can be enjoyed by the unliterary, and his verse has much to offer to a fastidious taste.

There are two ways in which a great writer can be condemned

unheard without being forgotten. He may be put on a pedestal, praised as a classic, and read only for examinations and for self-improvement. Or he can be relegated to the sickroom and the sleepy fireside and read without effort by people who wish to be soothed into forgetfulness of the world. The second method is less common, but perhaps more deceptive than the first.

Finally, to look at a book through its author's eyes is a useful preliminary exercise, but if persisted in is a hindrance to sound judgment.

2. Technique

THE LONGEST novel is only an account of a few selected events in the lives of a few selected characters. One of the novelist's most difficult problems is to suggest the connection between these few events and the multitude which are not mentioned at all. On this point more than any other Trollope concentrated his technical skill. Nearly all his humorous scenes suggest the world of silent figures outside the novel's boundary; his farce is very rarely pure farce. When Lord Dumbello is at cross-purposes with his hostess at Mrs. Proudie's conversazione, the implications are beyond laughter—the complexity of the social forces which drive into the same orbit people so diverse in birth, means, ability, tastes and opinions. Mid-Victorian writers were fond of proclaiming that one half of the world did not know how the other half lived. Here and in the scene between Bishop Proudie and Bertie Stanhope, the son of one of his own clergy, it is suggested that people do not even know how their own set live.

Another favourite form of humour arises from the social act, which though trivial in itself, causes an intense and humiliating concentration of the public gaze. Though the reader generally identifies himself with the helpless victim in the centre, the implied ranks of staring eyes suggest by their very anonymity, the pressure of life outside the book's confines.

Frequent, too, is the sudden switch from a detailed study of a character's thoughts to a description of the place where he is walking, and of people who care nothing for him, and whom he may not even notice. Such is the account of Charles Tudor's despair in *The Three Clerks.*

" He walked from Norfolk Street into the Strand, and there the world was still alive, though it was now nearly one o'clock. The debauched misery, the wretched outdoor midnight revelry of the world was there, streaming in and out from gin-palaces, and bawling itself hoarse with horrid, discordant, screech-owl slang. But he went his way unheeding and uncontaminated. Now, now that it was useless, he was thinking of the better things of the world."

Other minor touches often contribute to the same effect. One is the interlocking of one setting with another; Rufford and Ufford, scene of *The American Senator,* appear for a moment in *Ayala's Angel* and the Proudies are mentioned in *The Claverings.* Another is the misreporting which inevitably occurs whenever the affairs of the protagonists are discussed in general society. Lady Laura Kennedy is slandered by truthful people who are correct in their view of most of the facts. Everything is too complex to be understood from the outside.

The novels rarely end with a climax. Like Excalibur, the characters sheer off into the darkness from which they emerged, suggesting, as they disappear, the vastness of the unknown. Thus Augustus Scarborough accepts £25,000 in lieu of his lost inheritance and departs into the labyrinths of the city without leaving a hint of his future success or failure.

Sometimes a very minor character, often a servant, will sum up in a sentence the commensense attitude to something which has caused endless thought and argument to the others. Such is the encouragement offered to Mr. Crawley by the brickmaker of Hogglestock, and such is the scene in *Ralph the Heir* after the death of Squire Newton with all his loving plans for his illegitimate son disastrously uncompleted. The son is standing with the butler beside the dead body. " ' He would have given me his flesh and blood;—his very life,' said Ralph to the butler. ' I think no father ever so loved a son. And yet, what has it come to? ' Then he stooped down, and put his lips to the cold clay-blue forehead.

' It ain't come to much surely,' said old Grey to himself, as he crept away to his own room; ' and I don't suppose it do come to much mostly when folks go wrong.' "

A superficial reading might mistake the butler for a mask of the author's conventional moralising. The meaning lies rather in the sudden alteration of the point of view. It is like reversing a telescope. What has been examined during many chapters in all its complexity is now dismissed in one monumentally simple sentence from an uneducated man. The author does not side with or against him; each view of the question is allowed to react on the other. The butler's speech suggests that in all their plans the Newtons have disquieted themselves in vain, disguising from themselves the irrevocability of the one central fact of the case. On the other hand, the complex effects of illegitimacy on all the characters cast suspicion on easy gnomic summaries. The reader, probably without formulating it, will draw the conclusion that behind every platitude of a disinterested onlooker there lurks a situation as subtle as that of the Newtons. Once again the horizon is enlarged beyond the book's actual characters and events.

A slightly different device is used in the first chapter of *The Belton Estate*. After the suicide of the heir to the property, the only son of the owner, comes this passage: " It was full summer at Belton, and four months had now passed since the dreadful tidings had reached the castle. It was full summer, and the people of the village were again going about their ordinary business; and the shopgirls with their lovers from Redicote were again to be seen walking among the oaks in the park on a Sunday evening; and the world in that district of Somersetshire was getting itself back into its grooves."

Here there is the pathos of the individual lost in the crowd. Even the most desperate acts reverberate faintly amid the multitudinous concerns of men. Again a rich, unknown context for the book's events is briefly suggested, so as to increase their significance. The passage introduces also a recurrent theme. Things are not what they seem; the calm and ordinary mask violence and despair, and yet the calm and ordinary are not a sham. It is characteristic of Trollope's mind that he should call the richest and most comfortable college in Oxford " Lazarus." His whole style of writing contributes to the same effect. Often his style seems to be no style at all. Most of his sentences are made up of ordinary words, with a fair sprinkling of clichés. They seldom have a single memorable operative word, such as Thackeray uses so effectively. But much of what he loses in detail by his un-exciting style, he gains back when his books are considered as a whole. His paradoxes and subtleties take hundreds of pages to work themselves out, and they stand out all the more sharply, through the persistence of the droning conversational voice and the absence of the paradox of epigram. Nor, as an article by E. W. Parks has shown,[1] is the author's continual obtrusion of himself as the storyteller altogether useless. Henry James, who found this very discouraging, did not perhaps realise that the author himself plays a part similar to that of James's favourite watcher and narrator. This is not to deny Trollope's faults of style, but only to suggest, that none of them, except his occasional long-windedness, is without its compensations. Incidentally, only his descriptive and analytical passages are marred by this fault, partly due, perhaps, to the modesty of a man who does not feel confident of being read with careful attention. In accounts of speech or action, economy is his greatest stylistic virtue. Thus, in *Orley Farm*, when young Orme is driven to despair his state of mind is indicated in one sentence. He forces his horse to a dangerous jump which is safely accomplished. Then " ' Ah-h! ' said Peregrine, shouting angrily at the horse, as though the brute had done badly instead of well." Tom Towers, the unostentatious potentate behind *The Jupiter* newspaper, can strike terror into M.P.s and almost cause a general election merely by whispering at a party, " ' By the by, Sowerby, what do you think of this threatened dissolution? ' " Lady Kingsbury in *Marion Fay* hears of an accident to her stepson, the obstacle to the inheritance of the marquisate by her own son Frederick. Her mixed feelings are conveyed in the sentence " She leaned over them and kissed them

[1] *Nineteenth-Century Fiction. March, 1953.*

all [her children]; but she knelt at that [bed] on which Lord Frederick lay and woke him with her warm embraces."

2

Sub-plots were common form during most of Trollope's writing life, so it was tempting for a man not much given to reflection upon the principles of art, to leave the question of their real purpose in abeyance. Moreover, he often drove himself so hard that mere change of personalities in his story would have been a relief to his overtaxed imagination. It is only in the later works that sub-plots pull their weight, and even in those not always. *Mr. Scarborough's Family* provides examples both of relevant and irrelevant sub-plots. The Brussels episodes are no more than a cumbrous device to remove one of the characters from the orbit of the others. But the story of the Prosper inheritance contains a series of ironic contrasts with that of the Scarborough inheritance.

First there is the obvious contrast between the characters of the two landowners. Scarborough is clever, self-confident, fascinating, or terrible to others, and able to bend everyone to his will. Prosper is dull, timid, and conscious of being a joke to his nephew and to the woman he attempts to marry. Each has violent antipathies; Scarborough's arise from large private theories about matters within his experience, such as rent and inheritance. Prosper's are only protests against the unknown. Each frets under the compulsion of an entail, but while Scarborough attacks it with subtle long-drawn-out schemes, Prosper's attempt to disinherit his nephew is a fiasco. Though they never meet, their fortunes are interlocked by the quarrel between Prosper's nephew and Scarborough's sons.

Yet, utterly different as they are, there is a curious similarity in their histories. The calculations and the quiet, insatiable anger of Scarborough cause two separate reversals of the entail, so that in the end justice is done and the original heir receives the property. Prosper in his muddled resentment fails in his attempt at disinheritance, and once again the original heir is the heir at last. His failure is comprehensive and ignominious, for his plan requires that he should have a son, and he cannot even find a wife. Scarborough acts from a broad and intense judgment of life, Prosper from caprice and irritation, and yet both are driven to contemplate a thoroughly conventional action—disinheritance.

All this is very strange. Sub-plots are normally intended to strengthen the argument of the main plot. This one seems to weaken it, and yet there can be no doubt that the contrast was deliberate and carefully contrived. What precisely was Trollope aiming at? First he desired to place the fantastic and terrible Scarborough in a context of the ordinary—even the petty. The best way to do this was to show us another man doing the same things with the most trivial motives. But the thing goes deeper than this, and takes us close to a fundamental and most unusual quality of the author's mind. The main plot of the book is a satirical inquiry into the nature of honesty and the various ideas of it held in the world. Mr. Scarborough himself is the chosen instrument of the attack. The Prosper story tends to neutralise the irony created by the Scarborough one. If the Scarborough story criticises society, the Prosper story criticises the criticisms. In one sense it is satire turned against the author himself. Few writers would have conceived such an idea; it is a product of a rare compound of engrained mental qualities, moderation, bitterness, and self-distrust.

3

In the Barsetshire novels Mr. Harding is used as a moral touchstone for the other characters. To give this function to one character in a novel is not, of course, uncommon; what is, is the way he is portrayed. The typical character of this sort is Robert Elsmere, an active hero who influences everyone by his zeal and his persuasive arguments. Such a hero is often an idealised version of the author. But Harding is elderly when the story begins, weak, troubled, and lacking in energy. Not only is he unlike Trollope, but he is unlike anything Trollope ever wished to be or imagined that he was. Rather it is the book's other characters who resemble the author, in being vigorous and hearty. The Barsetshire world is crowded, individualist, and purposeful. Cloister, close, and parish church are battlegrounds. Mr. Harding moves among the born fighters like Grantly and Slope with an apologetic air, casting doubt on the validity of ambition and the importance of money. After reading the Autobiography it is strange to find implicit in every line of *The Warden* and its successors the conclusion that Harding is justified. Was this self-criticism, or did Harding emerge from a totally different level of his mind?

The sixteenth chapter of *The Small House at Allington* has considerable technical interest. Crosbie is on his way to Courcy Castle where he will betray his betrothed for the sake of rank. Though he has not yet looked this action in the face, the tenor of his thoughts is already tending towards it. By accident he meets an unknown clergyman who turns out to be Mr. Harding. The experienced reader of Victorian fiction will know just what to expect—an impassioned plea for fidelity from the old man to the young, or a touching story of days long ago which will mysteriously fit the present situation. But he will find nothing of the sort. There is a little rambling conversation, and only a chance mention of a lady with a large family recalls Crosbie for a moment to his own pre-occupations, influencing him, if at all, slightly in favour of the dishonourable course. The effect of this simple-seeming scene is complex. First and most obviously, it is the moment before the horror, a glimpse of innocence, ironical because not understood by the characters. To Harding it is ordinary. To Crosbie it has the sweet and sentimental flavour of an interlude irrelevant to the main concerns of his life. This is the great crisis of his existence and he has no idea of the fact. The cleverness of the scene lies in the implicit contrast between what actually happens and what is not stated. The stage is set for a drama that never takes place. As we shall see this idea of the undramatic crisis, of a void at the centre of things, is much more for Trollope than a technical device. It reflects the settled temper of a man determined not to be deceived, almost pathological in his dread of illusions. The goodness of Mr. Harding is powerless either to impress Crosbie or to understand his dilemma. Neither good nor evil can understand themselves, and still less can they understand each other. The indifferent subjects of the conversation are symbolical of a deeper failure of communication.

Mr. Harding's idle chatter about the past makes Crosbie, man of the world though he is, seem too young to be taking momentous decisions. By Harding's scale of time, he is not far from the cradle. The innocence of old age is confronted with the corruption of youth. But Harding's appeal to a distant past which he remembers with a gentle melancholy will soon be balanced by Crosbie's appeal to a past only a few weeks' old, but equally remote and irrecoverable. Finally, the scene has disturbing implications about the nature of moral decisions. In this sunny, quiet interlude when he is thinking of other things, the most important decision of Crosbie's life is being taken for him by his unconscious mind, and will only emerge into daylight some days later. So the crisis for which the stage was set occurs after all, though hidden at the time from the protagonists and the reader; all of them are the victims of a kind of double bluff.

The theme of the passive centre, which first occurs in the character of Harding, occurs later in more extreme forms. However passive, Harding is an interesting character. In *Is He Popenjoy?* the centre is a baby who dies in infancy. Because of the circumstances of his birth, he is the motive of action for all the characters, but none of them considers him as a human being. Once again a deliberate ambiguity is placed at the heart of the book. That the boy with all his disputed titles and honours should disappear without a trace suggests the futility of all the interest shown in him. On the other hand, there is a mystery; he is always discussed but seldom seen; even his parents know little of him. His death, which is the climax of the plot, is marked by the same absence of drama as we have observed before. There is no one to grieve, and no one likes to feel glad. There is no deathbed scene; only a telegram tells the news. His epitaph is pronounced by his father: " ' He has got away from all his troubles—lucky dog.' " But this emptiness at the centre does not produce a wholly negative effect. The absence of pathos, the absence of any majesty or mystery of death, the absence of all explanations insensibly suggest all these things to the reader. There is pathos in the father's insensibility, and in his regret at his own want of feeling. The marquis feels older and more aimless than ever before, and instead of grief for his child, has the grief of knowing that he will never again feel a strong emotion.

He says, " ' I don't understand much about what people call grief. I can't say that I was particularly fond of him, or that I shall personally miss him. They hardly ever brought him to me, and when they did, it bothered me. And yet, somehow it pinches me—it pinches me.' " Whatever the child's value and meaning clearly no one was aware of it. Nevertheless, he controls the plot, and the two events of his life—birth and death—are enough to nullify all the plotting and planning about the inheritance. Action is fruitless; unconscious stillness is alone effective. In an age when emotions were freely bludgeoned by the imagined death of children, this is an original, and even brilliant technical device.

Round this centre is established an equilibrium of forces which may seem, according to the point of view, satisfyingly complete or merely frustrating. In any case, it is very characteristic of the author's outlook and methods. The book is mainly concerned with the position of women. This favourite controversial subject of several generations customarily arouses the strongest feelings. But in Trollope's treatment of it we see the neutral, anonymous attitude which underlay his boisterous public personality; it led him to unusual technical expedients.

The story of Mary Lovelace is, in the main, an analysis of the suffering inflicted on women by mild and well-meaning men. She submits to endless sewing with her sisters-in-law. Lord George Germain, her husband, and uncle of the disputed Popenjoy, is sombre in his pleasures and perpetually preoccupied with imaginary business duties. As the brother of an absentee peer he feels responsibility but has no power. In London he bores his wife by reading the local paper from home. He is involved in an insincere flirtation with a married woman, which through pure carelessness he causes his wife to discover. On the other hand, the story of Jack de Barton shows what women suffer through gay, thoughtless men who are prepared to promise anything in the conviction that no one will expect them to keep their word. This bald summary of course does no justice to the subtlety or to the strength of the indictment.

Two kinds of remedy are considered, a feminist insistence on women's rights, and the domination of men by coquetry and feminine arts. Mary is involved in both because persuasive friends drag her to feminist meetings, and Mrs. Houghton uses the feminine arts on her husband. Both Mrs. Houghton and the feminists make use of the case against male stupidity and male privileges which the main plot has carefully built up. Mrs. Houghton uses it insincerely as a coquettish weapon, while the feminists only succeed in spreading jealousy and bitterness amongst themselves. The case built up in one part of the book seems discredited in another.

The satire on feminism is somewhat obvious, but this weakness does not prevent feminism from playing its appointed part in the book's structure. In one sense the total effort is negative. A three-cornered antithesis (between women's wrongs, and the two opposite methods of repairing them) produces a frustrating equilibrium. The main object of satire turns out to be different from what we thought. Male selfishness, feminine deceit, feminist passion, all these are secondary. Just as the Popenjoy baby is a passive figure at the heart of the plot, so there is a void and a denial at the centre of the conflict of ideas. The answer to the woman problem is that there is no answer. Yet just as Popenjoy, the passive centre, is seen at last, when he dies, to have an unsuspected value, so here the negative statement has a positive corollary. The commonplace idea of endurance and acceptance of necessity acquires a strange richness derived partly from this deep harmony between plot and ideas. In part, also, it is due to the fact that the commonplace, like " il faut cultiver notre jardin," is reached only by a long winding road. *Is He Popenjoy?* is not a masterpiece because this fine organisation is not always maintained in detail. Trollope became too interested in one character, Mary Lovelace, at the expense of strict maintenance of his original plan and purpose. Nevertheless, the book reveals an artistic potential and a subtlety which contrast strangely with the ordinariness of the author's purely intellectual powers.

4

The old Duke of Omnium appears in no less than seven of the Barsetshire and political novels. He is seldom prominent, but always important. His importance is satirical, though for a long time the satire is comparatively mild. It may be that at first the author did not comprehend the character's full possibilities. But on the other hand, the diffusion of satire is certainly deliberate. He had not yet reached the point where he would launch a full-scale satirical attack as he would more than once in the 1870s. But the Duke is all the time a moral touchstone, unobtrusive at first, savagely obvious as his death approaches. From this point of view, he is the obverse of Mr. Harding.

There is a good reason why the Duke should not be memorable as a character; he is more of a symbol than a character—a symbol of all the powers of the world. He is twice compared to a mountain, magnificent in quiescence. On another occasion he is called the lama, a description which exactly fits him. For his business is to be silent, invisible, and worshipped by the whole world. The adulation of his power is a kind of religion. Madame Goesler, who had refused to injure him by marrying him in his old age, and had afterwards nursed him in his last illness, finally realises this. " She had devoted herself to this old man who was now dead, and there had been moments in which she had thought that that sufficed. But it had not sufficed. . . . After that she

reflected whether it might not be best for her to become a devotee
—it did not matter much in what branch of the Christian religion,
so that she could assume some form of faith. . . . She had tried to
believe in the Duke of Omnium, but there she had failed."
Incongruous senses of the worlds " devotee " and " believe " are
deliberately juxtaposed.

The man is brought before us very gradually and his legend
always precedes him. In *Dr. Thorne* and *Framley Parsonage* he
is viewed from the point of view of someone who would never
think of speaking to him, but who watches him with awe. At this
stage the Duke is all taciturnity, remoteness, and effortless power.
He is always saying two or three words, and we are not even told
what they are. " He was very willing that the Queen should be
queen so long as he was allowed to be Duke of Omnium. Nor had
he begrudged Prince Albert any of his honours till he was called
Prince Consort. Then indeed, he had, to his own intimate friends,
made some remark in three words, not flattering to the discretion
of the Prime Minister." Likewise he obtained ecclesiastical pre-
ferment for Mark Robarts by means of two words to the Prime
Minister, which went a great way even with Lord Brock. Of
course the intimate friends to whom the Duke spoke never appear.
The only one who is mentioned by name is Lady Hartletop, and
she and the Duke never meet within Trollope's pages, though their
relationship is a source of scandalous amusement to society.

Nothing must be done too soon to make the Duke too human.
For the satire is twofold, and two parts need to be well separated.
In the Barsetshire series, and the first part of the political, the
satire is not directed against the Duke himself, but against his
admirers, whenever they think of him. At last, in *Phineas Redux*
we see him from the point of view of the slightly contemptuous
women who look after him in his illness and put up with his
whims. When we see him face to face, the implication (far more
effective for the long delay), is " This is the man whom they have
all worshipped and never known." In the past he had never
concerned himself with details; when he wanted to ruin his
neighbour Sowerby who owed him a large fortune, he had merely

" notified to Fothergill [his agent] his wish that some arrangement should be made about the Chaldicotes mortgages," and Fothergill had understood what the Duke meant as well as though the instructions had been written down by a lawyer. But in *The Eustace Diamonds* and *Phineas Redux* his Olympian calm gives way to a childish interest in little things. He complains that arch-bishops take rank of him (" ' quite absurd nowadays, since they've cut the archbishops down so terribly ' "). He is fascinated by the story of Lady Eustace's jewels, hoping that the thief is one of his own order. He is driven almost to tears by complaints about the poisoning of foxes on his land. His movement had been so secret and well guarded that even Sowerby had not been able to obtain an interview (" ' He never speaks to anyone about money ' "). Now he is discussed by Madame Goesler and Lady Glencora thus: " ' Wants to go to bed, does he? Very well, I'll go to him.' "

A clear contrast is pointed between Frank Gresham's two meetings with the Duke. As the eldest son of a squire, he is invited to a large party at Gatherum Castle. On the way he wonders what he will say to the Duke and resolves to allow him to choose his own subjects, only reserving the right to criticise West Barsetshire as hunting country. But he finds that the Duke puts in only a brief appearance, speaks to no one, except Fother-gill, and that the real purpose of the entertainment is the drinking which takes place after the Duke has left the gathering. When he meets the Duke again, he has married an heiress, and the Duke receives him with courteous flattery. Disraeli would have treated this change as a triumph. Trollope uses it to satirise one of his favourite heroes. The attack is partly against himself. He had vowed in his misery at Winchester and Harrow, that he would make the great accept him. He had already largely succeeded when he wrote this second scene, and now cast scorn on his own enduring ambition.

But he is analysing something else beside ambition, the attitude summed up in the phrase, " Here again, that don't apply." Everyone feels that the Duke is too great to submit to the ordinances of God or man. He can create his own rules.

Even in this last scene, where it is necessary to give the Duke
a speaking part, he says little beyond ordinary courtesies. One is
reminded of Henry James's acute remark in his preface to *The
Turn of the Screw*: " One had seen in fiction, some grand form of
wrong-doing, or better still, of wrong-being imputed, seen it
promised and denounced as by the hot breath of the Pit, and then,
all lamentably shrink to the compass of some particular immorality, some particular infamy portrayed; with the result, alas,
of the demonstration's falling sadly short." James avoided this
danger by means of critical reflection. Trollope, more instinctive
and less analytical, avoided it too. The Duke does become a
character to be known and remembered, but only when the
satirical plan demands it; that is, when he is dying, when his
capacity for wickedness is past, and he becomes a thing to be
pitied.

The end of his life and the events that follow his death make
one long logical contrast to what has gone before. The one partly
generous desire of his life—his wish to marry Madame Goesler, is
thwarted by his nephew's wife, who remembers how her own love
had been thwarted to enable Mr. Palliser to marry her according
to the Duke's wishes. Not that she is taking revenge on him, but
he has, unfortunately for himself, succeeded with the help of time
and circumstance, in converting her to his own view. The
romanticism of youth and of old age alike are checked by the
calculating strength of middle age. But the Duke does not see
the irony of this, for he does not understand his own history and
cannot see its relation to any other. The prolonged, intermittent
satire, spread over nearly half the author's writing life, is endowed
with great cumulative force in the last scene before the Duke's
death. The sting in the last words of the passage I now quote
is weighted with a labyrinthine Proustian significance. " A clergyman attended him, and gave him the sacrament. He took it, as
the champagne prescribed by Sir Omicron, or the few mouthfuls
of chicken broth which were administered to him by the old lady
with the smart cap; but it may be doubted whether he thought
much more of one remedy than of the other. He knew that he

had lived, and that the thing was done. His courage never failed him. As to the future, he neither feared much nor hoped much; but was unconsciously supported by a general trust in the goodness and the greatness of the God who had made him what he was."

As the Duke is dying, there is a clever scene of cross-purposes between Madame Goesler and old Mr. Maule who tries to win his way into her affections by praising the Duke. The man who has never met him praises him for his magnificence and aristocratic disdain. The woman who had known him and been fond of him " remembered how he had looked with his nightcap on, when he had lost his temper because they would not let him have a glass of curaçao." The contrast here is not as simple as it may appear. It is suggested that the people who approved the Duke's way of life did not regard him as a human being at all, but as an emblem. It takes some degree of affection for the man to reveal the horror of his life. In the clubs the old Duke is praised because he was above doing anything with his life, and his nephew is blamed for working too hard. The worshippers of ducal greatness are really exacting taskmasters. They require a duke to behave like a duke, which means not behaving like a man. In one sense therefore, adulation is a form of contempt, and Madame Goesler's criticisms and undignified recollections come nearer to true praise and respect.

Even after his death circumstances prevent the Duke from benefiting anybody. The inheritance of the title causes sorrow to his heir, because it is a check to his political career. His bequest of love to Madame Goesler is refused, and she acknowledges to herself that, though she has been fond of him, on the whole he has been a trouble to her. Mr. Maule is left, like an actor addressing rows of seats, lamenting that " there is nothing left like it now. With a princely income, I don't suppose he ever put by a shilling in his life. I've heard it said that he couldn't afford to marry, living in the manner in which he chose to live. And he understood what dignity meant."

It is interesting to compare this satirical effect with those of some of the purely satirical novels of the seventies; to compare the Duke with (say) Melmotte and Trevelyan. It is not that corruption is more general in *The Way We Live Now* or in *He Knew He Was Right*. For who is more generally admired than the Duke? The difference is as much social as moral. For the aristocratic code, however much misused by the Duke, retains some validity. The Duke of Omnium represents evil incorporated into a system, like faulty stones in a building. It may be the lesser evil to leave them as they are. But Melmotte is an alien figure of evil, disturbing a system, threatening to destroy it and replace it with his own. The worship of the Duke is largely a failure of logic; and some of those who practise it, like Frank Gresham, contrive to be reasonably innocent and happy when they forget the Duke. Melmotte's impact on others is haunting and obsessive.

Omnium's failure is personal, Melmotte's greatness implies the failure of a whole society. A benevolent duke is conceivable; but to occupy Melmotte's position one would need to be like him.

Technically the Duke's history is used as a weapon for a wide and sweeping yet temperate and unobtrusive criticism of a whole society. Its desultory character and intermittent appearance are exactly suited to the object in view. A comparison with the technique of pure satire in books like *The Way We Live Now* and *The Eustace Diamonds* leaves one with an appreciation of the versatility of the author's satirical imagination and of his technical powers alike.

5

In the story of the Duke's nephew, Plantagenet Palliser, Trollope made his only detailed study of a marriage. He also examined, with an ambiguity by now familiar, some of the unexpected consequences of the cynical marriage market about which his contemporaries had written with such blunt indignation. Trollope discovered the possibilities of Palliser only gradually. At first he seems only a dull politician. But in the abortive affair with Lady Dumbello before his marriage, we are told that he is

" trembling with expectant ruin." This phrase gives the key to his character. He has an inverted conscientiousness which finds an almost irresistible attraction in whatever is against his own interest. His coldness to his wife for a long time after their marriage is due partly to his natural reserve, but mainly to the fact that she seems to be all most men would wish for in a wife. She is attractive, affectionate, very rich, and approved by his uncle, the Duke, and all his friends. Nothing is to be lost, he thinks, by marrying her.

But when he discovers that she has seriously intended to leave him for Burgo Fitzgerald, when he fears that she will never give him an heir, when he is forced to refuse the cabinet office he most desires on her account, he begins to behave like a loving husband.

He tries to live simply, but aristocratic disdain will sometimes break out to the dismay of a man who has presumed on his friendship. He can be magnanimous but not grateful, because he hates to be under an obligation. He is so honest and devoted to facts that he often appears rude.

His wife is interested only in feelings. Even when she becomes a great political hostess and interferes in the making of cabinets, political theories remain for her only attitudes to be used in the service of personal relationships. One thing the two have in common and that is more damaging than any difference. She, too, is morbidly attracted to ruin, not out of conscience, but through a desire for constant sensation. Burgo Fitzgerald appeals to her because he is dissipated, and would probably ill-treat her, perhaps with physical violence. From this time on, the ideas of love, wickedness, and joy are associated in her mind.

Trollope attempted to reinforce this story with the parallel one of Glencora's friend Alice Vavasour. There is the material for an interesting contrast here. For whereas Glencora's desire for destruction is based firmly on a normal passion for a handsome man, Alice is moved by suppressed feminism. She feels that her fortune and political acumen can contribute largely to the career of her ambitious cousin, if she marries him, while she will make no mark in the world by marrying a county landowner. Even as she acts upon this feeling she finds her cousin physically repulsive. So though neither Glencora nor Alice can understand her own perversity, each can give the other good advice. But the contrast is too little pointed, and Alice's state of mind is too obscure. The force of the comparison is largely lost and what might have been one of Trollope's best technical effects is almost a failure. This failure, however, is only incidental to the success of the Palliser story itself.

That story begins in an atmosphere of satire. At first sight it is very like numerous descriptions of the marriage market in Thackeray and others: " Mr. Plantagenet Palliser had danced with her twice, and had spoken his mind. He had an interview with the marquis [Glencora's guardian] which was pre-eminently satisfactory, and everything was settled." But an original use is made of this familiar material. This cynical beginning is a grave handicap to the marriage, but not as Thackeray would have made it, necessarily fatal. The main difficulty lies not in Glencora's previous love, nor on their slight acquaintance before marriage, but in the obvious suitability of the match. " ' Why should he love me? We were told to marry each other and did it,' " says Glencora. Palliser's natural shyness adds to her scepticism.

Another obstacle lies in their two different kinds of sensitiveness. Palliser needs comfort, encouragement, and a shield against the pinpricks of public life. His wife needs to be caressed and praised. Each is as ill-suited as possible to give the other what is needed. Each in a different way is contemptuous of the other's intelligence. Palliser thinks anyone stupid who cannot understand the simplest points of parliamentary procedure; he does not realise that a woman can refuse to understand things which bore her. Glencora's contempt is more complex. It is partly the irritation of a subtle and accommodating spirit at a man whose ideas are fixed for ever. She cannot imagine inability to express feelings which really exist. She is irritated too, by his tendency to indulge in useless regrets and to blame himself for every misfortune. But most of all, she despises him for his unsuspicious attitude about Burgo Fitzgerald. He knew that she had loved

Burgo before her marriage, and had good reason to suppose that he was trying to entice her away afterwards. To her mind, a man who is not prepared to fight for a woman cannot care for her or be worth caring for. If he takes no precautions he deserves to be deserted. He sees it differently; to doubt his wife or to set a watch on her would be as great a dishonour as to lose her. She partly understands this scruple, but loving to be dominated finds generosity and forbearance a provocation.

Their mutual understanding, at first so slight, is always stimulated by disagreeable things. For it is only in the stress of strong irritation that Palliser can be eloquent about his affection. The two turning points are the crisis of the Fitzgerald affair and the public outcry against Palliser for his wife's machinations in the pocket borough which he had sincerely renounced. In each case the expressions of love, made incidentally in long tirades of criticism, astonish and profoundly impress her.

Glencora's machinations in the former pocket borough make necessary a payment which will seem to the public like a bribe. This is the sort of situation that rouses his dormant energy and gives his wife a rare insight into his feelings. " ' I shall know [he says] why I pay this £500. Because she who of all the world is the nearest and dearest to me '—she looked up into his face with amazement, as he stood stretching out both his arms in his energy —' has in her impetuous folly committed a grievous blunder. . . .' " Misfortunes and lapses from morality and prudence by Glencora are all needed to override the circumstances of the marriage. The effect of the marriage market is not what we thought. Typically, Trollope's most ambitious psychological studies involve the subtilising of a literary platitude.

6

Trollope's deceptive mildness is nowhere better illustrated than in *Orley Farm*. An example, trivial in itself, but revealing, is provided by Mr. Leonard Cooper in his book on Surtees (page 86).

Comparing the hunting scenes of Surtees with those of Trollope he claims that the former are far more realistic. Perhaps this is true; certainly Trollope does not rival Surtees as a sporting writer. But Mr. Cooper's example is unfortunately chosen. He refers to a passage in Chapter 28 of *Orley Farm* where the fox is called a " good-natured beast " because he had " consented to bless at once so many anxious sportsmen, and had left the back of the covert with the full pack at his heels." Mr. Cooper's comment is " Mr. Jorrocks on hearing the ' thief o' the world ' described as a good-natured beast would surely have given vent to his favourite grunt of ' Ookey Valker! ' " But anyone who reads the whole passage will see that the word " good-natured " is ironical—a gentle tilt at the idea that the fox loves to be hunted. Why did Mr. Cooper miss this? Probably because he knew Trollope to be a keen hunting man, and a defender of the sport against the charge of cruelty. He did not expect, and therefore did not see, irony on that subject from that quarter.

Orley Farm deals with law and justice. Once again there is a three-cornered antithesis between law as it is in practice, real justice, and theoretical ideas of law and justice. Stated in this way the subject may seem narrow. But the legal issue has wide general ramifications. The book is really an analysis of the inter-action of convention, theory, and instinct. Thus Felix Graham, who is a theorist of law, is dissatisfied with more than legal procedure. He is having a girl trained to be his wife because he is repelled by the normal haphazard way in which people marry. From this point of view the story of the Ormes and the comic relief of the commercial travellers have a relevance which they would not possess if law were the book's central theme.

Orley Farm is a story of a young widow, Lady Mason, who has acquired large property for her infant son by forgery of her husband's will. After twenty years of undisturbed possession, new evidence is brought to light which leads to her trial for perjury. All connected with the case know or strongly suspect her guilt, but she is found not guilty. She then on behalf of her son, surrenders the property to the rightful owner, Joseph Mason, her husband's son by a former marriage.[1]

As the immorality of normal legal procedure was a permanent bugbear for Trollope, his treatment of law would be surprising if we were not familiar with his method. In the first instance, law and legal procedure are seen as simply part of the way of the world. Chaffanbrass, the clever advocate who appears in several other books, expounds the principles of his life in cynical fashion. He has prevented malefactors from being a charge upon the community when they were well able to provide for themselves. The whole story deals with the time, money, and traditional subtlety expended to make out that a guilty woman is innocent. And yet the book is very different from ordinary social satire. In the first place, no great sufferings are caused. The injustice lies rather in sparing the guilty. The inconsistencies of law coincide in a curiously exact way with popular prejudices. For Moulder, the commercial traveller, the buying and selling of justice, and the bullying of witnesses are " the fairest thing that is," and " the bulwark of the constitution." When the system makes nearly everyone happy, righteous indignation becomes a much more precise emotion than in Victorian fiction it normally is.

Thus we find that this legal tradition is not, as it may have seemed at first, a simple machine for injustice. It works in several different directions at the same time. The system is designed to prevent any consideration of the question at issue among the lawyers taking part. Felix Graham, the theorist and one of Lady Mason's junior counsel, asks, at a meeting of counsel and solicitors, " ' I suppose there can really be no doubt as to her innocence? ' " It is like a sudden indecency at a polite gathering. On the other hand, the system, if its aim were to defeat justice, is hindered by its own rules. The crucial point in Lady Mason's trial is the cross-examination of two witnesses, both of whom must appear to be

[1] Trollope's knowledge of the law was sketchy, and several legal writers have detected errors in his treatment of it. Moreover, he failed to appreciate the strength of the arguments in favour of the system of advocacy. It is best as in reading *Bleak House* or *The Trial* to treat the book's legal system as a self-contained entity, and its points of contact with real legal procedure as accidental.

lying or mistaken if she is to escape. Mr. Chaffanbrass, in the opinion of the solicitors, can make anyone swear to anything, but etiquette forbids that he should cross-examine both witnesses and leave none to his colleagues.

But after all legal etiquette affects what is said more than what is done or understood. Those who tilt at it, like Felix Graham, fail to achieve anything, and they end in theories as remote from practical justice as the institutions they attack. It is the just, plain-spoken man, impatient of legal quibble, like Sir Peregrine Orme and Graham, who are mistaken about the facts of Lady Mason's case. The crafty legal men arrive at them effortlessly, in spite of themselves and their system. For those who know how to use it, etiquette is a flexible thing. Thus Mr. Furnival, a personal friend of Lady Mason, who undertakes her defence, was embarrassed and even shocked by Graham's tasteless question, but at a pinch, he is willing to nullify this legal procedure, without going against the letter of it. "He was to undertake the whole legal management of the affair. He must settle what attorney should have the matter in hand, and instruct that attorney how to re-instruct him, and how to re-instruct those other barristers who must necessarily be employed on the defence in a case of such magnitude."

The quotation illustrates the real function of legal traditions. They enable all connected with the law to think in two separate and inconsistent ways without discomfort. Thus Mr. Round, the attorney on the other side, is shocked as a lawyer when an indiscretion reveals Lady Mason's guilt to him. As the revelation comes from outside the legal system he agrees to make no use of it on behalf of his client. But in proportion as he is disconcerted as a lawyer, he is interested and excited as a man. The legal profession is insulated from a continual search after justice and from the passions and crimes which are the raw material of its work. Who shall say that this is not desirable? Graham, who does not accept the arbitrary division, only succeeds in worrying himself without achieving anything, while the great congress for the reform of law is an emblem of futility. The reformers cannot even understand each other, let alone agree. Trollope was unlike most writers (and strangely unlike his public self) in that anger gave him a special stimulus to be impartial. These strange paradoxes were the fruit of his abiding anger at what he considered the thoroughly dishonest system of advocacy.

But the relations between law and justice appear in the last analysis even more complex. It is true that Lady Mason was a forger and that the courts say she was not. But one's view of the verdict will depend on one's idea of justice. Could a verdict in favour of the grasping and vindictive Joseph Mason be just? In a remarkable scene which forms the book's unexpected climax, the ideas of law and justice are turned on their heads, yet in no irresponsible way. For in the court room scene (Chapter 64), the two antagonists, Lady Mason and Joseph Mason, who have been fighting at a distance for so long, are confronted. " As she thus looked, her gaze fell on one face that she had not seen for years, and their eyes met. It was the face of Joseph Mason of Groby, who sat opposite to her; and as she looked at him her own countenance did not quail for a moment. Her own countenance did not quail; but his eyes fell gradually down. . . ." Guilt and long-suffering have brought understanding to one; the consciousness of being defrauded has hardened the other. It is the just man who feels shame. The decision of the courts falsifies facts but answers to the feelings of the protagonists in this crucial moment.

Technically this is one of the most interesting paragraphs in Victorian literature. Its effect is felt throughout the book, looking backwards as well as forwards, subtilising every antithesis between law and justice, probing every assumption. But characteristically, this is achieved in a few ordinary sentences, which out of their context would never be noticed.

3. *The Drama of Loneliness*

I T IS a discouraging fact that Trollope was apt to be most vulnerable technically just when he was imaginatively at his best. *Mr. Scarborough's Family* and *The Last Chronicle*, two of his finest books, contain a high proportion of irrelevant matter. This is not surprising, though Trollope would have been angry if anyone had told him the reason. His strict self-discipline in keeping to a timetable of work made no allowances for a temporary failure of imagination. Instead of pausing, he turned (perhaps without knowing why) to the Brussels episodes in *Mr. Scarborough* or the London part of *The Last Chronicle*. This is not a criticism of his methods; for it is doubtful whether without them, he could have written effectively at all.

The sub-plot of *He Knew He Was Right* is not on all-fours with the others just mentioned, for it has some artistic justification. The main plot deals with the consequences of a baseless obsessional jealousy. As a logical analysis of a situation it stands beside the Casaubon part of *Middlemarch* or the history of old Dorrit in the Fleet as a monument to a kind of art seldom attempted by Victorian writers.

As in *Cousin Henry* deadlock was the essence of the situation. The story needed what Mr. Percy Lubbock found in *Esmond*, " layers of time in which the recorded incidents sink deep." It must be long enough to suggest the weary monotony of two broken lives, but it must not be tedious through lack of incident. For Trollope, a sub-plot provided the natural escape from this dilemma; and this time the sub-plot is relevant. All the threads of the story deal with obstinacy and loneliness—ranging from the obstinate integrity of Nora Rowley and Priscilla Stanbury, to the partly selfish, partly heroic obstinacy of Jemima Stanbury and Mrs. Trevelyan, to the closed mind of Trevelyan, ordered chaos, the formal garden of madness.

Loneliness never failed to stimulate Trollope's imagination. But only here and in *Cousin Henry* did he analyse it in detail. The analysis shows loneliness as inherent in certain natures, and little influenced by circumstances. " Thinking of the key, each confirms a prison," and there are no compensating ethereal rumours. It is no accident that the gloom of Dartmoor momentarily shadows the story. Trevelyan's loneliness is that of a weak man, with a desire to dominate others, but conscious of his wife's stronger will. This is why he feels bound so closely to the odious Bozzle whom he has hired to watch and report upon on his wife. " He was very wretched, understanding well the degradation to which he was subjecting himself in discussing his wife's conduct with this man; but with whom else could he discuss it? " In spite of his shame this is for him an unanswerable argument. The universal conspiracy to deceive him which he imagines, masks his real terrors of loneliness and of having no one to dominate. Conscious of his own weakness, he can yet feel secure in his superiority to a man who receives his pay. His attitude to his child is governed by the same weakness. Though he retains a father's normal affection, he cannot resist the temptation to use his son as a bargaining counter. By promising to give him up to his mother, and then pretending to reconsider his promise, he can taste power.

Spinsterdom causes a similar terror. Miss Stanbury, the elder, though naturally generous and good natured, is driven to extravagant antipathies to give some meaning to her aimless life. When in her old age generosity finally conquers, and she is at last on good terms with all her relations, it seems to her that all the reality of her life has passed away, and this leads her to realise for the first time how vain it has been. In Trollope's world, there is no remedy for loneliness. The happiest of those afflicted by it are those who surrender to its first attack. Priscilla Stanbury, who has no desires except to eat and drink as little as possible and then to die, is happier than those who struggle. Complete boredom is more tolerable than partial, and the least miserable are those who best understand their predicament. These gloomy and impressive estimates of loneliness are implicit in every chapter of the book. They represent the conviction of a man who always felt that he had been delivered from this fate through no merit of his own.

It could be argued that of all the periods of English fiction the mid-Victorian best held the difficult balance between character and environment. For Fielding, Mr. Allworthy and Mr. Western are just two contrasted characters; the similarity in their social status is irrelevant. In some of the best-known novels since Hardy a man is only the resultant of social forces. But Dickens could show us that while the debtor's prison left an indelible mark on all the Dorrits, each was marked in a different way, and according to his nature. For Trollope neither character nor social circumstance is sufficient alone to consummate the defeat of the Trevelyans. If this chapter concentrates on the social forces, that is only because they are less obvious on a casual reading and because they better repay analysis.

All the central characters, Trevelyan, Colonel Osborne the suspected friend of the family, Lady Milborough the kind counsellor, are victims of the same plague, aimlessness. From one point of view, the book is a study of the dangers of unearned income without the balancing responsibilities of property. Trevelyan's inherited wealth gives him too much scope. We are told in the book's first sentence that he had all the world before him where to choose; only gradually does it appear that this blessing is a curse to a man who needs, in order to preserve his balance, discipline, routine, and a regular occupation for his mind. What can such a man do with his day? He is serious and has few pleasures. He goes to his club, but only to read the papers and brood. He is fond of family life, but that cannot take up all one's time. He is bookish, he sits in the library, he imagines that he is devoted to science, but in fact he only desires to raise a needless dispute about waves of sound. Time is his curse; it ticks itself away, and beats an endless, maddening rhythm in his mind. He is not one of those who think deeply about their souls. So he has only one remedy—he must quarrel with his wife and, if possible, bring himself to suspect her virtue. There is a deep unconscious irony in his final claim, when all his self-inflicted troubles are complete. He says, " ' It has been my study to untie all the ties; and, by jove, I have succeeded. Look at me here. I have got rid of the trammels pretty well—haven't I?—have unshackled myself, and thrown off the paddings, and the wrappings, and the swaddling clothes. I have got rid of the conventionalities, and can look Nature straight in the face.' " He does not realise that he is congratulating himself on achieving by terrible efforts and sufferings the position from which he began. Not his own effort, but his father's will has given him this destructive freedom.

His wife also is affected by his inherited money. Her pride is wounded by the thought that he has bestowed wealth on her, while she had nothing to give. She is always on her guard against any attempt of his to dominate her, because she vaguely fears that it might turn out to be based on money. She has not enough respect for money to submit to its power, nor enough contempt for it to ignore her husband's financial superiority. Money is influencing her feelings even as she dismisses it as irrelevant. The law takes a hand in stimulating her resistance and her pride. By giving her no standing against her husband and no rights over her child, it makes her feel, as soon as discord begins, that a potential tyrant, justified by law, lurks in every husband. So she is quick to read tyranny into his actions. We may note in parenthesis that Trollope stands apart from the two main streams of Victorian thought about feminism. It was customary to argue either, on the one hand, that women's legal disabilities were justified by their natural inferiority or, on the other, that they should have legal equality because of their natural equality. But he felt that a man ought to be too certain of his dominion over his own household to require any assistance from the law. The paradox in his attitude to feminism is not really a failure of logic. He would have welcomed the passage of the legislation desired by feminists in the same spirit in which a boxer, confident of his superiority over his opponent, would prefer him not to have one hand tied behind his back. He would have welcomed it also for the more subtle reason illustrated by the case of Emily Trevelyan. But he despised and distrusted the feminist movement because he disagreed profoundly with its conception of female functions, and especially because he detested its ideal of the professional woman, celibate, independent, and unfeeling.

If the protagonists in the book are eager for battle, the audience is no better. Even Lady Milborough, the sincere and kindly family friend, is led by the tedium of social life, and love of administering large doses of sensible advice, to respond eagerly to the first signs of marital discord. In these circumstances the strangest fact about the story—the extraordinary passivity of the trouble maker, Colonel Osborne—becomes intelligible. He has only to visit Mrs. Trevelyan and call her Emily, as befits an old friend and contemporary of her father; to reflect that she is pretty and that her husband is rather a bear; to share with her an innocent secret about political influence used to help her father. Then his work is done. He is no lover, for he is playing a game according to elaborate rules of his own. He, too, is a little bored, and finds a temporary remedy in creating trouble for other people, as the Trevelyans find theirs in creating trouble for themselves. Lady Milborough, though she speaks sincerely of her detestation of him, respects him as the man without whom the game, which all four of them are playing, could not begin at all. They are like men pretending to fight a duel, not knowing that their pistols are loaded.

The pathos of the story springs not so much from the sufferings of the characters as from the absurd inadequacy of their greatest efforts to restore peace. Emily is driven by a mixture of pity and desperation to confess that all has been her fault. " They had the carriage to themselves, and she was down on her knees before him instantly. ' Oh, Louis! Oh, Louis! say that you forgive me! ' What could a woman do more than that in her mercy to a man? ' Yes; yes; yes,' he said; ' but do not talk now; I am so tired.'" Their great dramatic scenes inevitably fade into greyness.

This insincere confession is interpreted by Trevelyan as a confession of adultery. When each is trying to be the soul of generosity, they only succeed in adding to their troubles. Part of the damage is repaired at last, but there can be no happy ending; only a " white melancholy," a slight relief after the preceding gloom. As at the end of *The Wings of the Dove*, the practical issues fade away at the end, and an intangible one proves to be the most momentous of all. The approach of death startles them with the gift of the dignity which has so long evaded them both. The last wandering thoughts of a madman become monumental and realities pale by comparison.

Indeed, the book raises the whole question of the value of truth and the importance of words. From the first chapter, when Trevelyan idly wonders whether to go to his wife and take back his unconsidered criticism, till the moment of Trevelyan's death, words have a power of their own which the protagonists constantly undervalue. " ' Let all this be as though it had never been,' " says Trevelyan at an early stage in the quarrel. They all betray a similar overconfidence. Only in the final deathbed scene does it dawn on one of them at least that words, once spoken, are the common possession of the speaker and the hearer, and that neither alone can effectively recall them. Because they have not understood this, all their previous attempts at reconciliation are vain, and leave them with an added sense of injury.

After Emily's plea for forgiveness has been interpreted by Trevelyan as a confession of adultery, an interesting contrast between two valuations of truth is presented. In different ways, both Emily and her sister hold it supreme. To Nora, the sister, all seems simple. Of course Emily is innocent, she thinks, and if her husband has been misled, his mistake must be explained to him even if he is ill and mentally unbalanced. To tell the truth is a simple rule, and she has never paused to examine its implications. And so, when it seems that Trevelyan is slipping beyond the reach of argument and expostulation, she is willing to abandon the attempt to convince him. If people cannot hear, she feels that the obligation to speak must lapse.

But for Emily truth gradually becomes a subject not for simple rules, but for overmastering passion. At first, it is true, the grief of allowing him to remain in his misconception seems less than the horror of speaking of such a matter, and the fear of exciting him to violence which might hasten his death. But as she watches his strength ebb, the desire for truth becomes paramount. Her sister points out that if her husband after his death can know anything of earthly life, then he will know the truth, whether or not he had learnt it while still alive. But this argument only shows that she does not comprehend her sister's preoccupation. Emily is anxious, not so much to convince him as to recall her confession; which is impossible without his help. She is inclined to read back into her request for forgiveness the interpretation which he has unwarrantably given it. It is as if his suspicions have placed a retrospective and momentous lie in her mouth, and only by forcing him to retract can she be cleansed from it. Before all these disasters had begun for her, words were for her what they still are for Nora, instruments of meaning, governed in their use by rules of thumb. Now they have the vividness and power of material objects, or worse, of spectres. The desire to recall them, to rectify them, turns her almost into a monster. Truth is no longer a duty, but an engulfing self-indulgence.

Trevelyan himself, along with Josiah Crawley, is Trollope's most careful psychological portrait. He has the solidity which a character possesses when he is seen in the author's mind as a whole, but revealed to the reader by a long series of details. The method of the mystery story has been applied to psychology. He has the philosopher's stone of madness, the power of transmuting all new facts into evidence for his fixed idea. But the frightening thing about his crazy mental processes is their ordinariness. His vanity is ordinary; he can be proud in the midst of his grief of his skill in writing long, affectionate, argumentative, and exhaustive letters. His jealousy is largely the consequence of a normal, if exaggerated, self-pity. Having once made an accusation, even if he did not fully mean it, he has to create imaginary facts to justify himself. He can feel justified in making terrible charges, without believing that they are true; words are for him the current coin of prestige and injury rather than indications of objects and events. This aberration also is an extension of something normal. Most people in their anger say things they do not mean, and thoughtlessly answer one insult with another. But instead of ceasing to do this when anger and the argument end, Trevelyan continues it in long tedious dialogues inside his own mind. And self-pity makes him proud of his misery. " But Trevelyan did not turn or move. There he stood gazing at the pale, cloudless, heat-laden, motionless sky, thinking of his own sorrows, and remembering, too, doubtless, with the vanity of a madman, that he was probably being watched in his reverie." Towards the end, this mood is varied by a fantastic levity and carelessness.

Trevelyan's psychological failing, his inability to grasp the full meaning and effect of words, is balanced by a social factor, the reticence customary in speaking of a wife's unfaithfulness. All the lengthy marital dialogues skirt round and round the point. Trevelyan does not really mean to charge his wife with un-chastity, but the words he uses, when interpreted in the light of this customary reticence, seem to contain the accusation. The wife's instinctive reluctance to call things by their real names, prevents her until near the end from asking the questions which would force him to be precise. When he says, " ' You must repent,' " he means repent of her disobedience, but for her the word resounds in a narrower yet vaguer sense, suggesting, no doubt, Magdalens and houses of correction. But reticence even prevents her from revealing her horror of the implied charge. This verbal misunderstanding tends to effect her with a share of his monomania. The accusation, which has never in reality been made at all, festers in her brain to the exclusion of all other feelings. In the end, knowing that her husband's death is near, her only desire is to obtain from him an explicit clearing of her character; and though she has never ceased to love him, the night of his death is a time of triumph, because she has achieved her aim at the last possible moment.

At first sight Jemina Stanbury is an ordinary novelist's character—sour in words, generous in action. But she is nevertheless interesting as a pointer to Trollope's outlook on several questions. She is the avowed enemy of novels, even stipulating that her niece shall not read any while she is staying in her house. This attitude was no mere curiosity; Trollope himself had suffered from an attitude only slightly less rigid when *Rachel Ray* was refused by the magazine that had commissioned it. All Miss Stanbury's other prejudices went directly against the author's own professed opinions. Yet he did not need to struggle to be fair to such people. There were deep psychological reasons why Trollope, the Liberal, sympathised with the outlook of a stone-age Conservatism. The casual reader is apt to assume that he was a Conservative, and is surprised when he comes upon Trollope's bitter attacks on political Conservatism and on traditionalism in private life. But, though the conclusions he draws may be incorrect, the casual reader's instinct is not so wide of the mark. By thought and choice Trollope was a Liberal, an internationalist, and a satirist. But there is a deep-rooted emotional Conservatism in him, the strength of which he hardly understood himself, which affects his treatment of characters like Miss Stanbury and Miss Thorne of Ullathorne, and of issues like the Hospital controversy in *The Warden*. He liked to write Liberal journalism and at the same time to identify himself with the splendid prejudice which made Miss Stanbury write: " ' I don't think that writing radical stuff for a penny newspaper is a respectable occupation for a gentleman, and I will have nothing to do with it.' " There was an elementary violence, a pure assertion of the will in such an attitude, and Trollope rejoiced secretly even as his intellect rejected it.

Mr. Gibson, the clergyman, who with the best intentions jilts one girl after another, is unusual among Trollope's characters because he receives no sympathy from the author. His mind turns every personal experience into a platitude. In the midst of his matrimonial blunderings he reflects that the manner in which unmarried men are set upon by ladies in want of husbands was very disgraceful to the country at large. But with delightful inconsistency he can persuade himself that his vacillation is a sign of the true Lothario spirit.

" ' I fancy sometimes ' " (he says) " ' that some mysterious agency interferes with the affairs of a man and drives him on— and on—and on—almost—till he doesn't know where it drives him.' As he said this in a voice that was quite sepulchral in its tone, he felt some consolation in the conviction that this mysterious agency could not affect a man without imbuing him with a certain amount of grandeur—very uncomfortable, indeed, in its nature, but still having considerable value as a counterpoise. Pride must bear pain; but pain is recompensed by pride."

Even the sense of purpose and meaning in life is parodied. Indeed, the list of assumptions of civilised life questioned in the book is a formidable one. Truth, independence, the law of inheritance, the value of leisure, each in turn is laid bare to ridicule or doubt. It would seem that the book is primarily a satire. But this plausible conclusion would be mistaken. Trollope did not foresee in 1868 that in a few years with *The Eustace Diamonds* and *The Way We Live Now* he would become a satirist in earnest. *He Knew He Was Right* marks a half-way stage which the author was not aware of having reached. Satire was beginning to take a grip of him, but he had not as yet found a grip on satire. At this date his attitude to the accepted truths which the book questions was parallel to his view of feminism. He is so confident of male supremacy that he can look benevolently on " women's rights "; he is so confident that truth-telling, inheritance, and the rest can always be vindicated that he can turn a searching light on their limitations. He can afford to play with his cards on the table.

Perhaps he deceived himself; perhaps his distrust of institutions and of standards of conduct was already stronger than he would admit. A man is never the best judge of the direction in which his own mind is moving. Most conversions begin with a revulsion from the thing which in the end will prove irresistible. At the end of his life, in writing *Mr. Scarborough's Family*, he would discover many different kinds of honesty and all of them vulnerable. He was to live to be less assured, more angry with others, less satisfied with himself. But in 1868 the most serious criticisms could be left to the mad Trevelyan to voice; and the rest overshadowed by the fascinating operation of his mental disease.

4. 'The Eustace Diamonds'

T HE MAIN intention of *The Eustace Diamonds* is satirical, and, written in 1870, it is perhaps the first of Trollope's books of which this is true. The gloom of *He Knew He Was Right* had been solid; the characters enlist sympathy. But now the hollowness of people and of institutions became a leading theme, never afterwards wholly abandoned. The most obvious thing about this book (and the most surprising to a reader familiar only with Trollope's previous works) is that the central character is worthless. But as we shall see, this blatant woman, Lady Eustace, occupies the circle of ice in a finely-graded inferno.

Let us consider first the impersonal " characters," the law, public opinion, and the diamonds. The book is not primarily a satire on law and respectability, but these are tainted with a share of the same inaccuracy and unreality which corrupts the more obviously shady characters. The law is represented mainly by three of its servants. Frank Greystock is a rising young barrister, destined for high office and success, who allows personal feelings to overcome his legal sense and so supports Lady Eustace, his cousin, in her fraudulent retention of the diamonds which had belonged to her dead husband. The process is gradual; at first he says that as a lawyer he has no opinion on the case, and that he is merely honouring the ties of blood and friendship. But he insensibly slips into the position of giving his opinion as a lawyer of a case in which he has heard only one side, and where he is clearly biased by personal feeling. Both the rigidity of the law and the deceptiveness of impulses and feelings are part of the subject of this book. But here is a man whose fault is that he so confuses the two that he does not know which is guiding him at any moment. His equivocal attitude to promises of marriage is in keeping with this. His own neglect of the girl he has promised to marry is contrasted with his severe judgment of Lord Fawn who hesitates to carry out his engagement with Lady Eustace. As Fawn's hesitation is mainly due to a doubt about her right to the diamonds, Greystock's second error follows naturally from his first. In these two cases, legal training and knowledge fail to produce justice because of the unconscious desires of the lawyer himself, which nullify the normal effects of the legal system.

But what of the system itself? It is represented by the Eustace family solicitor, Camperdown, and by the final judgment of the courts about the ownership of the diamonds. Camperdown is convinced that Lady Eustace has no right to her late husband's diamonds, and tries to recover them for the husband's male heirs. He is polite and judicious; he writes to Lady Eustace at intervals in terms which grow very gradually more severe. His slowness allows two separate robberies to occur before he can formulate a clear legal claim.

Though the diamonds are recovered and the true circumstances of their theft known, justice is not done, either by the courts or by public opinion. For in the first robbery an empty container only is stolen, and Lady Eustace states on oath that the diamonds are gone too, when they are still in her possession. The thieves, being members of the officially criminal class, receive heavy sentences, while Lady Eustace's perjury escapes retribution. At the same time, the public is lost in admiration for the thieves, who have incompetently failed to capture anything of value.

Ironically, though, Lady Eustace is punished for perjury at the hands of someone who has no moral objection to it at all. Outraged society may be dumb, but a fellow-liar exacts the penalty; for Mrs. Carbuncle refuses to pay her financial debts to Lady Eustace on the ground that she can have no dealings with perjurers.

The failure of Camperdown, the champion of law and order,

is neatly countered by the hideous success of strict justice where it has no place, where generosity only should rule—in the giving of presents. Lady Eustace and Mrs. Carbuncle bargain fiercely about the length of their stays in each other's house, and even about paying for horses' feed and servants' liveries. " Mrs. Carbuncle assented at last to finding the double livery—but like a prudent woman, arranged to get her *quid pro quo*. ' You can add something, you know, to the present you'll have to give Lucinda [her niece, whose wedding day is near]. Lucinda shall choose something up to forty pounds.' ' We'll say thirty,' said Lizzie, who was beginning to know the value of money. ' Split the difference,' said Mrs. Carbuncle, with a pleasant little burst of laughter—and the difference was split."

Mrs. Carbuncle even goes to the length of writing to a friend to whom she has given a wedding present years before, to beg for one in return for her niece. When a very cheap one is sent in response to this request, she writes again to say, " ' You must remember that when you were married, I sent you a bracelet which cost £10.' " She does not behave in this way entirely without self-reproach, but consoles herself by thinking that " it is no good mincing matters nowadays." The Victorian idea of of progress had many facets.

But the striking part of this episode, which shows Trollope's skill as a satirist, lies in the friend's reply. In his bitterest vein, Trollope was like Swift in loving to carry an absurdity to its logical conclusion. He was not satirising Mrs. Carbuncle only, but a whole society, and no indignant retort would be so effective for this purpose as the letter which comes in reply. " ' I quite acknowledge the reciprocity system, but I don't think it extends to descendants, certainly not to nieces. I acknowledge, too, the present quoted at £10. I thought it had been £7 10s. At your second marriage I will do what is needful; but I can assure you I haven't recognised nieces with any of my friends.' "

One can express the calculated shock Trollope here inflicts upon his readers by a comparison. It is as if one had been listening for an hour to a man in a lunatic asylum claiming to be Napoleon, and was then told by his doctor that he was really Julius Cæsar. In Trollope's eyes, it was a sign of the gravest moral confusion when the proper spheres of justice and mercy were interchanged. Greystock's generosity to his cousin involves injustice to others. The sinister justice of the bargaining between Lady Eustace and Mrs. Carbuncle deprives social life of all its spontaneity.

But if the courts fail to enforce the justice of the law, one may still ask, " What is the value of this justice? " Trollope has an ambivalent attitude to it, as to many things in this book, which presents a series of standards of value. Each of them, except the lowest, is justified within its own limits, but most are found wanting in comparison with a higher one. Mr. Dove, the solitary legal expert, implicitly judges Camperdown's devotion to abstract justice. For him a squabble between two rich people about diamonds is a squabble about trifles.

The diamonds have two functions in the plot. They are the still centre round which all the characters and events are gathered. They are the point without magnitude which alone permits the ample circle of the story to be drawn. Every character is related to the diamonds in a different way. For Mr. Camperdown they are in the wrong hands, and so are an emblem of an outrage upon justice. They appeal both to the obstinacy and the avarice of Lady Eustace. To Lord Fawn they are a possible stain upon his honour, if he marries the woman who is perhaps retaining them illegally. Frank Greystock sees them as a symbol of the persecution his cousin has to endure. For the Duke of Omnium they are the cause of an enjoyable scandal and for Lady Glencora a godsend for relieving the boredom of his invalid old age.

Trollope is at his best when his purpose appears not gradually by the light of common day, but instantaneously, as when a flash of lightning gives a sudden memorable distinctness to the dim shapes which have been watched in the twilight. Throughout most of the book the second function of the diamonds is concealed. We are encouraged to regard the diamonds only through the eyes of the characters, each of whom, in his different way, thinks them highly important. Then, at last, Mr. Dove brings us face to face with the question, " What are the diamonds, and what is their value? " The answer is " Nothing." If this question had been asked and answered at the beginning of the book, it would merely have been trite. Coming where it does, after Trollope has skilfully led us to evade it for so long, it casts a piercing satirical light on all the characters. An agreed error lies at the heart of all their disagreements.

From this point of view the best parallel that I know to *The Eustace Diamonds*, both morally and technically, is *The Revenger's Tragedy*. There in an often-quoted speech, addressed to the skull of his dead lady, Vendice seems to cast doubt on the worth of the only two motives of action recognised in the play—sexual desire and revenge.

Now this speech has won a place in anthologies simply as poetry and has been praised by many who have not understood its crucial position in the play. Mr. Dove's speech, which has a similar function in *The Eustace Diamonds*, has never been quoted or remembered. Out of its context it is as ordinary as any speech could well be. Yet it is the keystone of a great arch of satire. This contrast may help to explain why the novel has for so long been regarded as an inferior form of art. Artistically, it is normally much more difficult to appreciate than poetry or drama; but unlike these, novels can be read with enjoyment by people who never suspect their artistic purposes. For many people, story and character (important though these are for the total artistic effect) have acted as a screen to prevent the appreciation of other qualities. The exceptions, of course, are the novelists who have been altogether delivered over to the highbrows, like Richardson, Melville, and Henry James. They and their like share one or both of two qualities. Either they cannot be read for the story alone without exciting the desire, attested by Johnson, to hang oneself; or they have at times a highly-wrought prose style which, however far it may be from prose poetry, has the same kind of memorableness as poetry has. Melville's chapter on " The Whiteness of the Whale," like the speech of Vendice in *The Revenger's Tragedy*, draws attention to itself as an artistic climax, by its whole manner. Compared with these, the prosaic novelists of greatness are difficult to appreciate, for, where the ordinary interest of a good story is so strong, an inadequate appreciation has a way of seeming adequate. If you do not fully appreciate the Whiteness of the Whale, you will merely be puzzled, but perhaps hundreds have enjoyed Walter Scott for every one who has appreciated him.

The forces of convention and average opinion are represented in the book by Lord Fawn and his sister, Mrs. Hittaway. Lord Fawn is an honest and conscientious man, who takes an official attitude to everything—even to his engagement with Lady Eustace. Timid and cautious though he is, moderate and reasonable though he imagines himself to be, he expects to have it both ways—to marry for money, and then to have all that he might have had if he married from choice. Mrs. Hittaway, though a minor and ordinary character is important because of her position in the story. She needed to be drawn with care so that the everyday, unreflecting assumptions of society might seem neither too much nor too little justified. Her behaviour is hard and artificial, and her ambition is to help her husband, a civil servant, to cut a formidable figure. An essential part of this programme is the August shooting in Scotland, but their income makes it necessary to have this at someone else's expense. Hittaway's only merit as a sportsman is that he never shoots a keeper, and his wife is so bored in Scotland that she writes to her sister, " ' If it wasn't for Orlando and the children, I'd brazen it out [in London] and let people say what they pleased.' " Hard, selfish, careerist, humourless, and censorious, she is an ordinary enough character, such as many novelists might draw. But almost always she would be used in a different way. Here, having shown us all this woman's faults, he surprises us by using her as a positive moral standard.

Trollope, in his later years, tended to see good and evil as a series of layers, not as simply antithetical. But the possibilities of evil, as he saw them, are far greater than those of good. His moral system is like a staircase, which originally had ten stairs; but the top three have mysteriously disappeared. There is Do-Well even

ANTHONY TROLLOPE

in his gloomiest books, represented here by Lucy Morris and others but there is no Do-Better or Do-Best. The scale stretches downwards to damnation, but never approaches sanctity. Nor is this merely because sanctity is a more difficult literary subject than damnation. In some writers, renowned for their gloomy view of human nature—in M. Mauriac for instance—the upper stairs exist at least by implication. But Trollope never seems to suspect that the moral centre of gravity has been displaced. In this, perhaps, he was typical of the more eminent early and mid-Victorian writers, while the lesser ones avoided this defect only by falling into a greater one—by sacrificing the lower steps of the stair as well as the higher.

In this case, then, it turns out that Mrs. Hittaway is perfectly justified in her condemnation of the more sympathetic Lady Eustace. Why? Because Mrs. Hittaway, following Society's standards, and knowing no others is at least faithful to these. There is genuineness in the obvious insincerity of her desire to be in Scotland in August. But Lady Eustace's insincerity in marrying a vicious and dying man for his money leads only to further insincerity, and to the betrayal even of this standard of conduct. She lies to him, and it is suggested that the shock of sudden insight into her character hastens his death. Afterwards, she attempts to add to her ample inheritance by stealing the family diamonds. The difference between the two women is most obvious in their attitude to lying. Mrs. Hittaway considers herself bound not to be shocked by the behaviour of her own class, for otherwise she would forfeit her position as a knowing woman of the world. She takes it for granted that a poor man, able and ambitious, like Frank Greystock, will not keep his promise to marry a governess. Mrs. Hittaway knows about such things, and mildly deprecates them. But Lady Eustace "liked lies, thinking them to be more beautiful than truth." She finally agreed to marry a fortune-hunter, suspected of being married already, who has a prepared patter of bogus poetical phrases adopted for women's benefit. But in a final scene of large satirical implications, she almost rejects him for not being bogus enough.

At the same time, Trollope shows how wide is the practical moral agreement between the two women. In many respects the weary cynicism of the one becomes equivalent to the other's delight in illusion. Each, though selfish, acts aimlessly. It is typical of Lady Eustace, that when the empty diamond box is stolen, she performs what looks like a clever and daring crime in a fit of absence of mind. Acting always on the spur of the moment, she is frightened when the full implications of what she has done are explained to her. This is where Trollope's conception differs most radically from Thackeray's Becky Sharp. He need not have feared that Lady Eustace would be regarded as only a poor copy of her. Becky Sharp is always a careful calculator; Lady Eustace is spiritually an innocent, and her wickedness is the wickedness of a child. She has as much affinity with Chaucer's Criseyde and Middleton's Beatrice as with Becky Sharp.

But Mrs. Hittaway's brisk air conceals the same aimlessness. When she sends for Gowran, Lady Eustace's steward, to come to London and give evidence against her, she allows him to travel all the way back to Scotland without having a real chance to give it. Unlike Lady Eustace, though, Mrs. Hittaway understands that there are limits to the cynicism of society. She is no more hypocritical than she feels that circumstances force her to be. Lady Eustace projects her own immoralism back on to society, wishfully believing it much worse than it is. She reflects that the countenance of the great Lady Glencora Palliser will be as valuable to her as another lover. She is utterly unrealistic in her conception of the way she is judged by others. The relationship between Lady Eustace and Mrs. Carbuncle reveals a gradual subsidence of moral standards. At first, each imagines herself to be free from moral restraints, yet each discovers her mistake in the shock of watching the debasement of the other. Paradoxically, these shocks stimulate the watcher to a further debasement. They are " united in the strife which divides them."

Lady Eustace's ideas of love and pleasure are especially interesting. Her extravagance is all wasted because she buys not what she likes but what she thinks the fashionable world expects her to like. In this, she is like Mrs. Hittaway and many, perhaps too many, characters in Victorian novels. But all the same, her case has some unique features. It does more than illustrate the power of convention and Trollope's own lifelong conviction that trying to enjoy oneself is the hardest work of all. So far as I know, Lady Eustace provides the only important study by a male Victorian novelist of masochism. No woman actually analysed it effectively, but one or two unconsciously revealed it in pouring their own temperaments into their heroines. Rhoda Broughton's *Not Wisely But Too Well* is a notable example. For a psychiatrist a work of this last type would be more interesting than an external analysis, but by literary standards the reverse is true. Literature can deal effectively only with what an author can see, and partly control. Even autobiography, if it is to qualify as literature, involves the subject seen as object. Even literature of the unconscious mind is only literature because Joyce can be pictured with his ear to the skull of the sleeping man, reading his dreams.

In terms of masochism, Lady Eustace's bewildering changes of affection become intelligible. For instance, she first feels drawn to Lord George Carruthers when he sneers at the institution of marriage. Mrs. Carbuncle, who has no real belief in marriage, feels it incumbent upon her to be shocked. If she considered the question simply as a moral one, Lady Eustace would probably respond in the same way, and equally insincerely. But her imagination is gripped by the man's brutality and contempt. She reflects that he has " eyes that could look love and bloodshed almost at the same time," and concludes, " To be hurried about the world by such a man, treated sometimes with crushing severity, and at others with the tenderest love, not to be spoken to for one fortnight, and then to be embraced perpetually for another, to be cast every now and then into some abyss of despair by his rashness, and then raised to a pinnacle of human joy by his courage—that, thought Lizzie, would be the kind of life which would suit her poetical temperament." (It would be an interesting experiment to ask a number of English scholars, if they did not recognise these quotations, to guess their author.) In the same way, Lady Eustace feels a sudden attraction towards the Scotland Yard detective, Major Mackintosh, when he comes to tell her that he knows she has committed perjury.

It might be objected of course, that as a study of masochism Trollope's picture is woefully incomplete, because of the reticence which contemporary standards and his own views agreed in demanding. But, as we have seen, one of Lady Eustace's leading characteristics is unconsciousness of self. It is arguable that her concealed masochism is quite as overt as it could be and remain consistent with her character. Any suggestion of physical perversion was ruled out just as clearly by her nature as by literary convention and principle.

Her scene with Major Mackintosh, just mentioned, indicates the innocent strain in her wickedness. When he tells her that after her previous perjury she will now be required to tell the truth in court, she promises to do so in the off-hand manner of a woman agreeing to a minor change of plan. There is no moral change involved in her new decision. She does not even realise the practical difficulty of contradicting on oath all that she has previously said on oath. Self-deception is as natural to her as breathing. She can persuade herself equally easily that she is a *femme fatale*, or a lady of fashion, or a born recluse. All her poses are sincere. This Byronic quality gives an added irony to her association with Lord George Carruthers. For she habitually associates him with Byron and thinks of him as " the corsair." But she does not know that she is far too Byronic herself to need Lord George's help in reaching this delectable state, or that he thinks so meanly of the world that he deliberately adopts this immoral pose to impress people. Artificial as the Corsair ideal of love may be, it can be real enough to lead to death and crime. Lord George is only a feigned version of this artificial character.

At heart (the reader discovers this only gradually), Lord George is a cautious man, and he is alarmed when his pose of immorality is taken too seriously and he is suspected of having stolen the diamonds himself. It is typical alike of his character and of the book's whole ironical method that he should say, " ' If it turns out that she [Lady Eustace] has had a couple of bravos in her pay, like an old Italian marquis, I shall think very highly of her indeed.' " This is the instinctive respect paid by the weak unprincipled man to the determined criminal. But of course the object of his respect is really as vacillating as himself and has planned nothing.

His remarks on marriage reveal him more clearly than anything else. He attacks marriage laws in a lofty tone reminiscent of Shelley's *Epipsychidion*. " ' I assert,' he says, ' that if men and women were really true no vows would be needed,' " and attacks the cynicism with which women break their oath to love for ever and ever. This tirade takes its point from the nature of his hearers. There is Lucinda Roanoake, who is due in a short time to make this vow to love a man physically and morally repulsive to her. There is Lady Eustace who has married for money and hastened her husband's death by her falseness; and there is Mrs. Carbuncle, a woman separated from her husband and involved in an undefined relationship with the moralising Lord George himself. His company seems to justify him up to the hilt, and Mrs. Carbuncle's protest seems only an insincere, conventional response. But Trollope was not satisfied with this ordinary level of satire. For the circumstances show that this moralising crusade of immorality, rejecting convention in favour of truth, is really just as immoral and self-seeking as Mrs. Carbuncle feebly pretends to think. For what is advanced as tending towards a higher kind of fidelity has really two very different motives. Lord George hopes that if marriage vows and conventions are weakened it will be easier for him to have a rapid series of affairs, each, during its few weeks' duration, an eternal and immutable union of souls, and he correctly judges that this blend of cruelty, cynicism, and romantic high principles will be peculiarly appealing to Lady Eustace's masochistic temperament, and so help him towards the control of her fortune. By a further irony he intends to achieve this by means of the marriage ceremony which he is denouncing. He is acute enough to see that such an inconsistency will only improve his chances with such a woman. Finally, the man who is trying to shock Mrs. Carbuncle by casting stones at female infidelity is the same man who has incited her to break her own vows.

It will be clear from all this that the relation between the unconventional and the conventional in the book is not simple. A final twist is given by the affair of Lucinda Roanoake and Sir Griffin Tewett. For this illustrates the result of following the normal behaviour of society without possessing the feelings appropriate to it. As always for his scenes of pure horror, Trollope prepares his effects carefully. Lucinda is introduced as the niece of the doubtfully respectable but moderately fashionable Mrs. Carbuncle. She is eighteen, but looks twenty-four; she does not trouble to talk; her background and early history are enigmatic. An Eton boy is heard to remark that, " ' She's a heroine, and would shoot a fellow as soon as look at him.' " This expresses in naïve epigram what many dimly feel. She is admired because she does not appear to want a husband, and treats rich bachelors and everyone else with the same fatigued rigidity. She is admired for rejecting the materialistic standards of those about her and for not bothering to explain that she does so. The fashionable do not listen to moral lectures, and ignore those who leave or remain outside their own circle, but they are intrigued by a young girl who walks through all their traditional round of pleasure untouched by enjoyment or desire. When people try to sound her by speculating on her opinions in her presence, she is silent; when it rains during hunting she says that she likes to be wet. She is animated only about points of fact. She fiercely contradicts a false statement about hunting. " ' I've been out all day without finding at all,' said Lucinda who loved the truth." This judgment of character, while remaining valid, will be given an ironical twist by the events that follow.

Her story is placed in contrast with Lady Eustace's to which it has a superficial similarity. For Lady Eustace, after deciding to follow worldly or Hittaway standards, breaks away from them through her ingrained love of lying. Lucinda also decides to follow these standards and rebels at the last moment through her love of truth, her only virtue. The old theory of the tragic flaw is here reversed; her one redeeming virtue is the only thing out of harmony with the moral gloom of the situation and so brings about her downfall. Again Lady Eustace is a shallow character fully revealed; Lucinda, much less described, suggests unexplored profundity. This contrast contributes much to the book's structure.

But Lucinda's strange hardness is not inborn. Her affection for her horse and her passion for hunting show a nature capable of affection; her reckless riding shows determination coupled with a half-conscious desire for a fatal accident. Her love of truth, supported by no other generous feeling, leaves her poised helpless, unable to desire, or to enjoy, or to reject. She is saddened by the marriage presents of the rich, who do not care for her, because she feels they are empty of meaning, but her thirst for a state of poverty where every symbol might have significance, is abortive. " ' Oh, if I were marrying a poor man and a poor friend had given me a gridiron to help me with my husband's dinner, how I could have valued it! ' " But she cannot impugn the justice of her aunt's retort, " ' I don't know that you like poor things and poor people better than anybody else.' " Her longing is no more than a daydream which would dissolve if she tried to act upon it. Dialectically the priestess of mammon always has the advantage over her.

The Eustace Diamonds is in part a study of sexual aberrations. The story of Lucinda and Sir Griffin Tewett, a study of aberrations within the conventional framework, balances those of Lady Eustace, and Lord George who revolt against convention and moral decency at the same time. The ambiguity about the value of convention is deliberate as it is in many great satirical works, including *Don Quixote*, *Gulliver's Travels*, *I Promessi Sposi*, and *The Possessed*. This part of the book presents custom and convention, not as mischievous, but as inadequate. Trollope never believed in the noble savage, but he shows here the results of conventional behaviour when the humane spirit which should inform it is absent.

Sir Griffin appears at first as a very ordinary young man of the lower aristocracy. It seems natural that he should be attracted by Lucinda's beauty and by her air of queenly pride, and that he should be intrigued by her refusal to flatter him. Sir Griffin's experience of life is narrow, and he regards it as a law of nature that men in his position must invariably be chased by all marriageable girls except the few who are of higher wealth and status. When he enters the story, we are told that he is weak, mean, and fond of alcohol, but that he has one redeeming quality, an honest desire to marry Lucinda for her beauty. At this stage no hint is given of the strange shape which this redeeming quality will take.

Sir Griffin's love is a strange, contradictory, inextricable mixture of cruelty and conventional romantic feeling. He is repelled by the continuance, after the acceptance of his proposal, of the unyielding coldness which had originally interested him. It becomes a point of honour with him to break down Lucinda's spirit and force her to love him. Every failure increases his determination to go through with the marriage so that he can afterwards avenge himself for the terrible injury of not being loved. Repeatedly he feels that he would break the engagement himself if only he could be sure that she would regret him; he is always cowed and made almost ardent by her serene and sincere assurances that she cares nothing for the honour of marrying him. In spite of all his roughness and all his determination to take a cruel revenge, he submits involuntarily to a stronger character and he thinks, perhaps rationalising the motives of this distasteful submission, that if they quarrel and break off the match it will seem to others that she has rejected him. Yet for all his anger and frustration at her treatment of him, it is clear that if Lucinda had shown any feminine softness he would not have wanted to marry her. He is one of those unfortunate beings in whom anger, submission, and sexual desire are so closely linked that the last cannot long survive without the others. Finally, Sir Griffin is gifted with a complete lack of self-knowledge and he still subscribes sincerely to the ordinary romantic ideas of love which are so out of keeping with his tortuous character. He desires to be told that he is loved;

he expects from this granite woman the very exhibition of tenderness which, if she had really been capable of it, would have prevented him from ever desiring her. Love within a conventional framework can be very strange indeed.

The effect of strangeness is heightened by the exaggerated ordinariness of all the preparations for a fashionable wedding. Lady Eustace who in her own way deviates as far as Lucinda from the spirit of the marriage service, at first treats the affair as an ordinary and touching story of a pair of young lovers. " ' Has Lucinda told you? ' " Mrs. Carbuncle asks on the day of the engagement. " ' Do you think I've got no eyes.' " Lady Eustace replies, " ' Of course it was going to be. I knew that from the very moment Sir Griffin arrived at Portray.' " But a moment later she shows how easily conventional romantic ideas blend with conventional cynical ones. " ' She likes him, I suppose? . . . Not that girls ever really care about men now. They've got to be married and they make the best of it. She's very handsome and I suppose he's pretty well off.' " Each of these blending though contrary attitudes is equally remote from Lucinda's stern spirit; and all three attitudes are equally far from any sane conception of sexual morals. The moral confusion which is the book's real subject here reaches its climax. Cross-purposes are complete; the lost souls cannot communicate with each other.

Confusion reigns also in the mind of Mrs. Carbuncle. As soon as Lucinda has accepted Sir Griffin, she hurried to separate them so that they may not have time to quarrel before the engagement has been thoroughly ratified. On the very same day she hears Lucinda protest that she hates Sir Griffin above all men. The grimness of the situation impresses her but does not alter her purpose. Not that she is unfeeling towards her niece; she hopes to gain nothing for herself from the marriage. Grieved by Lucinda's horror, she is also sorely harassed by Sir Griffin's consistent rudeness, his threats (never altogether serious) to break their engagement, and his innuendoes about matrimonial traps laid to catch him. Yet in spite of all this the sweetness of a fashionable wedding lingers in her unreceptive mind. She still works hard without any help or encouragement to secure every possible present. The final sudden failure of all her efforts for Lucinda nearly breaks her heart. In this portrayal of Mrs. Carbuncle we can see clearly where Trollope diverged from every other English novelist of the first rank, except Sir Walter Scott. Fielding, Dickens, Thackeray, Conrad, and the rest would have conceived such a character as hard and deliberately cruel. Mrs. Carbuncle, tender and un-selfish in many ways, acts without any intelligible purpose. She is incapable of altering time-honoured reactions when facts have clearly shown them to be inappropriate. In one respect, Trollope occupies the place among novelists which Webster holds among dramatists—he has a universal pity.

The motives of Lucinda's final refusal to go to church for her own wedding are compounded of personal dislike of the bride-groom, disgust at the cynicism exhibited in fashionable weddings, a despairing delight in suffering, and a slight but definite sexual abnormality. Mrs. Carbuncle knows her niece well but not well enough. She succeeds for a long time in avoiding an irrevocable rupture by preventing the engaged couple from being much alone together and by appealing to Lucinda's courage, asking her to bear his caresses as if exhorting her to be brave in the hunting-field. This for a time is successful. But Lucinda's acceptance of Sir Griffin's offer, superficially similar to that of the time-honoured " bartered bride " is really very different. She is too determined to yield to duress, too pessimistic to yield to ambition or the romance of wealth. She acts throughout with a despairing automatism. A common, but seldom described feeling is conveyed very exactly. Under the influence of despair (or desire) the will seems to lose all control, and control passes to an apparently alien, irresponsible and inhuman force. A quotation will illustrate this. Mrs. Carbuncle, fearing that Lucinda will lose Sir Griffin after all, asks, " ' Will you, then, just have the kindness to tell me what it is you propose to yourself? '

" ' I don't propose anything.'

" ' And where will you go when your money's done? '

" ' Just where I am going now! ' . . .

" ' You don't like anybody else,' suggested Mrs. Carbuncle.

" ' I don't like anything or anybody,' said Lucinda. . . .

" ' And now, when there's this great opening for you, you won't know your own mind.'

" ' I know my own mind well enough.' "

In this last phrase Trollope resorts to that deliberate verbal ambiguity which has become so popular since. Such a departure from his usual methods indicates a key passage.

A clue to her inconsistency in hating and accepting the man at the same time is provided by the scene in which Sir Griffin tries to kiss her. Her hatred is not in the main personal. " Never before had she been thus polluted. The embrace has disgusted her. It made her odious to herself. And if this, the beginning of it, were so bad, how was she to drink the cup to the bitter dregs? " This passage with its suggestion of final physical union (rare in Trollope) is crucial. She has accepted Sir Griffin in the abandon of pure despair, caused by her abnormal revulsion from sex, combined with her position as an impoverished society girl who ought to be trying to win a husband. The book's cycle of sexual aberrations is complete, and here as always their analysis is inextricably linked with that of social forces. This applies even to the apparently irrelevant and certainly fantastic lightning wooing of the policeman Gager and Patience Crabstick, which is the result of their common link with criminals. Lucinda's final volte-face in refusing to go to her wedding is dictated by the same despair which originally induced her to promise to marry Sir Griffin. It is natural to her despairing mind to choose deliberately the worse of two bad alternatives. So she had accepted the man; so now she delights to smash a great wedding feast with a word and ruin her reputation for ever

5. 'An Eye for an Eye': A New Phase

THE FIRST crisis of Trollope's writing life occurred when he abandoned the Irish scene and turned with *The Warden* to the field that would give him enduring fame. The second is marked by the appearance of *He Knew He Was Right* in 1869, the beginning of a new kind of writing, of his greatest artistic achievements, and perhaps also of the loss of popularity, which was soon to become apparent. The new atmosphere is unmistakable, tinged with gloom, sometimes with madness, a world of internal inner feelings, and rare but often terrible external events. Works like *An Eye for an Eye, Kept in the Dark, The Way We Live Now*, and *Cousin Henry* are claustrophobic. To turn to these after *Barchester Towers*, full of active humorous characters and unquestioned assumptions, is like the change from the broad horizons of *War and Peace* to the intensity and darkness of *Crime and Punishment*.

In reading *He Knew He Was Right* we can watch the change taking place under our eyes. The central situation, a husband's maniac brooding on the conduct of his innocent wife, is typical of the later works. But the crowded world, the mirror of life seen from a distance is there too. The Close at Exeter is less gay and less memorable than the Close at Barchester, but it is drawn in a slightly acidulated version of the same style. The result is most curious. It is as if this long book had been written by two different people, or rather by the same man at two widely separated periods of his life. But in reading it I think it would be easy to guess which line Trollope would follow in his subsequent work. The social comedy, the everyday world, though portrayed at length in this book, are perfunctory. They read like what they are, the work of a man who is not fully concentrating because of the new ideas in his mind. But the psychological portrait of Trevelyan, the self-injured husband, reads like the work of a man who has made a new and important discovery.

An Eye for an Eye was unpublished until 1879, but written about 1870, and so followed close upon *He Knew He Was Right*. Here we find for the first time Trollope's new world unmixed with the old. It is true that the break was never complete. In the later political novels which were written after this time, there is only a slightly increased emphasis on the psychological as against the practical. *Ayala's Angel*, published in 1881, is similar in many ways to what he had been writing in the early sixties. Nevertheless, the change about the year 1870 is marked and sudden, and thereafter the new methods always predominate over the old.

It is tempting to try to account for this change. But the memory of the " mythical sorrows of Shakespeare " must make the bravest hesitate. One could point out, for instance, that within the two years previous to the publication of *He Knew He Was Right*, Trollope had left his work in the Post Office and had buried his political ambitions after his unsuccessful attempt in the election at Beverley. In the years which followed, Trollope worked hard by ordinary standards, but hard work, as we have seen, was a term that did not mean to Trollope what it does to most of us. The prospect of a few hours with nothing to do and no one to disturb him, so pleasant to most people, was horror for him. He would have agreed with John Webster's character who said:

> " There's nothing of so infinit vexation
> As mans owne thoughts."

When, near the end of his life, he was in failing health Trollope would still say (in a letter to his son) that work was his one comfort. So, if we choose, we can ascribe the gloomy tone of the later books in part to the comparative leisure afforded by retirement from the Post Office. Partly, also, it was due, as I shall suggest in dealing with *The Way We Live Now*, to a general and belated understanding of the changes that were coming over Victorian England. Perhaps it is true, too, that men who have had an unhappy and insecure boyhood, tend in their later years to revert to their early outlook. As an illustration of this, I have been told of the case of a rich self-made business man who had lived for many years in luxury. As he grew old and infirm he gradually became more parsimonious, until one day he saw the food left over from a meal being thrown away, and furiously complained that if things were wasted like this, there would be nothing to eat next day. He mentally reverted to the early days when the next meal had been uncertain.

Whether these considerations do anything to explain the change must be a matter of opinion. It may be objected that Trollope was not a doddering old man in 1870, but in his active fifties; and the critic must always reckon with sudden literary changes for which no biographical explanation can be found. But, in any case, the nature of the change here is clear.

The plot of *An Eye for an Eye* is simple. A young officer, who by the death of his cousin has unexpectedly become the heir to an earldom, falls in love with a poor Irish girl who becomes his mistress after a promise of marriage. He hesitates between his loyalty to her and his loyalty to the property and title, until, when he finally decides to reject the girl he is pushed over a cliff by her infuriated mother. The cast is strictly limited, the action takes place in two places only, the country house in Dorset and a West Irish coastal village. Except for the violent ending there is little action; even the mental struggle of Nevill is played down. The moral choice seems in the end to make itself with no real decision on his part. It seems inevitable that the claims of rank and wealth must triumph. It is true that Nevill is a man who takes his colour from his surroundings, and as he moves from Ireland to Dorset and back he undergoes corresponding mental oscillations. But he can never think of his Irish Kate, even in his moments of greatest devotion to her, as a future countess and lady of an English estate. His plans for marriage all involve living abroad, unknown. This is a symptom of the gulf in his eyes between the two worlds in which he has lived. But Trollope contrives to suggest how small the difference is in reality, however great psychologically. One is a land of riches, the other of poverty, but both are tedious, one, as Mr. Michael Sadleir says, with " the portentous, stately, tedium of feudal Dorset," the other with " the untidy, reckless tedium of Western Ireland." The bleakness of useless wealth is like the bleakness of poverty, and both produce loneliness. But birth and upbringing have made Nevill see a momentous contrast where the impartial judge would see only a pale similarity.

The hero is not a memorable character; he is hardly meant to be. He is just an average young Englishman of his class, with a taste for adventure and a liking for people with a culture entirely different from his own. His uncle the Earl and his aunt are religious, self-denying, and impressed with the duties rather than the pleasures of high rank. The point of the book is the way an average good-hearted young man and two conscientious older people can be corrupted by the idea of wealth and rank. They are not tempted by its pleasures, but by what they conceive to be its duties. Trollope puts his finger on the terrible consequences of their high-minded doctrines in this passage, describing Nevill's thoughts as he decides to follow his uncle's advice after the latter's death, when he has succeeded to title and property.

" ' Sans reproche ' was the motto of his house, and was emblazoned on the wall of the hall that was now his own. If it might be possible to him, he would live up to it and neither degrade his order nor betray his country." This is the authority he invokes for desertion and the breaking of a solemn promise.

The point here is the *unconsciousness* of temptation. Nevill can feel the pull of loyalty to his love and to his promise of marriage. He can feel the pull of loyalty to what are held to be the duties of his order. But he feels both intermittently. He cannot connect them, or weigh one against the other. They belong to different categories in his mind. The irony of the situation, the irony of the motto, is that Nevill himself cannot see the irony.

Parallel with the temptation of Nevill is the temptation of his aunt, the countess. For in spite of her instinct as a lady of rank and her feminine contempt for the supposed feminine scheming of a nameless Irish girl, she cannot escape from her religious principles. After advising her nephew with the most passionate entreaties to abandon the girl, she is left face to face with her conviction that to break one's pledged word is a grave offence against her religious code and against the code of gentlemanly conduct. At the last moment, therefore, she recants and, just before her nephew sets out for Ireland for the last time, contradicts her previous advice to him. When she hears of his death she characteristically blames herself, because of her original advice. Her mental conflict only becomes important near the end of the book, and this perhaps is a fault of technique. But when it does appear it is powerfully drawn, and provides an interesting sidelight on Nevill's own. Her heart-rendings have a dignity which Nevill's lack, for, basing herself on moral truths, she can see the whole issue and repent her error. But Nevill is a drifter who allows circumstances to take the place of his conscience.

The plot here is at once simpler and more important than, say, in *Rachel Ray* (1863). The books of the fifties and sixties are full of incident, but seldom have a clear, single issue on which the whole story turns. The simpler a plot is the more it is likely to dominate a book's every sentence, and that is what happens here.

With the Irish side of the story Trollope is not so successful. Mrs. O'Hara, the murdering mother, is hardly more than a conventional picture of " wild Irish." Her attitude to the rich stranger is never made clear, and though its contradictions are possible they do need to be explained. For she takes the seduction extremely calmly and then goes into a murderous frenzy when she finds that the marriage will not follow. We are given no preparation for her eventual violence. Like all the Irish characters in the book she is a Catholic, and one wonders whether Trollope remembered this sufficiently. For she is shown ending her days as a madwoman continually repeating the words " an eye for an eye and a tooth for a tooth." This sounds much more like the Protestant fanaticism which Trollope portrayed so well in Mrs. Bolton of *John Caldigate*. It would seem that Trollope here used religious fanaticism as a device for the plot without seriously considering its appropriateness. But the flaw is not a great one and the effectiveness of the ending almost atones for it.

In the character of Father Marty, the priest who is first Nevill's friend and then his accuser, Trollope did better. Compared with the other characters he is insensitive to the importance of rank. He cannot see Nevill's difficulty. But we are not allowed to be sure why this is. Is it because, as he says himself " his bishop is the only lord that matters to him "? Or because he is foreign and ignorant? In either case his attitude seems natural. But there is an absurdity in his position as a priest. For it is as if he has only two parishioners. " ' While I live I will follow you,' " he says to the recreant Nevill. He is a very Doctor Watson of parish priests—his practice is never very absorbing. It would be interesting to know why Trollope made this mistake. Did he simply sacrifice probability to a rhetorical scene? Or did he think of the duties of a poor Irish priest in terms of the rich unattached Anglican clergy about whom he had so often written? Well as Trollope knew Ireland, he was apt to lose his hold on probability in dealing with its people in a way he never did with his English characters.

A very similar error is made by Charles Reade in *Griffith Gaunt* where two priests are apparently at the beck and call of a simple family without reference to their supporters. Perhaps this type of anomaly goes deeper than a casual inconsistency, suiting an author's convenience. The average Victorian did not think of the Catholic Church as it actually appeared before him in his everyday life—a growing body, quietly organised into parishes, very British, very loyal, and lacking any united political interest. He thought of it much more in terms of the historical accounts of its Elizabethan period which he had read at his first school. Priests were so romantic or so sinister that ordinary verisimilitude was not considered. He no more asked if a Catholic priest could arrange to desert his work without notice than he wondered at Byron's Corsair for not earning a steady weekly wage.

There is one further point about the Irish setting of *An Eye for an Eye*. Why is so little fuss made about Kate O'Hara as a fallen woman? The contrast with *The Vicar of Bullhampton* is very marked. For there Trollope makes profuse apologies for introducing Carrie Brattle at all. And the two works were written (though not published) very nearly at the same time. One can only guess at the answer. But it would seem that the rule-of-thumb morality of the great British novel-reading public in 1870, though very fierce, was also very easily placated. There might be an objection to Carrie Brattle, but there was none to Tristan and Isolde, nor to Launcelot and Guinevere. The Irish background gave the average reader just the salve his conscience needed. It gave a tinge of romance and remoteness, and enabled him to reflect pleasantly that good old England was not like this and that, anyway, little better could be expected of Papists. Trollope, without any conscious effort, understood these prejudices.

6. 'The Way We Live Now'

IT IS one of the drawbacks of Trollope's casual artistic methods that some of his characters and incidents seem only to occur when they do because he happened to think of them when he did. But this book has a unifying theme—the collapse of standards and of social order before new methods of finance—which unites almost all of it in a satisfying whole.

In many of his books, though his subject was ostensibly the present, Trollope had been influenced by memories of the past. In the Barsetshire novels, England is still an agricultural country in spite of the railways. *Dombey and Son* represents a later stage of social development than *Barchester Towers* though it was written about ten years before. Now for the first time Trollope chose to be contemporary, even perhaps prophetic, and though he was all the time producing one or more books a year *The Way We Live Now* has the appearance of a great leap forward in time.

He never had spared the vices of the rich. But in the Barsetshire novels, money and rank still bore some relation to each other. The occasional *nouveau riche*, like Miss Dunstable, was easily absorbed by society, and partly adopted an aristocratic point of view. And so there was an element of responsibility even in the misuse of power. But now, almost everyone is tending to become irresponsible. Huge sums are won and lost in a moment and fortunes can be made out of non-existent enterprises. The origin of Melmotte, the central figure, is known to nobody, the source of his wealth is unknown, and his greatness so blinds with excess of light that people imagine that neither normal moral nor practical laws apply to him.

In outline, Melmotte's story is the great traditional story of fortune's wheel, the rise, the grandeur, and the fall of a great man. But the treatment has unique features which illustrate this disturbing suspension of ordinary laws. For neither his unprecedented commercial greatness, nor his collapse, represent much objective change in his prosperity. Credit makes him and loss of credit breaks him. The new financial system is a concourse of intangibles.

Credit is paradoxically separated from its own origins in personal confidence in a man's worth and solvency. Everybody is following everybody else's lead in accepting Melmotte. Excessive deference is paid to public opinion, and the result is that public opinion ceases to exist. Who is to say who the leader is when everyone is walking in a circle following the man in front?[1] Most disturbing of all is the indirect power of money to influence people unawares. Thus a prince of the blood goes to Melmotte's ball simply as one of the normal duties of his station; but the real reason for his presence is the recovery of a lady's jewels at Melmotte's expense.

As credit becomes at the same time omnipotent and devoid of meaning, people trust Melmotte's bare word for large sums of money. It is ridiculous to trouble him to sign a cheque; and so money almost disappears from the dealings of a man whose only business is financial manipulation.

The same charming vagueness shows itself in the deliberations of the directors of Melmotte's great American railway enterprise. " Mr. Longestaffe was astonished to find how soon the business was done, and how very little he had been called on to do. Miles Grendall had read something out of a book which he had been unable to follow. Then the chairman had read some figures. Mr. Cohenlupe had declared that their prosperity was unprecedented; —and the Board was over." But as the functions of ready cash

[1] There is a parallel here with Newman's analysis of generally-accepted prejudices in *The Present Position of Catholics*—especially interesting as Newman is dealing with the strength of unreasoning traditions, Trollope with the spread of new ideas.

decline, the domination of economics grows stronger. The story of Melmotte's party, given for the Chinese emperor, shows business methods encroaching on social life. The party tickets are openly sold, and they rise and fall in value just like stocks and shares, and with as little reason. Here, too, credit becomes an absolute but phantom monarch, allowing no appeal. Though for a long time credit works only in his favour, Melmotte cannot control it. " He had contemplated great things; but the things which he was achieving were beyond his contemplation." These involuntary achievements bring about his fall; he is all the time a servant, not a master.

If, amid all these fluctuations, his real wealth does not alter much, his conduct and the generally accepted judgment on his character hardly alter at all. Here is no case of concealed villainy unmasked. It is true that at the height of his success he becomes a little more overbearing; when his fortunes begin to totter he is a little more reckless, though not more unscrupulous in his crimes. The time when the dinner for the Emperor of China is being planned is the apex of his career. But, endlessly discussed, endlessly admired though he is, no one suggests that he is, in the ordinary sense, honest. Some excuse dishonesty, some ignore it, some are faintly ill at ease, but very few, and they not people of fashion or importance, are surprised at the high honours he receives.

But in the few days before the banquet a great change occurs. There are rumours that Melmotte is not financially sound; it is hinted that he has committed forgery and may be arrested. Mysterious paragraphs, mentioning no names, appear in the Press. In describing the dilemma of all the invited guests, the author makes this comment, " No one wishes to dine with a swindler." An obvious remark, but its implications are wide. In his fall, as in his prosperity, Melmotte is always judged by unreal standards. As the case of Oscar Wilde would later illustrate in the realm of fact, wickedness, elegant or monstrous or magnificent, is one thing in the public mind, but the police court is quite another. The revulsion against Melmotte which leads to his disgrace and suicide is caused by the mere suspicion that he will turn out to be what he had always been supposed to be. A false signature is concrete; it recalls aristocratic minds, bemused by the contemplation of apparently unlimited wealth and power, to ordinary moral categories and definite legal penalties.

It is not only moral standards that are vitiated. Lady Monogram, who has exerted herself to secure tickets for Melmotte's evening party, is worried by the rumours. She would be bitterly ashamed of having gone if the Emperor and the English Prince have stayed away. Unwilling to entrust such a delicate matter to a servant, she asks her husband to find out if they are there.

" Sir Damask was the most good-natured man in the world, but he did not like the job. ' What can be the objection? ' asked his wife.

" ' Go to a man's house and find out whether a man's guests are come before you go yourself! I just don't see it, Ju.'

" ' Guests! What nonsense! The Emperor and all the Royal Family! As if it were like any other party.' "

Without knowing it, Melmotte has rendered the social code also void.

As Melmotte's success and failure alike depend not on facts, but on reputations, newspapers play an important part in the story. Indeed, the book opens with an account of the three editors; the corruption of the word comes first. The semi-smart world of literary reviews is ruled by the same code as the commercial, which it imagines to be so different. Venal reviewers comfort themselves with the reflection that " If I didn't somebody else would." Lady Carbury finds a title for her novel before considering its plot, just as, in the Vera Cruz railway project, the shares were real, but the trains are imaginary. The newspaper leaders about Melmotte hedge like the speculators on the stock exchange. In the same way the Beargarden set unconsciously imitates Melmotte's business methods with their gambling and cheating.

A series of inappropriate ideas about money poisons family life. Lady Carbury is driven to desperate and shady schemes by her son's gambling and extravagance until finally the two separate altogether. Melmotte's wish to buy a title for his daughter leads to cruelty which even prevents her from mourning his death. The joint schemes of Nidderdale and his father Auld Reekie for carrying off the heiress end by making them despise each other. The Grendalls form a sinister alliance in their parasitic attendance upon Melmotte, until they become accomplices, and the relationship of father and son is extinguished and forgotten by both.

What is the connection between this new commerce and the latter-day representatives of Barsetshire? They do not obtain the unqualified approval which we might expect; they can be corrupted too. There is Roger Carbury certainly, the honest Suffolk squire with his air of conscious virtue in decadent times. Trollope seems to have intended him to be the standard by which the other characters should be judged. But he made the mistake of allowing his own creation to be aware of the part assigned to him, and so he seems to be almost a prig, which was certainly not intended. Perhaps it was a mistake, though a very natural one, to give him a dual rôle of virtue, for he is both the old-fashioned and responsible squire, hating flashy finance, and the constant and injured lover. But he does have one difficult problem in casuistry, which helps to relieve the impression of an effortless and censorious virtue. His successful rival in love, Paul Montague, is one of his closest friends, and he resents what he considers Montague's treachery in intervening, as a late-comer, between him and a cousin of his own.

But when the girl Hetta Carbury has accepted Montague, rumours reach her of a disreputable incident which might throw doubt on his affection for her. Roger Carbury, both as an old friend of the family and a man in Montague's confidence, is asked to give an opinion on this. He refuses to speak on the ground that he is an interested party and that he has heard of Montague's affairs in confidence. At first sight this seems to himself and others the only honourable course. But he gradually comes to see that the appeal to honour really conceals an injustice. For though he knows Montague has been to blame, he knows also that he has never been false to Hetta.

But though this difficulty helps to redeem Roger Carbury from mere facile uprightness, it does not do so completely. The implications are not stressed, and in spite of all this Roger Carbury seems to stand over the other characters with an air of academic moral correctness.

It would be natural to suppose from this that Trollope was merely lamenting the half-imaginary glories of the past. But this would be a great mistake. Anyone, of course, would prefer the abuses of the Barsetshire system to those of the Melmotte system. But the latter are not entirely revolutionary or even wholly new. In some ways they only accentuate what the unsuspecting might consider the grand old anomalies of the past. The inequality of the sexes, instead of being lessened, has actually increased; whereas, under the old system women were expected to be quiet and almost idle, they are now bullied and insulted just because they are weak. The growth of ruthless competition is not confined to commerce.

Almost everyone in the book however degraded can strike an attitude and appeal to the good old days. Sir Felix Carbury, Hetta's dissolute brother, without a moral scruple to bless himself with, can still speak in the language of ancient chivalry in defence of his sister and believe in it himself. An appeal to the good old days is made by the members of the Beargarden Club when it has to close down. It strikes none of them as incongruous, though the club has been short-lived, and its traditions were only drinking and gambling all night, cheating and unpaid debts. Rootlessness can only be detected from outside. There is the same confusion in the opposition to Melmotte as in his supporters. " Just at this moment, there was a very strong feeling against Melmotte, owing perhaps as much to his having tumbled over poor Mr. Beauchamp in the House of Commons as to the stories of the forgeries. . . ." One of the editors opposes him simply out of perversity and the knowledge that blame sells better than praise, while some people support him in honourable ignorance of his nature.

It is the same with the lawyers. It seems at first sight that in his revulsion from Squercum, the sharp and disreputable lawyer of the new civilisation, a gentile masquerading as a Jew so that he may gain an advantage by working on Sundays, Trollope will grow almost sentimental about the stately delays of Slow and Bideawhile. These two had been satirised in the Barsetshire series, but with an easy, pleasant satire reserved for the incidental absurdities of a system, supposed at that time to be permanent and reasonably good. But we discover later with relief that we are not meant to be taken in by their venerable air. Their obstinate conviction that no one, least of all Squercum, can teach them anything about transacting legal business leads to serious loss for their clients. They hand over title-deeds to Melmotte on forged authority and without even receiving the purchase money. This is more culpable because, though hard in their ordinary dealings, they regard Melmotte as a being of a different order, far above being watched with ordinary commercial suspicion. These ardent traditionalists have, without realising it, underwritten Melmotte's business methods. They are more closely linked to the despised Squercum than they know. Their inconsistency gives Squercum just the pretext he desires for abandoning all the best traditions of law and commerce, for he is quick to point out that he is only developing ideas suggested by the practice of one of the oldest and most respected legal firms in London.

But all this is subsidiary to the case of the elder Mr. Longestaffe and his daughter. The Longestaffes are an old family with a fine estate and a large income, who are embarrassed financially through their own foolishness. The head of the family fancies himself as a traditionalist, and is accustomed to blame everything on one single terrible departure from ancient standards of British virtue—the admission of the Jews into Parliament. " Whenever creditors were more than ordinarily importunate, when Slow and Bideawhile could do nothing for him, he would refer to that fatal measure as though it was the cause of every embarrassment which had harassed him." Having issued this charter of irresponsibility, he takes to dealing with Melmotte to raise the ready money he needs, and even welcomes social intercourse between the two families. He is far more modern than he realises, and in consequence he is confronted with what seems to him a story of horror.

Georgiana, his daughter, has been looking for a husband for ten years, always aiming a little too high in the social scale, annually lowering her sights, but never enough to allow for the passing of time. Now she is further handicapped by her father's inability to afford the London season. Melmotte introduces her to a rich Jewish merchant called Brehgert, a widower with grown-up children. Physically he is the very Platonic idea of what a Jew is popularly supposed to be, " a fat greasy man of fifty, conspicuous for hair-dye." Bertrand Russell has called Trollope anti-semitic. If, as seems probable, he was judging on this character, he might have read more carefully. For apart from Roger Carbury, Brehgert is the only genuinely honest man in the book, and behaves throughout with intelligence and forbearance. Instead of being a symbol of anti-semitism, Brehgert's disagreeable appearance helps to rehabilitate not only a Jew, but—a much more difficult matter—the popular idea of one.

The Longestaffe aversion to Brehgert—even Georgiana regards him only as a last resort—reveals the sort of moral confusion which Pope epitomised in the words:

" Puffs, Powders, Patches, Bibles, Billet-doux."

" An old fat Jew," says Mr. Longestaffe, unaware that in this brief phrase he is making three entirely different kinds of objection to the marriage. By lumping them all together, as if old age or fatness were a natural consequence of belonging to a national or religious group, he forfeits all claim to a reasoned opposition.

The contrast in delicacy and reasonableness between Longestaffe and Brehgert is underlined by their last meeting after the proposed marriage has been abandoned. Longestaffe who has spoken with such thoughtless violence and even insulted Brehgert personally, is shocked and distressed that the other should refer to the past affair at all. In his unreal reticence as in his previous unwarranted outspokenness, he is out of touch with facts. Brehgert maintains throughout a calm and dignified attitude. Longe-staffe, annoyed first by the man's calmness, then by his out-spokenness, is like a weather-cock reproaching a compass needle for pointing first too far to the east, then too far to the west.

Georgiana herself has been worried by the synagogue, and has planned to get him to go nowhere so that she might pass him off as a Christian. Her mother's comment epitomises a type of mind for which religion and conscience can always be used to support caprice or passion. " ' It seems to me that it can't be possible. It's worse than your wife's sister. I'm sure there's something in the Bible against it.' " There could be no more telling comment on the mentality which Arnold satirised in *Culture and Anarchy*.

The Longestaffes may be driven into this ecstasy of shame and anger, but they are not ashamed of dealing with Melmotte. They can abandon moral considerations almost completely and then manufacture the fiercest indignation out of a mere prejudice. It is suggested that a suppressed feeling of guilt about one point leads to a louder outburst about the other. But, really, Georgiana's defection is the logical consequence of her parents' actions. For if they had had nothing to do with Melmotte, she would never have met Brehgert, and if they had not squandered their large income until they were unable to keep up their position, she would have been able to look for a husband among the aristocracy. But if Mr. Longestaffe cannot visit London, his daughter is inevitably cut off from the fashionable world, and that is the offence of which he is accusing her. By a further irony, Mr. Longestaffe, who considers himself so ill-used, is really very fortunate, for one would never expect that a man introduced by Melmotte would be either honest or courteous, and Brehgert is both. His anger is doubly futile.

To understand Trollope's intention here, it is useful to consider the two permanent and opposite errors into which the satirist may fall. The more obvious is triteness. The more important vices are limited in number and in interest. To find an original method of attacking them is almost as difficult, after the achievements of the past, as to find a new way of writing blank verse. Some writers, like Oscar Wilde, take refuge in what may prove an equally damaging error. They turn all the normal satirical judgments on their heads, and sometimes achieve no more than an irrelevant firework display. For satire devoid of its moral content is inevitably trivial. The story of Brehgert and the Longestaffes provides an example of Trollope's method of avoiding the dilemma. He takes what is in outline an ordinary story—similar to the plot of Thackeray's *Philip* and of several other well-known novels of the time. There are the same issues; the marriage market, wealth placed before love, disparity of age in marriage, and the sinister flirtation of a needy aristocracy with rich commercial upstarts. Then slowly and calmly, without self-conscious paradox, without any suggestion that moral categories can be neatly interchanged for literary purposes, the author proceeds to falsify a number of time-honoured assumptions. The attempt to sell the girl for money is made by herself, instead of by her parents. The insolvent parents, though they are mercenary and care little for their daughter, are horrified, not for her sake, but for their own. The elderly man, with nothing but his money to recommend him, is in reality far superior to the proposed young bride in understanding and generosity. Finally, and this is the crucial point, all these surprises follow naturally from the original situation. Society and contemporary satirists are satirised at the same time; Trollope's indictment is formidable without being familiar, and avoids altogether the derivativeness of pure parody.

The Way We Live Now is among other things a sociological novel. It shows how part of the aristocracy and the gentry is drawn into the orbit of the financiers. Mr. Longestaffe sits for hours in Melmotte's antechamber while the nephew of a duke gives him soothing explanations. Trollope does not analyse this situation as Scott would probably have done. He is, so as to speak, a pictorial sociologist, not a scientific one. His mind was not given to weighing complicated sets of causes. His aristocratic characters do not ask themselves how they come to be in this strange position. But one reason emerges clearly. The insistence on useless luxuries, like powdered footmen, to copy men even richer than themselves, leads men of ample inherited wealth into financial difficulties as soon as circumstances cease to be ideal for the landed interest.

But Longestaffe still has a sort of code; and in an interesting passage we see how it contributes to his troubles. " He was a silly man, who had no fixed idea that it behoved him to be of use to anyone; but, yet, he had compassed a certain nobility of feeling. There was very little that his position called upon him to do, but there was much that it forbade him to do. It was not allowed to him to be close in money matters. He could leave his tradesmen's bills unpaid till the men were clamorous, but he could not question the items in their accounts. He could be tyrannical to his servants, but he could not make inquiry as to the consumption of his wines in the servants' hall. He had no pity for his tenants in regard to game, but he hesitated much as to raising their rent." He gains none of the practical advantages of honesty or of dishonesty.

And of course, he is bored. The characters do not enjoy, or even expect to enjoy their own extravagances. A pervading boredom is indicated, without being stressed, by passages like this, as Melmotte, now a member of Parliament, approaches bankruptcy and death. " There were a great many members present, and a general feeling prevailed that the world was more than ordinarily alive because of Melmotte and his failures." There is domestic boredom as well, grey winter afternoons, dull tea-drinking and meaningless flirtation. Perhaps there was a change in the author as well as in his subject. The middle-aged Trollope had never been bored, and the Barsetshire characters were like him in this. Now, though he was only sixty, he felt old age coming on before its time.

Formally, Trollope came near to writing a masterpiece. That he did not is probably due to the fact, noticed by Mr. Michael Sadleir, that he had not fully prepared for Melmotte's central position when the book was begun. Still, the main characters are closely grouped round Melmotte. Their various connections with him do not strike us as contrived, complicated though they are.

For they all depend in some way on the book's main subject—
money, and every twist of plot is intended to illustrate the per-
meation of society by Melmotte's standards of conduct. In one
case only does the connection seem forced—in Paul Montague's
affair with Mrs. Hurtle. It could be argued that this is relevant
because Mrs. Hurtle is the feminine version of the *Americanism* of
the Vera Cruz railway, and because she contributes to the study
of the unnatural by reversing the normal rôles of male and female.
But this defence will not hold. One can never be satisfied with
a purely intellectual link between different parts of a novel.
Considerations like these have to be thought up deliberately, they
do not suggest themselves of their own accord. Besides this part
of the book contributes nothing to its varied and subtle study of
money. All the elements of a masterpiece are here except the
editor's scissors.

At times there is a skilful use of detail. The impression made
by the Emperor of China is conveyed in a few phrases like " the
awful quiescent solemnity of the celestial one." Double inter-
preters are needed before he can hold any conversation, for he
does not deign to speak Chinese and his esoteric language must
be translated first into Chinese and then into English. Melmotte
is suitably introduced, so as to speak, as a camp-follower behind
his money and the magnificence of his entertainments. More than
a page is devoted to an account of the ball that is to be held at
his house in Grosvenor Square before his name is mentioned for
the first time. No doubt Trollope meant that this unusual device
should anticipate Melmotte's final scene when, deprived of his
wealth, he becomes merely an unimportant suicide's corpse.

The Beargarden Club illustrates how ideas of money are
modified by idleness and good nature. The principle of its
existence is the combination of profligacy and parsimony. It has
no morning papers, no library, no expensive front for other people
to look at. But all this economy is devoted to the cause of reckless
gambling. The members hate trouble and fuss so much that they
give plenary power in all money matters to an agent so that they
shall be cheated only by one man. The same dread dominates

their relations to each other. No one expects Miles Grendall
to honour the IOUs he regularly issues for large gambling
debts.

" ' Won't Mr. Grendall pay it? '

" ' Oh, dear no. How the devil should he? '

" ' Then he shouldn't play.'

" ' That'd be hard on him, poor fellow. If you went to his
uncle, the duke, I suppose you could get it. Or Buntinford might
put it right for you. Perhaps he might win, you know, some day,
and then he'd make it square. He'd be fair enough if he had it.
Poor Miles.' "

These passages illustrate a main theme of the book—that
money, when it becomes the centre of a man's universe, continually evades realisation. Mr. Longestaffe's embarrassments are
due to money spent on powdered footmen, and the like, whom
nobody enjoys.   Melmotte's gigantic dealings are concluded
without money transactions and make nonsense of work. So here
these young men, whose life is devoted to making money at
games of chance, are driven by habit to play with a man from
whom they cannot win. For all of them money proves to be a
phantom.

But the Beargarden scenes have another purpose also. Trollope
understood very well the principle of literary relativity. When
Othello strikes Desdemona, the act is as shocking as the blinding
of Gloucester, because *Othello* presupposes a much higher level
of civilisation than *King Lear*. Trollope made use of this psychological fact in *Miss Mackenzie* where he succeeds in making the
harmless dissipations of maiden ladies seem extremely daring.
So here, but more effectively still, by comparison with Melmotte
the somnolent good nature of the Beargarden seems almost
sublime.

From this point of view the behaviour of Nidderdale is important. He is a modest man who moves among the Beargarden
group without identifying himself with them. He gambles but
without the real gambling fever. As the eldest son of a peer who
wants money, he had had his fling and has now settled down with

good-humoured pertinacity to his appointed task—marrying an heiress, Melmotte's daughter, Marie. But for all this, he becomes, relatively, a symbol of virtue.

Without probing into the moral nature of the proposed marriage, he sees it as a sound bargain, which he tries to perform in an honest spirit. When Melmotte is near to disgrace, and as it proves to death also, Nidderdale finds himself sitting next to him in the House of Commons. Disliking Melmotte personally and already abandoning the marriage in his own mind (because of the disturbing financial rumours about Melmotte), he still will not snub his neighbour. It " did not suit the turn of his mind." After Melmotte's suicide he says with a curious uncomprehending sincerity, " ' None of you fellows will believe me, but, upon my word, I liked that girl and I'd've stuck to her at last,—only there are some things a fellow can't do. He was such a thundering scoundrel.' " In the end, though the marriage project has been abandoned, Marie comes to trust him as her only reliable friend. Nidderdale stands for fair dealing on an unquestioned basis of cynicism. On his lips and on others the word " love " echoes emptily, showing that it is much easier to alter ways of conduct than habits of thought.

Dolly Longestaffe is the central Beargarden figure, and he is the most apathetic of them all. Informed by Felix Carbury that Grendall has been cheating when they three and Nidderdale have been playing for high stakes, he is unimpressed.

" ' I wish you hadn't told me. Why did you pick me out to tell me? Why didn't you tell Nidderdale? '

" ' He might have said, what didn't you tell Longestaffe? '

" ' No he wouldn't. Nobody would suppose that anybody would pick me out for this kind of thing. If I'd known that you were going to tell me such a story as this I wouldn't have come with you.'

" ' That's nonsense, Dolly.'

" ' Very well. I can't bear these kind of things. I feel all in a twitter already.'

" ' You mean to go on playing just the same? '

"'Of course I do. If he won anything very heavy I should begin to think about it, I suppose.'"

Trollope shows us the consequences of Melmotte as they are mirrored in this placid spirit. Vague disquiet in him is as startling as the destruction of empires. Melmotte is the first person he has ever taken the trouble to despise. He is driven to write letters, almost to fancy himself as a man of business, even to make a moral reflection. "'I've a sort of feeling,'" he says, "'that I don't like a family property going to pieces. A fellow oughtn't to let his family property go to pieces.'"

It is fitting that this moron should be the first to see through Melmotte. While all the clever people still believe in him, Dolly argues "'When I buy a thing and don't pay for it, it is because I haven't got the tin.'" He has not the brain to be hypnotised like all the others by the bogus mysteries of credit. He alone is stupid enough to see the obvious truth.

7. ' Dr. Wortle's School' and 'Kept in the Dark'

TWO MISUNDERSTOOD NOVELS

TO-DAY THE Victorians are no longer unfashionable; their ideas are considered worthy of serious discussion. But in books written about them between the wars, in Sir Harold Nicolson's book on Tennyson, for instance, any admiration of them is expressed tentatively and defensively. It was natural that men who wished to recommend Victorians to an unsympathetic period should seize on what seemed most modern in them and brandish it triumphantly before the public. That is what Sir Hugh Walpole did in 1928 with *Dr. Wortle's School*. To him and to many others the book seemed modern because they thought it questioned the sanctity of marriage.

The plot of the book turns on the marriage of a supposed widow, whose husband is really still alive. The second marriage has been entered into with good faith on both sides, as convincing but misleading evidence had been found of the death of the first husband, Ferdinand Lefroy. He is a drunkard who has consistently ill-treated his wife, and when they discover the truth, she and Mr. Peacocke, the second husband, decide to remain together. Peacocke is a clergyman and a fine scholar, an Englishman and an Oxford man, who has met his wife during a visit to America. They return to England and Peacocke is employed by Dr. Wortle, also a clergyman and the headmaster of an expensive and successful school. When he first engages Peacocke as a teacher, Wortle has no suspicion of the facts, but he soon hears them both from Peacocke himself, who begins to feel that he is practising deception, and, in a garbled version, from the first husband's brother.

This is how Sir Hugh Walpole describes the book, " He [Trollope] says to the world, ' I have paid attention to your social hypocrisies long enough. I care as much as you do for good conduct and right living, but I care still more for honest common sense.' . . . He is advancing now to the modern view of greater consideration for the individual case. . . . ' These people [the Peacockes] are right,' says Dr. Wortle-Trollope, ' so let's have no more nonsense.' " This passage represents, perhaps in a slightly exaggerated form, a very general view of the book's intention.

But in fact the moral problem of the book is subtler than this. The real point lies not in the conduct of Peacocke and his wife, but in that of Dr. Wortle on discovering the facts. Only once, and that very early in the book, does Trollope ask himself how the Peacockes should have behaved, and then he answers the question unequivocally. He says, " Every day passed together as man and wife must be a falsehood and a sin. Though their hearts might have burst in the doing of it they should have parted." He even says (what is certainly an exaggeration), " There is no one who reads this but will say that they should have parted." Trollope would not have thought it worth while to discuss at length a question which, in his eyes, was capable of a certain and obvious answer. The first essential for the understanding of *Dr. Wortle's School* is to realise that it was written in the conviction that marriage is always and everywhere binding for life.

The book is a study of the clash between an unquestioned morality and the character and circumstances of the man who is forced to act as a judge. If a doubt were admitted about the moral issue, the book would be one-sided and Dr. Wortle's dilemma unreal; his decision would be a foregone conclusion. Orthodox moral teaching provides the one and only argument against the Peacockes. Every other consideration points in their favour. If moral agnosticism were even contemplated, the book's central conflict would be a battle in which one side run away before a shot was fired.

Like several of Trollope's later works, *Dr. Wortle's School* is a study in the grotesque. How did it come about that a clergyman of the Church of England condoned adultery? To-day this might not seem such a grotesque question, but to understand the author's purpose, we need to realise that for him and for many of his readers no imaginable question would have been more grotesque.

Everything that happens in the book is designed to throw light on this question. The doctor's character is displayed gradually and with the utmost care, and even the scenes in which he does not appear contribute to it. For instance, the American scenes, in which Peacocke is searching for evidence of Ferdinand Lefroy's death, are designed to reveal the horror of Mrs. Peacocke's former life, which is an important part of the data for Dr. Wortle's decision. And why is the love affair between Wortle's daughter and Earl Bracy's son left without a conclusion? As a rule, the final chapters of Trollope's books are full of marriages and tedious brief sketches of the future lives of the characters. But the exception here is easy to explain, for in this case the love is incidental to something else. What matters is the doctor's attitude to it. It gives him the opportunity to reveal himself in the character of the proud freeborn Englishman of the middle class, who admits no superior. From this point of view the outcome of the affair is unimportant. The key to the doctor's character is a proud impatience of all restraint. In his correspondence with Earl Bracy he shows himself to be in the tradition of Dr. Johnson's levellers; he believes in class distinctions below himself, but not above. He despises those who are not " gentlemen " while asserting his equality to an earl. He uses the useful word " gentleman " as a banner of middle-class revolt.[1]

Several writers have detected a likeness between Dr. Wortle and Trollope himself. Their case is a strong one, and it may well

[1] The obverse of this appears in *The Duke's Children* where the Duke of Omnium dismisses as irrelevant his daughter's claim that her poverty-stricken suitor is a 'gentleman.' " ' So is my private secretary,' " he says.

be that Trollope was aware of the resemblance. But the wrong conclusions have been drawn. It has been assumed that Trollope must necessarily approve of Dr. Wortle, if he created him in his own image. But if Dr. Wortle is a portrait of Trollope there is just as much reason to suppose that Charles Tudor, John Eames, and Mr. Whittlestaffe are also. In each of these, if they are self-portraits, there is abundant self-criticism. It is odd that the plentiful indications of a satirical attitude towards Dr. Wortle in the book's first chapter should have been so generally over-looked. In the very first sentence we are told that " he was much esteemed by others—and by himself." Within a page or two we learn that " he liked that people under him should thrive—and he liked them to know that they throve by his means," and that he was " an affectionate tyrant." Trollope exposes his faults with the loving care an unillusioned man feels for his own.

All the circumstances make a powerful appeal both to Dr. Wortle's virtues and to his inflated ideas of himself. Since he sees himself as a beneficent provider of all good things for his household and servants, the very fact that he has employed Peacocke influences him in his favour. Then he is warm-hearted and generous and he cannot bring himself to expose a woman to the world's contempt. Moreover, her case has many extenuating circumstances. She had evidence of her husband's death and the doctor has been able to guess his nature through meeting his brother, who came to the school in search of a price for his silence. The joy of disappointing this monster's expectations about the effect of the revelation to an English clergyman is another motive for clemency. Again, he is almost insanely jealous of interference, and so the admonitions of his bishop only incite him to disobedience. But perhaps the decisive factor is the lure of the disadvantageous course and the desire to offend those who have the power of injuring him financially. For rumours of the affair, spread and exaggerated by one of the doctor's enemies, cause a sharp drop in the number of his pupils. This attitude is generous, certainly, but it springs also from pride. In his heart he resents being paid by the parents of his pupils. Just as his loud assertion of equality with a lord is mingled with a snobbish devotion to the aristocracy, so is this proud independence mingled with a strong interest in money. Snobbery and avarice are combined in his desire to amass a dowry large enough to allow his daughter to marry above his own rank. But pride is his ruling passion, and he would rather sacrifice any money or ambition than abide an insult.

In spite of all these powerful inducements he cannot bring himself to allow the Peacockes to remain at the school together. He compromises by sending Peacocke to America to find evidence about the death of Ferdinand Lefroy; for an unguarded utterance of his brother Robert has suggested to both Wortle and Peacocke that this death has now at last really occured. But he allows Mrs. Peacocke to remain where she is, treats her very kindly and holds out the hope of the restoration of Peacocke's position in the school if they are finally able to marry according to law. By this course, as it turns out, the doctor exposes himself to loss of reputation as well as to financial loss. It is not long before a newspaper called *Everybody's Business* suggests that the attractions of Mrs. Peacocke have moved him to act in this way. Without associating himself with this idea, the bishop refers to it in a letter to the Doctor, as an instance of the scandal which he is causing. The Doctor's reaction is very characteristic; his anger against the newspaper, though strong, is as nothing compared with anger against the bishop for noticing it. Indeed, as soon as he has convinced himself that he could win an action for libel against the newspaper, his anger against it cools altogether. When he hears that the newspaper is willing to make a public apology and pay his legal expenses, he instructs his lawyer to tell them " that they will oblige me by putting in no apology, and as for your bill, I would prefer to pay it myself." But his anger against the bishop, who has merely referred to the newspaper's accusation, is still extremely bitter. Puzzling as this is in itself, it is easily intelligible in the light of the Doctor's character. For as soon as anyone is in his power the benevolent instincts of the patriarch predominate in him. Hot-tempered though he is, he never once reproaches Peacocke, who caused all the trouble by concealing the facts on his original appointment to the school. He feels no anger at being deceived for one reason only, because, it would be so easy to punish the man. In the same way, once he is assured that he has the newspaper in his power (if he chooses to bring a libel action), he is full of generosity. Before he was certain of this, his anger against it had been strong, and those who are outside his control, like the bishop and parents of his pupils, cannot be forgiven even imaginary injuries.

Even advice for which he has himself asked, carries with it a suggestion of superiority that is apt to infuriate him. His method of asking advice is characteristic; he would rather die than ask it of the bishop, and instead he goes to Mr. Puddicombe, a neighbouring clergyman of much lower standing than himself. When he is told by Mr. Puddicombe, albeit in a kind and friendly way, that he has countenanced immorality and deceit in a brother clergyman, he at once, naturally, takes a peevishly opposite line. Riding home, and imagining himself in Peacocke's place, he says to himself, " ' If it were me, I'd treat her as my wife in spite of all the Puddicombes in creation; in spite of all the bishops.' " In the same way he had said to Peacocke on first being told the story of his marriage, " ' I would have clung to her let the law say what it might.' " Both these remarks are inconsistent with his action in making the immediate separation of the Peacockes a condition of his help and countenance. But the inconsistency is very easy to explain. Only two feelings can shake his normal moral convictions, pity towards an inferior, a member, so to speak, of his own patriarchate, and resentment against his superiors, or against those who are presuming (even at his own request) to give him advice. These two impulses are the strongest in his life.

He is a man who delights in shocking and exasperating others. That is why, for instance, he says to his wife, " ' It is often a question to me whether the religion of the world is not more odious than its want of religion.' " Though not enthusiastic, he is really incapable of abandoning his religion, but he knows his wife will be shocked by this remark. When he remonstrates sternly with the bishop for referring to the scandalous London paper, the bishop's reply is studiously mild. It begins, " ' Your letter has pained me exceedingly, because I find that I have caused you a degree of annoyance which I am certainly very sorry I have inflicted.' " The rebuke for his strong language is as soft as possible, and the letter ends, " ' Under these circumstances, I trust that the affair may now be allowed to rest without any breach of those kind feelings which have hitherto existed between us.' "

This the Doctor calls a " beastly letter." Why? Because it shows that he has failed in his purpose of annoying the bishop and because it seems to leave no room for further controversy. Peace is the last thing he wants. And so his defence of the Peacockes is consciously paradoxical, a quixotic challenge to the whole world. Unfortunately for the general comprehension of this book to-day, changes of opinion have made it seem to some people more like a platitude.

Kept in the Dark, too, has been misunderstood, but the reason for the mistake has been different. For this book has come to seem yet more improbable with the passage of time, and its deliberate fantasy has been explained as reflecting the unconscious absurdity of a whole period, and its conventions. Though Dr. Wortle's conduct has appeared natural to many modern readers, and Western's in *Kept in the Dark* has seemed absurd, they have two things in common. Each seemed to his creator a solitary exponent of a fantastic idea; to twentieth-century readers each has seemed to advocate a doctrine generally accepted when the books were written.

Kept in the Dark is the story of a girl who marries without telling her husband that she has been engaged before. Western, the husband, is informed by Sir Francis Geraldine, the former fiancé, of the engagement. He then leaves his wife in disgust, but is finally reconciled to her. This bare plot is typical of Trollope's later works, and the whole interest is psychological. The book is not one of Trollope's best. The few obvious climaxes in the story are not sufficiently realised, and the motives of the characters are not always very clear; but it is a serious attempt to analyse an obsession. Both Geraldine and Western are interesting characters, and each gains from the mixed likeness and contrast of their two natures. Each has been jilted—Sir Francis by Mrs. Western herself. Western told his future wife the story of the girl who deceived him early in their acquaintance, and so it was partly out of delicacy that she did not recount her own much more justified treatment of Geraldine.

In some ways Geraldine comes near to being the traditional bad baronet of fiction. But there is more to him than that; he is a man in whose mind wounds can never heal, though he can carry them off with an air. He makes mischief between husband and wife, not out of jealousy, but from the desire for revenge masquerading as even-handed justice. That he is on the whole glad to have escaped marriage does not mitigate his indignation at being rejected. There is a fine scene where he is discussing the revelation he proposes to make to the husband with a friend who tries to dissuade him from it. The friend is not strongly individualised, and takes no high moral ground. His ideas are that one does not cause unnecessary trouble when one has nothing to gain by it, and that one should treat a woman with some forbearance. It is the average morality of the more stupid upperclass Englishman put at its lowest. Sir Francis replied, " ' Those are your ideas because you don't take the trouble to return evil for evil. But then you never take the trouble to return good for good. In fact, you have no idea of duty.' " The useless baronet suddenly reveals how seriously he takes life. And the ordinary unthinking morality of his friend has no answer to make.

Western, like Geraldine, is extremely sensitive. He trusts and idealises his wife so much that, when he has convicted her of the smallest fault, nothing is too bad for him to suspect. But whereas in Geraldine's character sensitiveness is an excuse for cruelty, in Western it is a kind of nobility. His cruelty to his wife in leaving her is unconscious, and he suffers as much as she does. When his mental balance is restored he is prepared to make ample amends.

The book is an analysis of the relation between sensitiveness and cruelty. Geraldine is sensitive through pride and this makes him deliberately cruel. Western is sensitive through shyness and timidity, and he is cruel without realising it. We see how their sensitiveness, the only thing they have in common, can outweigh all their immense differences, so that at the crucial point their conduct becomes indistinguishable. This one accidental resemblance leads them to co-operate in an injustice which neither of them alone could have achieved. Trollope knew well from his own experience the dangers of acute sensitiveness, and here as in several of his later books, he turned his satirical guns against himself. In this case sensitiveness has the power to make an honest man assist his enemies to harm his friends.

It is easy to make a great mistake over this book, to suppose that its central situation was due to the preposterously high standards of Victorian propriety. In fact, it has nothing to do with propriety. We miss the whole point of the book if we do not see that it is meant to be a study in an abnormal state of mind. To draw deductions about Victorian ethics from Western's conduct is like using Ophelia to prove that Elizabethan girls were inclined to wander in their speech. Trollope has enjoyed such a vogue as the " voice of the Victorian epoch " that his eccentricities has been overlooked. On the showing of some of his later works he is as little fitted to fill this exalted but limiting position as Dr. Johnson is to be considered the representative Augustan. In both men a cursory examination will reveal the way in which they were typical. Rather more care is needed to see that in important respects they were unique. Some critics have treated the dark, absurd, obsessed characters of these later novels like a barrister in a cross-examination dealing with a recalcitrant witness. Sir Hugh Walpole summarises them thus: " Little stories that depend for their interest in absurd situations as when in *Kept in the Dark* a lover dismisses his young lady because, before she knew him, she had been engaged for a short period to somebody else—there's gentlemanly conduct for you! " There are two misstatements in this passage. For the couple were already married, and Western left his wife, not because she had been engaged before, but because she had not told him of it, and because he suspected a plot. But more important than these comparatively slight errors is the standard of judgment applied. One can almost hear the reasonable voice of the barrister, " I put it to you, Mr. Western, was not this a very odd way to behave? " It is like asking Macbeth why he did not wait quietly for the witches' prophecy to be fulfilled, or King Lear why he did not keep the power in his grasp. It is an attitude which, if carried to extremes, would repudiate all imaginative literature as untrue to life.

More interesting than any refutation of this criticism of Walpole's is the question, Why did he make this mistake? Why did he think it enough to condemn a novel, to say that the main character did not act like a gentleman? He was not a stupid man, nor an unappreciative reader. If he had come across a character like Western in his favourite *War and Peace* he would probably have approved. But his friendly and genial contempt for Trollope, his engrained conviction that Victorian England was a time of no surprises, and its literature easy to master, put him off his guard. He wrote without thought, because he believed he knew what Trollope was going to say before he said it. He is not the only one.

8. 'Mr. Scarborough's Family'

IN THIS work Trollope not only invented a very good plot, but achieved a perfect harmony between plot and character. For the plot is a fantastic one and any failure of characterisation would have made the strain on credulity too great. Mr. Scarborough, having as a young man, inherited an entailed estate, decides early in life to make plans to defeat the entail. He therefore goes through a second marriage ceremony with his wife after the birth of his eldest son, and, as he hopes, another son is subsequently born. Both marriages take place abroad and secretly. When his elder son, Mountjoy, becomes hopelessly in debt, he announces and produces documents to prove that Mountjoy is illegitimate. With the agreement of his second son, Augustus, now apparently the legal heir, he buys up the Mountjoy debts at the cost of the money originally advanced only. The moneylenders reluctantly agree to waive the huge interest due to them, because they fear that, as Mountjoy has no expectations, they may get nothing if they refuse Mr. Scarborough's offer. The squire then disinherits Augustus of everything except the bare property. Finally, he produces documents to prove that his first marriage was valid and so land, house, money and all finally revert to Mountjoy.

Stated in this way the story seems too like a fairy-tale to be successful as ordinary prose fiction. Hundreds of objections occur to the mind at once. How could Mr. Scarborough have foreseen it all twenty or thirty years before? What was his motive in this elaborate deceit if he did? Why did the younger son spoil his own prospects by consenting to the redemption of his brother's debts? And so on, and so on. But the story is so arranged and the characters so drawn that none of these objections has any weight with the reader.

This was one of Trollope's last books. It was published posthumously. And there is abundant evidence that in his last ten years or so the more fantastic sides of human nature increasingly fascinated Trollope. There are few more fantastic characters than Mr. Scarborough in our literature, and yet it is not difficult to believe in him. Trollope shares with Dickens an exceptional power of making the fantastic seem indisputable, but their methods are different. Dickens does it in a moment by putting into the mouth of Mr. Mantalini or Mrs. Gamp some unanswerable and unforgettable remark. Trollope begins with the more ordinary facets of his character, but shows Mr. Scarborough as a man with a fixed idea about property. As this fixed idea is examined and unfolded throughout the book, the man's character appears more and more absurd. But every stage of absurdity is the logical consequence of the one before. There is no point at which we can say, " This is too much." For the author would reply with justice that it all hangs together.

It would be fruitless to declare one of these two methods superior to the other. But the method Trollope uses with Mr. Scarborough has at least one effect which the other has not. By showing us the slightly peculiar becoming the more and more fantastic, he suggests doubts about the ordinariness of the ordinary. If this is what a slight peculiarity leads to, the really humdrum, average, uninteresting character may be much rarer than we supposed. Trollope is considered by his detractors, even by some of his professed admirers, to be a photographer, a superficial chronicler of ordinary life. But if, as in the case of Mr. Scarborough, he can turn the ordinary into something " rich and strange," who cares how ordinary the material may be? Wordsworth's landscapes would have seemed ordinary—to most people.

Throughout the book Mr. Scarborough is on his deathbed. So he is never like a proud hero of tragedy defying the stars. His strong will and his cleverness are balanced by physical weakness. It must be remembered, too, that he is a gentleman. He finds it extremely easy to outwit everyone not only because of his foresight, but because of his position. Trollope suggests that the society he is depicting will always be led by the nose by such men, because it rests on the assumption that a gentleman will always behave like a gentleman. For instance, he will not defame his wife's character. But gentleman is a very flexible idea. Society may be shocked by Mr. Scarborough, but so is Mr. Scarborough shocked by the world around him. " He sets God and man at absolute defiance, and always does it with the most profound courtesy," says one character of him. In his own eyes Mr. Scarborough is completely justified. He claims to have done the best he can for both his sons. He hates entails, not simply because they interfere with his plans, but with the abiding metaphysical hatred of the political theorist. To him the law " consisted of a perplexed entanglement of rules got together so that the few might live in comfort at the expense of the many. Robbery, if you could get to the bottom of it, was bad, as was all violence; but taxation was robbery, rent was robbery, prices fixed according to the desire of the seller and not in obedience to justice, were robbery." He speaks with admiration of the man he considers truly honest; and we miss Trollope's whole point if we do not see that he is sincere in this. But it is his own kind of honesty. The honesty of the world—exemplified in the book by his lawyer, Grey—will indeed protect a man from being robbed by those who possess it, but to Mr. Scarborough it seems only a complicated form of self-interest. His denunciations are more like those of a Hebrew prophet than of an ordinary cynic. The second-best, the average, seem worthless to him.

How did Trollope mean us to take all this? We cannot swallow it whole, but we can hardly dismiss Mr. Scarborough as a madman. Like the fool in *Lear*, he hits the mark too often to be ignored. Trollope has taken care to show that he is vulnerable even by his own standards. Rent is robbery, but he owes his wealth to it. But then most people are inconsistent. I suggest that

Trollope's satirical aim was similar to that of Sir Thomas More in the *Utopia*. If the good heathen in his blindness can be as reasonable as this, what a commentary on Christian civilisation. So here, if Mr. Scarborough, throwing off every religious and moral restraint, can make such a good case for his subversive views, and show himself no less generous, no less true to his principles, no less self-denying than the world around him, what are we to think of the spacious days of Queen Victoria? But it should be noticed as well that this kind of satire is best written by those who value the thing they satirise, as Sir Thomas More did, and as Trollope did.

The two sons are not drawn in such detail as their father, but they are vivid enough. Mountjoy the elder is the born gentleman, conscious that he is bad and useless, but unable to alter his nature. He is a man of strong feeling and endears himself to his father by refusing to believe that his mother ever lived in sin.

Augustus is sober, industrious, and cold-blooded, the very embodiment of the worst side of the values of the world which his father attacks. They each, therefore, think the other incurably dishonest. Augustus's disagreeable nature is conveyed early in the book by his restraint. He is a practical man, who takes things as they come. He does not complain that he has (apparently) been defrauded before, or that his mother has been defamed. His father can never forgive him for this. For to Mr. Scarborough a man without righteous indignation is less than a man. Augustus secretly agrees with his brother in thinking that Mountjoy is still both the rightful and the legal heir. And, though he is right in this idea, by a notable stroke of irony, it is only this doubt which eventually prevents him from inheriting. For he is afraid that if Mountjoy's creditors are not satisfied, they may investigate the facts and be able to prove that Mr. Scarborough is lying and that Mountjoy is the true heir. For this reason he agrees to the payment of Mountjoy's creditors out of the estate. His father sees his motives and uses them to outwit him. For once Mountjoy is solvent and the estate unburdened, Mr. Scarborough can arrange for the property to pass to his eldest and favourite son.

The scene in which these plots and counter-plots come to a head is remarkable for its economy of means. Augustus's worldly wisdom is outmanœuvred by Mr. Scarborough, just as his worldly morality has previously been exposed by him.

Mr. Scarborough is speaking.

" ' Augustus is very anxious to pay these poor men their money. It is a noble feeling on the part of Augustus; you must admit that, Mr. Grey.' The irony with which this was said was evident in the squire's face and voice. Augustus only quietly laughed. The attorney sat as firm as death. He was not going to argue with such a statement or to laugh at such a joke. ' I suppose it will come to over a hundred thousand pounds.'

" ' Eighty thousand, I should think,' said Augustus. ' The bonds amount to a great deal more than that—twice that.' "

When he sees how Augustus conducts himself as the new heir, Mr. Scarborough gradually comes to hate him. He conceives the idea of leaving him the bare estate without any money to support it. Admittedly, Augustus has given his father some provocation, by inviting his friends to his father's house without consulting him, and by his unfeeling attitude to his father's physical sufferings. But Mr. Scarborough's growing detestation of him, like all his emotions, is obviously in excess of the facts. Now in the chapter entitled " Mr. Scarborough's Correspondence " he is revealed for the first time as a megalomaniac. The dual object of spiting his younger son and evading the spirit of the law has become more desirable than anything else. The contrast between the way he writes to Mountjoy to suggest his plan and the way he speaks of it privately is very instructive. In the letter to Mountjoy he says:

" ' Your brother has kindly interfered for the payment of your creditors, and as all the outstanding bonds have been redeemed, you would now by his generosity be enabled to enjoy any property which might be left to you. There are a few tables and chairs at my disposal, and a gem or two, and some odd volumes which perhaps you might like to possess.' "

Here Mr. Scarborough is preserving his dignity, still playing an elaborate single-handed game against the majesty of the law and the constitution. He wishes his son to enjoy the irony and acknowledge that his skill has been masterly.

But in the quiet of his own sickroom he says:

" ' Mountjoy is not a fool, and will understand very well what I mean. I wonder whether I could scrape the paper off the drawing-room walls, and leave the scraps to his brother, without interfering with the entail.' "

Here at last is the revelation for which Trollope has been carefully preparing us for nearly forty chapters. Beneath his plots, his sneers and his satire, the man is a maniac. He may be a Victorian landowner, but his spiritual ancestor is Sir Epicure Mammon. And such is Trollope's skill that not only does his character completely convince us, but we are forced to admit that the man is the same man we met in the first chapter. He has not changed. We have merely seen deeper into his mind.

As time goes on, he arrogates more and more to himself. He sets himself up as a judge over his sons and declares that he has tried them both and he knows them now. Finally, he declares (and proves) the validity of his first marriage and leaves everything to Mountjoy. At this point the reader may expect that his megalomania will only increase, and that he will die defiant. But now a new strain enters the narrative, a strain of tenderness. It is appropriate (even if unexpected) because he has planned and plotted for others and not for himself.

" ' You will do something, I suppose, for poor Gus? ' the old man said to his son one morning." In reading this sentence one can only admire once again the subtlety and economy of a writer who can indicate momentous and complicated states of mind by a remark so ordinary.

This prepares us for the surprising epitaph which Trollope pronounces upon him: " in every phase of his life he had been actuated by love for others." One of the other characters says of him after his death, " ' If you can imagine for yourself a state of things in which neither truth nor morality shall be thought essential, then old Mr. Scarborough would be your hero.' " That is the point. Trollope was prepared to imagine such a state, but it is clear from all his writings that he was not prepared to approve it. Why then all this adulation for Mr. Scarborough?

Mr. Michael Sadleir tells us that this book is a novel of property. Clearly it is concerned throughout with property, entail, inheritance, and primogeniture. But if this remark means that property is the entire subject of the novel, its *raison d'être*, then I disagree. The book's real subject, it seems to me, is honesty. Each of the main characters has a different standard of honesty, each is justified from one point of view and each is vulnerable. To Mr. Scarborough honesty means finding out what abstract justice demands, and then using any means, in defiance of morality and law, to bring it about. To Mountjoy honesty means behaving like a gentleman. For him it is all right to owe money which he cannot really pay, and to raise money on one's expectations, but it is wrong to lie or dissimulate or acquiesce in an attack on the good name of his mother. For Augustus honesty means simply keeping without the law and ignoring all generous feelings. For Mr. Grey it means doing your duty by your employer and con- forming to the ordinary usages of decent people. The point of the book is not that Mr. Scarborough's grotesque morality is justified, but that it is no more vulnerable than the others. " If you can imagine a state of things in which neither truth nor morality shall be thought essential. . . ." Yes, but if these words are understood in their deepest sense, none of the other characters follows them either.

If the ordinary honesty of the world satisfies you, Trollope means to say, you have no right to condemn Mr. Scarborough. If you do not condemn him, what becomes of your worldly honesty?

In fact, none of the other main characters acquires a right to condemn him. Augustus takes his stand on his own cleverness and self-interest; and had he been consistent he could have overcome his father. But his father lured him into a solitary act of generosity. As his father's supposed heir he gave his indispensable adhesion to the payments from the estate to his brother's creditors. Superficially this was just and generous; according to Augustus's calculations it was an act of self-interest, because it might prevent a law-suit. In its effects, through his father's cleverness, his action became even more generous than it appeared. For by freeing the estate it prepared the way for the real heir to inherit. By Augustus's standards, his father has proved himself the better man.

Mr. Scarborough's antics enable the moneylenders to enjoy the pleasures of injured virtue. But how can they condemn him? Legally, they have no case. The repayment is made freely by men on whom they have no claim. And in justice? They receive back what they have given, and the attempted injustice of exorbitant interest is frustrated.

A subtler case is that of Mr. Grey. It is no accident that for all his protestations, he becomes ever more deeply involved in Scarborough's machinations and ever more fascinated by his character. It is that fascination exercised by extremism over the moderate, by consistent principles over those who compromise. He is shocked that a man " on the very brink of eternity " should command such unlimited daring. But then Grey's own ideas about eternity are vague. He is dragged to church by his daughter and possesses neither the consolations of belief nor of disbelief. As a result of Scarborough's actions he comes to see that inconsistency extends to his everyday work as well. He has tried to serve the law and abstract justice at the same time, in the belief that their dictates were the same. But he is driven by Scarborough's manipulation of evidence to defend in the name of law what he knows to be unjust. His moral protest, which seemed at first unanswerable, gradually falters. As his father's hated schemes in the end save him from bankruptcy, Mountjoy's protests falter also.

The best satire encourages self-criticism by the reader. In a book whose characters and events are fantastic, it is peculiarly difficult to achieve this. Trollope overcomes the difficulty by making use of the handicap. The reader is encouraged to regard Scarborough and his plots as remote from his own ideas about honesty. This makes the sudden focusing of attention on Grey's deceptive ordinariness all the more disturbing. The reader tends to identify himself with Grey, and to share in the pillorying of Scarborough. Too late he discovers that Scarborough can hit back and that his supposed safe position by Grey's side is really a place of danger. Dr. Leavis's comment on Swift applies here: " It is as if one found him in the place—at the point of view— where one expected to find his butt."

Successful satire is rare. Perhaps the commonest reason for failure is the attempt to concentrate guilt on too few heads. Much toil, often the toil of great writers, has gone to the pre- paration of that artistically useless thing, a hell for other people. But for this one failing, for instance, Marcus Clarke might have written great satire in *For the Term of His Natural Life*. But because the reader only identifies himself with the sufferings of the innocent, never with the crimes of the system, the book, fine as it is, remains only brilliant melodrama.

Where Trollope's satire fails is where Swift's also fails. Universal and searching in his attack, the standards from which the attack is conducted are, like Swift's " reason," imprecise. But this criticism is not so severe as it may seem. Few even of the great satirists, but are open to the charge either of imprecision, or of narrowness, or of melodrama.

APPENDIX

APPENDIX

THE POLITICAL NOVELS AND HISTORY

IT HAS usually been assumed that Trollope's political novels are *romans à clef*. Mr. L. S. Amery is expressing the normal views of critics when he says in his preface to *The Prime Minister*, "No one can mistake Mr. Gresham and Mr. Daubeny for anybody else than Mr. Gladstone and Mr. Disraeli." A front-page article in *The Times Literary Supplement* in 1937 confirmed these identifications and added that of Turnbull with Bright. But it is surprising that no one, except Dr. R. W. Chapman, appears to have produced serious arguments for this view. For it involves startling corollaries; it would mean that Frederic Harrison who knew Trollope well completely mistook his intentions and that Trollope himself was a liar. In a letter to the *Daily Telegraph* in 1869 he said, "I depicted Mr. Bright neither in his private nor his public character, and I cannot imagine how any likeness justifying such a charge against me can be found." In the Autobiography he said that the Brocks, De Terriers, Monks, Greshams, and Daubenys were not portraits of living men. These are the statements of a man who in his life was a byword for frankness and whose Autobiography is full of confessions most damaging to his literary reputation. It is noteworthy, too, that he did not invariably deny the imputation of introducing real characters and institutions into his books. Take the case of *The Warden*. He did not object to the identification of Mr. Popular Sentiment with Dickens and of Dr. Anticant with Carlyle. *The Times* in an appreciative review had mildly rebuked him for caricaturing a leading personality of *The Times* in the character of Tom Towers. Trollope says in the Autobiography, "I had introduced one Tom Towers as being potent among the contributors to the Jupiter, under which name I certainly did allude to *The Times*. But at that time living away in

Ireland, I had not even heard the name of any gentleman connected with *The Times* newspaper, and could not have intended to represent any individual by Tom Towers. As I had created an archdeacon, so I had created a journalist, and the one creation was no more personal or indicative of morbid tendencies than the other. If Tom Towers was at all like any gentleman then connected with *The Times*, my moral consciousness must again have been very powerful."

I suggest that the same kind of mistake has been made with Trollope's political characters. It may be objected that this admission about *The Times* and the literary parodies in *The Warden*, by establishing that Trollope did sometimes glance at real people and institutions, make the traditional identifications in the political novels more plausible. But in fact all these established cases are caricatures done in passing. If the chapters dealing with Mr. Popular Sentiment and Dr. Pessimist Anticant were left out of *The Warden* there would not be a single loose end. Gresham, Turnbull and the rest are leading characters of their books, and though they have their amusing side, they are certainly not mere caricatures.

Let us examine Dr. Chapman's arguments on the other side. In the volume of essays presented to Humphrey Milford he notes that Lord Brock is the Liberal leader in *Can You Forgive Her?* which appeared in monthly parts in 1864-65, and that in *Phineas Finn* he has been replaced by Mr. Mildmay. Palmerston, with whom he identifies Brock, died in 1865; Lord De Terrier, the Conservative leader in *Phineas Finn* (1867-69) has given way to Daubeny in *Phineas Redux*. So he identifies De Terrier with Derby who resigned and died between the writing of these two books. Two things should be noted about these identifications. First, Lord Brock and Lord De Terrier, unlike Gresham and Daubeny, have no recognisable character. As their comic names suggest, they are simple party leaders, typical figures. With the exception of one anecdote about Lord Brock suggesting that he thought private life more important than public, nothing is said about either of them that could not be said of any two Victorian party leaders real or imaginary. Dr. Chapman's identification then in these two cases depends solely on the coincidence of dates.

But the coincidence of dates, if it is to carry any weight, should hold good throughout. It is not in itself a particularly striking fact that both Trollope's Conservative party and the real one should have changed its leader between 1867 and 1873. Dr. Chapman admits that the similarity breaks down. For instance, in his opinion, the most certain identification of all is that of Daubeny with Disraeli. *The Duke's Children* began to appear in 1879 when Disraeli was still Prime Minister, But Daubeny had given way to Lord Drummond. Even in *The Prime Minister* (1875-76) Daubeny sat for a time below the gangway.

Again, the whole question of the time scheme of the novels is more complex than Dr. Chapman seems to recognise. For instance he identifies (only tentatively, it is true) Trollope's Duke of St. Bungay with the third Lord Lansdowne. Now, the Duke was an active though senior politician in *The Prime Minister* and has a hand in the making of cabinets, and is still writing political letters in *The Duke's Children*. But the third Lord Lansdowne was crippled with gout in 1852 and died about ten years later. Not only was *The Duke's Children* not published till 1879-80, but Trollope actually gives the 'seventies as the date of its events. Perhaps this relative definiteness, or lesser vagueness, is due to the comparatively small importance of politics in the book. In *Phineas Redux* which is very largely political he is content to tell us on the first page of a " general election of 18—," any time in the nineteenth century. The political indications of time in the books as a whole are not as vague as this, but they are neither definite nor wholly consistent. At one moment the absence of party organisation, both in the House and in the constituencies, the enormous political influence of peers, and the rotten borough controversy, might tempt us to place the Phineas books not very far in time from the reform bill of 1832. At another there seems to be a reference to the reform bill of 1867. The attempt to date events by political organisation and atmosphere can at best give only an approximate answer. The attempt to date them by a comparison of ministries and measures will give no answer at all. Where is the historical parallel to the coalition in *The Prime Minister?* or to the Tory attempt to disestablish the Church? Dr. Chapman's time-scheme seems much too rigid to fit Trollope's flexible ideas. It is likely that, in starting to write *Phineas Finn* Trollope was nervous about his powers of achieving verisimilitude. We know that he remained always self-conscious about his failure to win a seat in Parliament, and as he sat in the gallery learning the usages and atmosphere of the House before writing about it, he may well have wondered if his outsider's descriptions could challenge those of practising politicians. He need not have worried. He had been proclaimed an expert on the life of the cathedral close without even meeting an archdeacon. Atmospheric verisimilitude was so strong as to seem to extend to persons also. His trouble proved to be the opposite of what he may have expected, and hence perhaps the greater freedom of political invention which he allowed himself in the subsequent novels. I do not think Daubeny would have been allowed even to toy with the idea of disestablishment in *Phineas Finn*.

Dr. Chapman points out that the names Gresham and Daubeny agree with Gladstone and Disraeli in their initial letters and in the number of their syllables. Here again it is only if such a correspondence ran through all the names supposed to represent real politicians that the argument would become strong. One would not necessarily expect the same kind of correspondence in each name. For instance, the personality of Bright might not have been indicated by a directly parallel treatment of his name, which would give Briggs or Bell or the like, but a name like Brilliant or Gray (*lucus a non lucendo*) or Sheen would give the hint. There must be a very large number of names which could suggest Bright in this way; but so far as I know, Turnbull is not one of them. Yet the *Saturday Review* in its article on *Phineas Finn* was more confident of the Turnbull-Bright identification than of any other, and even suggested that hatred of Bright was one of Trollope's dominating motives—a suggestion which reads strangely to-day. This identification is not a marginal one; to discard it would endanger the whole argument of Dr. Chapman and his supporters.

It is instructive to consider the similarities and the differences between the real Bright and the fictional Turnbull. Each was a Radical and a manufacturer, while Turnbull's " free trade in every-thing except malt " might be a reference to the Quaker and Temper-ance reformer. This is about the limit of the similarities. If anyone considers them very impressive, he might reflect how normal such a combination was in mid-Victorian times. Half of *Culture and Anarchy* deals with people who answer to this description. The three points of similarity are not three separate clues corroborating each other, like, say, a mole on the face, a passion for rowing and belonging to a family of fifteen children. They really form between them only one clue, like this group—very rich, large number of servants, thousands of acres of property. The similarity in fact hardly goes beyond the degree inherent in the author's original decision to write about the House of Commons and the actual political parties.

Of the differences between Bright and Turnbull, I would not give much weight to that of temper. Turnbull appears as a rough over-bearing man, whose wife and children must have a bad time of it. Yet Gladstone wrote in his journal on November 15th, 1871, " Fore-noon with Bright, who departed having charmed everyone with his gentleness " and Queen Victoria wrote in the same sense. But against this, one might say that Bright could be fierce in public life, and Trollope might have been depicting and exaggerating the man's public demeanour, neglecting or perhaps not knowing his behaviour in private.

More serious are the political discrepancies. It seems that in one part of his life Bright was very unpopular. Now, if Turnbull really was drawn from Bright, then Trollope cannot have thought very highly of the latter; and one would expect him to dwell on this unpopularity, even exaggerate it as, on this theory, he certainly exaggerated any harshness of manner that Bright may have had. But instead " Mr. Turnbull " was one of the most popular, if not the most popular politicians in the country. Poor men believed in him, thinking that he was their most honest public friend; and men who were not poor believed in his power, thinking that his counsels must surely prevail." Again the first article of Turnbull's political creed is that he must always be a freelance. There is never any question of his joining a government; he sneers at his old friend and colleague Monk for doing so. But Bright was included in several cabinets. Even when there is the casual similarity of policy which one would expect to occur between a real and fictional Radical leader, it is similarity with a difference. Bright's criticism of Disraeli's reforming legislation of 1867 recalls Turnbull's criticism of the reforms, not of a Conservative leader, but of the Liberal Mildmay, and though both bills were electoral reforms, their measures were very different. This theme of similarity with difference recurs all through Trollope's treatment of politics—identity of parties and physical setting, similarity of social and political types, dissimilarity of men and political issues. It is interesting to notice how different in style are the speeches of Bright and Turnbull.

As an example of the way people are apt to leap to conclusions when faced with this kind of unlikeness in likeness, we may return to the *Saturday Review* of March, 1869. It is taken for granted there that Bright and Turnbull are identical not only mentally and morally, but physically also. Yet the D.N.B. says that Bright was five foot seven inches in height; Turnbull was " nearly six feet and stood quite upright." Anyone who doubts that the passion for identification can run riot beyond all bounds should consult Sir Algernon West's *Recollections 1832-86* which furnishes several examples.

We find the same kind of difficulty if we try to equate Gladstone and Gresham. For instance, there is a reference in *Phineas Finn* to a quarrel and subsequent reconciliation between Gresham and Mildmay. The reader on the watch for parallels will naturally think of the reconciliation between Palmerston and Lord John Russell. Now Mildmay has been taken by some as a portrait of Russell, though one would have thought that Mildmay could never have written *No Popery* on Cardinal Wiseman's door. But to suggest that Gresham was meant for Palmerston would throw out the whole system of interpretation. There are after all only a limited number of possible political acts in a mid-Victorian parliamentary setting. Coincidences were inevitable; but examples like this, and that of Turnbull's attack on Mildmay's Reform Bill, suggest that when Trollope was aware of them he liked so to mix the personalities that no consistent historical interpretation would be possible.

Now in several respects Gresham's character agrees with Gladstone's. As Dr. Chapman puts it, " The case of Gresham is less clear (than Daubeny); but this commanding intellect, his abounding eloquence—perhaps also his arrogant manner and his ungovernable temper?—seem to point to Gladstone." But is this combination of qualities rare among public men? Can we not easily think of several politicians of to-day who might be described thus? No one, so far as I know, has yet credited Trollope with the gift of prophecy, or claimed that Gresham is a portrait of Mr. Aneurin Bevan. Yet one characteristic of Gresham, though it would doubtless be unfair to attribute it to Mr. Bevan, could be ascribed much more plausibly to him than to Gladstone. " For Mr. Gresham is a man with no feelings for the past, void of historical association, hardly with memories—living altogether for the future which he is anxious to fashion anew out of the vigour of his own brain."

Again if one were looking for a portrait of Gladstone in the political novels, one could fix with equal plausibility upon Finespun, the Chancellor of the Exchequer in *Can You Forgive Her?* True, he is a very minor character, but if we remember Popular Sentiment and Pessimist Anticant, that need be nothing against the identification. The description of him by the Duke of St. Bungay is just as consistent with

Gladstone as Gresham is. The only important incident in Finespun's brief history is a very close parallel to one in Gladstone's. For Finespun resigned the Chancellorship because his colleagues could not approve of the sweeping measures he wished to introduce. An entry in the Greville diary for 17th May, 1860, reads: "A queer state of things when the Prime Minister himself secretly desires to see the defeat of a measure so precious to his own Chancellor of the Exchequer (Gladstone)." There is no need to decide whether Greville was right; if he thought this, Trollope might have heard and believed the same story. This coincidence certainly does not prove that Finespun was meant for Gladstone, but it must throw doubt on the identification with Gresham.

So far there is no convincing evidence of any intention to copy real characters. But the case of Daubeny and Disraeli is more difficult. Daubeny, before becoming the Conservative leader, was, in Gresham's opinion, helped in his audacious policy by "a leader who, though thoroughly trusted, was very idle." It was natural that a contemporary reader should think of the relation between Disraeli and Derby. And while Daubeny is by no means a likeness of the real Disraeli, Dr. Chapman justly says that he is like what Trollope imagined Disraeli to be. For instance, speaking of Disraeli's own novels, he says, "an audacious conjurer has generally been his hero," and in *Phineas Redux* the dissatisfied Tories tell themselves that "Daubeny has ever been mysterious, unintelligible, and given to conjuring."

On the other hand, if Trollope had really wished to expose in Daubeny his conception of Disraeli as changeable and unprincipled, he did not do it efficiently. For the issue chosen to illustrate these traits in Daubeny is establishment. Even to a prejudiced man, it must have been obvious that this was a question upon which Disraeli never faltered. Except the monarchy, there was no part of traditional Conservative policy which Disraeli was so certain to maintain. Trollope was not given to wild exaggeration, and it is hard to believe that he missed the mark by so much. Incidentally, whereas Trollope's Daubeny supports the High Church, and his Liberals the Low, Disraeli's patronage usually favoured the Low Church, and Gladstone was a convinced High Churchman. The similarity between Daubeny and Disraeli is too great to be the result of accident, but the divergence is too strong to let us suppose that the similarity was seriously intended. Later on, I shall try to resolve this contradiction.

The general objections to historical identification are also strong.

We know that Trollope was interested in the character of Palmerston. Could he have dressed him in the colourless mask of Lord Brock? Dr. Chapman says that " it would be clumsy to mix fact and fiction by naming real politicians." Certainly, on his theory of identification, it would; though not if Gresham, Turnbull and the rest are purely imaginary. But Trollope repeatedly mixes fact and fiction in this way. Sometimes, as Dr. Chapman pleads, mention of real politicians occurs in unpolitical novels. But Palmerston is mentioned in the most political of all, *Phineas Finn*, and Gladstone is mentioned in the electioneering part of *Ralph the Heir*. In one of the few purely political chapters in *Framley Parsonage* a character called Sidonia is introduced. Now only average knowledge was needed to associate Sidonia with Disraeli. It is typical of Trollope's method with names to make their meaning obvious, where they have a meaning at all. Quiverful, Fillgrave, Fiasco, and many more have been setting the teeth of the fastidious on edge for three generations. And if it is unlikely that he would refer to Palmerston both in his real name and under an alias, it is surely incredible that he had two separate disguises for Disraeli.

It seems that one important general consideration has been over-looked. A clue to it can be found in T. S. Eliot's remark about the difficulty of avoiding Shakespearian echoes when writing blank verse to-day. The average poet, in composing blank verse, will write bad Shakespearian verse, though he may never consciously have thought of Shakespeare while he was writing. How much more strongly does this apply to political fiction. Trollope began by deliberately copying the House of Commons, its atmosphere and procedure, the general state of the parties, and the political clubs. Where imitation goes further than this it was unconscious. Disraeli, who afflicted Trollope with the fascination of horror, naturally had the strongest unconscious influence. Political measures, which have a slighter hold on the mind than personalities, did not influence him at all.

If this theory is correct, it would explain why Trollope was so irritated by the suggestion that he was copying real characters. If it had been true, why after all should he have been reluctant to have it known? There could have been nothing libellous in the identifications even if one or two of them might have seemed unkind. Apart from his inveterate truthfulness, one feels that Trollope would have enjoyed the stir caused by any caricatures he had really intended. But if he had been trying with all his might, like T. S. Eliot, to avoid the obvious models, his irritation is perfectly natural; and it is natural, too, that he should be the last to recognise any partial likenesses for which his conscious mind was not responsible. This explains, though it does not vindicate, the defiant tone of his letter to the *Daily Telegraph*, "I cannot imagine how any likeness justifying such a charge against me can be found."

Frederic Harrison in his preface to *Phineas Finn* wrote, "We read a page and say: ' Oh, Mr. Gladstone to the life! A photograph of Disraeli, of Bright!' But on the next page we find Mr. Gresham, Mr. Daubeny, or Mr. Monk[1] taking action, saying things which Gladstone, or Disraeli, or Bright never did, and could not have said or done." Knowing Trollope and the politicians of the day as he did, he had better means of judging than most.

Cardinal Newman in his preface to *Loss and Gain* said, " The principal characters are imaginary; and the writer wishes to disclaim personal allusion in any . . . At the same time, free use has been made of sayings and doings which are characteristic of the time and place in which the scene is laid. And, moreover, when a general truth of fact is exhibited in a tale, in individual specimens of it it is impossible that the ideal representation should not more or less coincide, in spite of the author's endeavour, with its existing instances or champions." This last sentence is even more true of political novels than of *Loss and Gain*.

Romans à clef may be much rarer than is generally supposed.

[1] One would expect the name Turnbull here, corresponding to Bright. Turnbull and Monk are utterly different, yet each, it seems, can be equated in different minds with Bright.

BIBLIOGRAPHY OF ANTHONY TROLLOPE

The Macdermots of Ballycloran. 3 vols. London. Newby. 1847.

The Kellys and the O'Kellys: or Landlords and Tenants. 3 vols. London. Colburn. 1848. (Oxford University Press, "World's Classics.")

La Vendée: An Historical Romance. 3 vols. London. Colburn. 1850.

The Warden. 1 vol. London. Longman. 1855. (Chatto & Windus, "Zodiac"; Dent, "Everyman's Library"; Nelson, "Classics"; Oxford University Press, "World's Classics," and "Illustrated Trollope.")

Barchester Towers. 3 vols. London. Longman. 1857. (Chatto & Windus, "Zodiac"; Collins, "New Classics"; Dent, "Everyman's Library"; Nelson, "Classics"; Oxford University Press, "World's Classics," and "Illustrated Trollope.")

The Three Clerks: A Novel. 3 vols. London. Bentley. 1858. (Oxford University Press, "World's Classics.")

Doctor Thorne: A Novel. 3 vols. London. Chapman & Hall. 1858. (Chatto & Windus, "Zodiac"; Dent, "Everyman's Library"; Nelson, "Classics"; Oxford University Press, "World's Classics.")

The Bertrams: A Novel. 3 vols. London. Chapman & Hall. 1859.

The West Indies and the Spanish Main. 1 vol. London. Chapman & Hall. 1859.

Castle Richmond: A Novel. 3 vols. London. Chapman & Hall. 1860.

Framley Parsonage. With illustrations by J. E. Millais. 3 vols. London. Smith, Elder. 1861. (Chatto & Windus, "Zodiac"; Dent, "Everyman's Library"; Nelson, "Classics"; Oxford University Press, "World's Classics.")

Tales of All Countries. 1 vol. London. Chapman & Hall. 1861.

Orley Farm. With illustrations by J. E. Millais. London. Chapman & Hall. 1862. (Oxford University Press, "World's Classics.")

North America. 2 vols. London. Chapman & Hall. 1862.

Tales of All Countries: Second Series. 1 vol. London. Chapman & Hall. 1863.

Rachel Ray: A Novel. 2 vols. London. Chapman & Hall. 1863. (Oxford University Press, " World's Classics.")

The Small House at Allington. With illustrations by J. E. Millais. 2 vols. London. Smith, Elder. 1864. (Chatto & Windus, " Zodiac "; Dent, " Everyman's Library "; Nelson, " Classics "; Oxford University Press, " World's Classics.")

Can You Forgive Her? With illustrations by " Phiz " and E. Taylor. 2 vols. London. Chapman & Hall. 1864. (Oxford University Press, " World's Classics," and " Illustrated Trollope.")

Miss Mackenzie. 2 vols. London. Chapman & Hall. 1865. (Oxford University Press, " World's Classics.")

Hunting Sketches. 1 vol. London. Chapman & Hall. 1865.

The Belton Estate. 3 vols. London. Chapman & Hall. 1866. (Oxford University Press, " World's Classics.")

Travelling Sketches. 1 vol. London. Chapman & Hall. 1866.

Clergymen of the Church of England. 1 vol. Chapman & Hall. 1866.

Nina Balatka. 2 vols. Edinburgh & London. Blackwood. 1867. (Oxford University Press, " World's Classics," with *Linda Tressel.*)

The Last Chronicle of Barset. With illustrations by George H. Thomas. 2 vols. London. Smith, Elder. 1867. (Chatto & Windus, " Zodiac "; Dent, " Everyman's Library "; Nelson, " Classics "; Oxford University Press, " World's Classics.")

The Claverings. With illustrations by M. Ellen Edwards. 2 vols. London. Smith, Elder. 1867. (Oxford University Press, " World's Classics.")

Lotta Schmidt: and Other Stories. 1 vol. London. Strahan. 1867.

Linda Tressel. 2 vols. Edinburgh & London. Blackwood, 1868. (Oxford University Press, " World's Classics," with *Nina Balatka.*)

Phineas Finn, The Irish Member. With illustrations by J. E. Millais. 2 vols. London. Virtue. 1869. (Dent, " Everyman's Library "; Oxford University Press, " World's Classics," and " Illustrated Trollope.")

He Knew He Was Right. With illustrations by Marcus Stone. 2 vols. London. Strahan. 1869. (Oxford University Press, " World's Classics.")

The Vicar of Bullhampton. With illustrations by H. Woods. 1 vol.

London. Bradbury, Evans. 1870. (Oxford University Press, "World's Classics.")

An Editor's Tales. 1 vol. London. Strahan. 1870.

The Struggles of Brown, Jones and Robinson: by one of the Firm. With illustrations. 1 vol. London. Smith, Elder. 1870.

The Commentaries of Cæsar. 1 vol. Edinburgh & London. Blackwood. 1870.

Sir Harry Hotspur of Humblethwaite. 1 vol. London. Hurst & Blackett. 1871. (Oxford University Press, "World's Classics.")

Ralph the Heir. 3 vols. London. Hurst & Blackett. 1871. Also 1 vol. (8vo). With illustrations by F. A. Fraser. London. Strahan. 1871. (Oxford University Press, "World's Classics.")

The Golden Lion of Granpère. 1 vol. London. Tinsley. 1872.

Australia and New Zealand. 2 vols. London. Chapman & Hall. 1873.

The Eustace Diamonds. 3 vols. London. Chapman & Hall. 1873. (Oxford University Press, "World's Classics," and "Illustrated Trollope.")

Phineas Redux. With illustrations by Frank Holl. 2 vols. London. Chapman & Hall. 1874. (Oxford University Press, "World's Classics," and "Illustrated Trollope.")

Lady Anna. 2 vols. London. Chapman & Hall. 1874. (Oxford University Press, "World's Classics.")

Harry Heathcote of Gangoil: A Tale of Australian Bush Life. 1 vol. London. Sampson, Low. 1874.

The Way We Live Now. With illustrations by Luke Fildes. 2 vols. London. Chapman & Hall. 1875. (Oxford University Press, "World's Classics.")

The Prime Minister. 2 vols. London. Chapman & Hall. 1876. (Oxford University Press, "World's Classics," and "Illustrated Trollope.")

The American Senator. 3 vols. London. Chapman & Hall. 1877. (Oxford University Press, "World's Classics.")

South Africa. 2 vols. London. Chapman & Hall. 1878.

Is He Popenjoy?: A Novel. 3 vols. London. Chapman & Hall. 1878. (Oxford University Press, "World's Classics.")

How the "Mastiffs" went to Iceland. With illustrations by Mrs. Hugh Blackburn. 1 vol. London. Virtue. 1878.

An Eye for an Eye. 2 vols. London. Chapman & Hall. 1879.

Thackeray. 1 vol. London. Macmillan. 1879.

John Caldigate. 3 vols. London. Chapman & Hall. 1879. (Oxford University Press, "World's Classics.")

Cousin Henry: A Novel. 2 vols. London. Chapman & Hall. 1879. (Oxford University Press, "World's Classics.")

The Duke's Children: A Novel. 3 vols. London. Chapman & Hall. 1880. (Oxford University Press, "World's Classics," and "Illustrated Trollope.")

The Life of Cicero. 2 vols. London. Chapman & Hall. 1880.

Doctor Wortle's School: A Novel. 2 vols. London. Chapman & Hall. 1881. (Oxford University Press, "World's Classics.")

Ayala's Angel. 3 vols. London. Chapman & Hall. 1881. (Oxford University Press, "World's Classics.")

Why Frau Frohmann Raised Her Prices: And Other Stories. 1 vol. London. Isbister. 1882.

Lord Palmerston ("English Political Leaders"). 1 vol. London. Isbister. 1882.

Kept in the Dark: A Novel. With a frontispiece by J. E. Millais. 2 vols. London. Chatto & Windus. 1882.

Marion Fay: A Novel. 3 vols. London. Chapman & Hall. 1882.

The Fixed Period. 2 vols. Edinburgh & London. Blackwood. 1882.

Mr. Scarborough's Family. 3 vols. London. Chatto & Windus. 1883.

The Landleaguers. 3 vols. London. Chatto & Windus. 1883.

An Autobiography. 2 vols. Edinburgh & London. Blackwood. 1883. (Oxford University Press, "World's Classics," and "Illustrated Trollope.")

An Old Man's Love. 2 vols. Edinburgh & London. Blackwood. 1884. (Oxford University Press, "World's Classics.")

Letters. 1 vol. Edited by Bradford Adam Booth. Oxford University Press. 1951.

Various minor items have been published in recent years.

INDEX